FAITH, HOPE, AND CHARITY

Inspiration from
the Lives of General
Relief Society Presidents

FAITH, HOPE, AND CHARITY

Inspiration from
the Lives of General
Relief Society Presidents

Janet Peterson
& LaRene Gaunt

Covenant Communications, Inc.

To my daughter, daughters-in-law, and granddaughters,
who will carry on the legacy of Relief Society in our family.
—Janet Peterson

To these "elect ladies," the general presidents of the Relief Society,
whose lives exemplify the joy and power of service.
—LaRene Gaunt

Cover images:
Bathsheba W. Smith by Lee Greene Richards, *Clarissa S. Williams* by Lee Greene Richards

Cover images:
Emma Hale Smith by Lee Greene Richards, *Eliza R. Snow* by John Willard Clawson, *Zina Diantha Huntington Young* by John Willard Clawson, *Emmeline B. Wells* by Lee Greene Richards, *Louise Y. Robison* by John Willard Clawson, *Amy Brown Lyman* by Lee Greene Richards, *Belle S. Spafford* by Alvin Gittins, *Barbara B. Smith* by Cloy Kent, *Barbara W. Winder* by Cloy Kent
© by Intellectual Reserve, Inc.

Cover images:
Elaine L. Jack, Mary Ellen Smoot, Bonnie D. Parkin
© by Drake Busath/Busath Photography

Cover design copyrighted 2008 by Covenant Communications, Inc.

Published by Covenant Communications, Inc.
American Fork, Utah

Printed in Canada
First Printing: March 2008

15 14 13 12 11 10 09 08   10 9 8 7 6 5 4 3 2 1

ISBN 10: 1-59811-520-0
ISBN 13: 978-1-59811-520-8

CONTENTS

ACKNOWLEDGMENTS

We express appreciation to Kat Gille and Kathy Jenkins of Covenant Communications for their faith and expertise in completing this project. We warmly thank the past five general presidents of the Relief Society—Barbara B. Smith, Barbara W. Winder, Elaine L. Jack, Mary Ellen W. Smoot, and Bonnie D. Parkin—for sharing their lives, experiences, and testimonies with us. We also thank their families, counselors, and board members for their help. We are grateful to the descendants and associates of the deceased presidents for their generous assistance many years ago when we embarked on the first edition of this book. We appreciate our families' love and encouragement in our various writing endeavors.

PREFACE

When we thought of writing a book on the general presidents of the Relief Society in the late 1980s, we did not even know who all the presidents were. Emma Smith and Eliza R. Snow were firm in our minds as the first two presidents, Zina Young seemed a hazy third, and Emmeline B. Wells and Amy Brown Lyman fit in somewhere down the line. The later presidents, Belle Spafford, Barbara Smith, and Barbara Winder, we knew from our own experiences in Relief Society, but the middle group of presidents were names we had little acquaintance with. We felt we were in company with many women in the Church.

As we researched the lives of the women who had served as general presidents from the Relief Society's beginnings in 1842, we came to know women with completely different personalities, but whose commonality involved many threads of likeness—faith, service, compassion, obedience, trials, heartaches, endurance. We learned how these sisters, working through inspiration, guided the Relief Society organization from a gathering of twenty women to now the largest women's organization in the world. We also gained an understanding of how each president was called to serve at a particular time to lend her particular strengths and abilities to Relief Society.

This book was originally published in the spring of 1990 under the title *Elect Ladies: Presidents of the Relief Society*. At that time, Barbara W. Winder had just been released and Elaine L. Jack sustained as the new general president. More than fifteen years later, *Elect Ladies* needed to be updated with an in-depth report of Elaine's administration as well as the biographies of the two most recent presidents, Mary Ellen Smoot and Bonnie D. Parkin. We feel all the Relief Society general presidents need to be known by Latter-day Saint women throughout the Church, for their lives instruct, inspire, and testify of the truthfulness of the gospel of Jesus Christ. While all of the women who have served in this capacity have certainly been "elect ladies," our publisher felt it appropriate to retitle the book since it has been substantially updated from the original version. Now under the title *Faith, Hope, and Charity*, this volume chronicles the lives, service, and testimonies of the fourteen exemplary sisters who have led the Relief Society to become one of the largest organizations in the world.

Sarah M. Kimball, who originated the sewing circle that eventually became the circle of Relief Society sisters, served as general secretary in 1881. She prepared a jubilee box of photographs, documents, and memorabilia to be opened fifty years later. In 1930, not only a jubilee year but also the centennial of the organization of The Church of Jesus Christ of Latter-day Saints, Louise Y. Robison, then general president, opened the box.

Sarah wrote to her successor:

> Hon. Secretary: This is dedicated to you with the fond hope and firm belief that you are enjoying many advantages and blessings that were not enjoyed by your predecessors.
> May God abundantly bless you and your labors.
> [Signed] Sarah M. Kimball
> Sec. Relief Society
> Salt Lake City
> April 1st, 1881

Now in the twenty-first century, we Relief Society sisters around the world are indeed "enjoying many advantages and blessings that were not enjoyed by [our] predecessors" in 1930, 1881, or 1842. We have received a rich heritage of sisterhood from thousands of Relief Society sisters who, often under difficult conditions, have served each other and the Lord faithfully, building the organization of Relief Society as we now know it. To these pioneering sisters, and particularly to the fourteen Relief Society presidents who have led the Relief Society from a group of twenty women to now more than five and a half million sisters worldwide, we owe an immense debt of gratitude.

1

EMMA HALE SMITH
1842–1844

Relief Society's Beginnings

On March 17, 1842, in the Masonic Hall in Nauvoo, Illinois, twenty women and two men listened as Joseph Smith, Jr., Prophet and President of The Church of Jesus Christ of Latter-day Saints, organized the women of the Church and read a revelation he had received twelve years earlier, in 1830. "Thou art an elect lady, whom I [the Lord] have called," Joseph quoted. Emma Hale Smith, the elect lady referred to, was "an elect lady," the Prophet explained, because she was "elected to preside."[1]

Just moments before, thirty-seven-year-old Emma had been unanimously elected by her peers as the first president of the new women's organization. Hers was not a token presidency because she was the wife of the Prophet; she was a strong, independent woman in her own right. Her peers chose her to lead the Relief Society, a society dedicated to ministering relief to others, not only because they loved her and respected her intellect, but also because they knew well her compassion for human suffering.

The Relief Society had its beginnings in the 1830s in Kirtland, Ohio, during construction of the Kirtland Temple. There was much to be done, and as the temple was raised stone by stone, sisters from Kirtland and surrounding areas joined in the work. Some churned butter to send to the workmen, others cooked meals, and still others cleaned and polished the woodwork as it was completed. One day Joseph Smith entered the temple and saw the women working together sewing the temple veils. "Well, sisters," he said, "you are always on hand. The sisters are always first and foremost in all good works. Mary was the first at the resurrection; and the sisters now are the first to work on the inside of the temple."[2]

When the Saints moved to Nauvoo a few years later, women again joined together to help with the building of the Nauvoo Temple. And again, there were many tasks to be done. Sarah M. Kimball, wife of nonmember Hiram Kimball, and her seamstress sewed shirts for the men working on the temple. Knowing that additional hands could produce more clothing, they invited several neighbors to join with them in the Kimballs' parlor on March 4, 1842. As they worked, the women discussed the idea of a ladies' society. Their enthusiasm grew as the hours went by, and before the day was over, Eliza R. Snow had been asked to write a constitution and bylaws to present to the Prophet Joseph Smith.

According to Sarah Kimball's account, Joseph told Eliza that although the constitution and bylaws were the best he had ever seen, "this is not what you want. Tell the sisters their offering is accepted of the Lord, and He has something better for them than a written constitution. Invite them all to meet me and a few of the brethren in the Masonic Hall over my store next Thursday afternoon, and I will organize the sisters under the priesthood after a pattern of the priesthood."[3]

When the twenty sisters met with the Prophet on Thursday, March 17, Elders John Taylor and Willard Richards of the Quorum of the Twelve Apostles were also present. Addressing the group, Joseph put in words the "object of the Society": "that the Society of Sisters might provoke the brethren to good works in looking to the wants of the poor—searching after objects of charity, and in administering to their wants—to assist by correcting the morals and strengthening the virtues of the community."[4] At a later meeting, he told them they were "not only to relieve the poor, but to save souls."[5]

The women chose Emma Smith as their president, and she then selected Sarah M. Cleveland as first counselor and Elizabeth Ann Whitney as second counselor. John Taylor ordained the counselors and then gave Emma a blessing in which he "confirmed upon her all the blessings which have been conferred upon her, that she might be a mother in Israel and look to the wants of the needy, and be a pattern of virtue and possess all the qualifications necessary for her to stand and preside and dignify her office, to teach the females those principles requisite for their future usefulness."[6] He then suggested that the new organization be named the Nauvoo Female Benevolent Society. Emma objected to the word *benevolent* because of its association with corrupt organizations. Eliza Snow agreed, noting that their society should not follow the popular institutions of the day and should set its own course. "We are going to do something extraordinary," Emma explained. "When a boat is struck on the rapids with a multitude of 'Mormons' on board, we shall consider that a loud call for relief; we expect extraordinary occasions and pressing calls."[7] Her remarks were persuasive, and the name chosen was The Female Relief Society of Nauvoo.

Joseph donated a five-dollar gold piece for the initial funding of the society, and additional contributions at that meeting brought the total to $10.62. Members of the new society elected Eliza R. Snow as secretary, Phebe M. Wheeler, assistant secretary, and Elvira A. Coles, treasurer. Seven women who were not in attendance were accepted into membership, making a total of twenty-seven official members of the first Relief Society. Emma then discussed the duties of the members as she saw them: to "seek out and relieve the distressed—that each member should be ambitious to do good."[8]

Forty-four new members joined the society at its second meeting. They included Zina D. H. Young, who would be the third general president of the Relief Society; Mary Fielding Smith, wife of Joseph's brother Hyrum; and Lucy Mack Smith, mother of Joseph and Hyrum.

Lucy addressed the group. "This institution is a good one," she said. "We must cherish one another, watch over one another, comfort one another and gain instruction, that we may all sit down in heaven together."[9]

Vilate Kimball, wife of Heber C. Kimball, expressed her desire to be "found aiding in every benevolent cause,"[10] and Elizabeth Ann Whitney stressed the need to avoid the appearance of evil and to pray for one another so that the work might succeed. Emma then led a discussion on the needs of the poor and outlined proposals to help women obtain necessities and employment. She also suggested establishing societies in other Mormon communities. Soon branches of the Relief Society were organized in the neighboring towns of Macedonia and LaHarpe, Illinois.

Each week additional women joined the sisterhood. Of the first testimony meeting, held April 19, 1842, Eliza R. Snow recorded, "The meeting was very interesting, nearly all present arose & spoke, and the spirit of the Lord like a purifying stream, refreshed every heart."[11]

Joseph Smith attended several of the meetings. On April 28 he told the sisters: "You are now placed in a situation in which you can act according to those sympathies which God has planted in your bosoms. If you live up to these principles, how great and glorious will be your reward in the celestial kingdom! If you live up to your privileges, the angels cannot be restrained from being your associates."[12] After giving them further instructions, he added, "And I now turn the key to you in the name of God and this Society shall rejoice, and knowledge and intelligence shall flow down from this time—this is the beginning of better days to this Society."[13]

By summer, membership was so large that no building in Nauvoo could accommodate the women, so the Relief Society held its meetings outdoors in "the Grove," near the temple site. The sisters had much to do in assisting the poor, welcoming the ever-increasing number of newly arrived Saints, caring for the sick, and contending with persecution from anti-Mormon forces. During the late summer, Emma Smith, Eliza R. Snow, and Amanda Smith presented a petition to Illinois Governor Thomas Carlin on behalf of the Relief Society to plead for protection from suits pending against the Prophet.[14]

With membership over eleven hundred and a lack of indoor facilities during the winter, the Relief Society did not meet formally from September 1842 to June 1843, but the women continued to help one another. The "necessity committee," forerunner of today's visiting teaching, was organized in 1843 to search for those who were "poor and suffering." Emma led the way in compassionate service, not only by virtue of her calling but also by her compassionate nature. Emmeline B. Wells recalled: "Sister Emma was benevolent and hospitable; she drew around her a large circle of friends, who were like good comrades. She was motherly in nature to young people, always had a houseful to entertain or be entertained. She was very high-spirited and the brethren and sisters paid her great respect. Emma was a great solace to her husband in all his persecutions and the severe ordeals through which he passed; she was always ready to encourage and comfort him, devoted to his interests, and was constantly by him whenever it was possible. She was queen in her home, so to speak, and beloved by the people, who were many of them indebted to her for favors and kindnesses."[15]

When the Relief Society reconvened on June 16, 1843, Emma was away from Nauvoo, so her counselor Elizabeth Ann Whitney conveyed her instructions to "not only relieve the wants of the poor but also cast in our mites to assist the brethren in building the Lord's House."[16] With four wards in Nauvoo by then, Emma suggested dividing the Relief Society into separate ward groups with one set of officers serving all four groups. Elvira A. Coles (later Holmes), treasurer, reported the financial status of the society: five hundred dollars had been received, and four hundred dollars had been spent. She noted that "much good had been done, and the hearts of many had been made to rejoice."[17]

During its second year, 1843–44, only fourteen Relief Society meetings were reported, most of them in private homes. The sisters again adjourned for the winter months, reconvening in March 1844.

Emma presided at two meetings—one in the morning and one in the afternoon—on March 9, 1844. Both meetings were too crowded for all of the sisters who wanted to attend, so two additional sessions were planned for the following week. At the March 16 meetings, Emma expressed her desire to have all the sisters gather again when they could find an adequate building—not knowing that there would be no more meetings of the Female Relief Society of Nauvoo. Over the next few months escalating turmoil in Nauvoo would result not only in the martyrdom of the Prophet but also in the eventual expulsion of the Saints from Illinois. Thus, nearly two years to the day after its organization, the Relief Society ceased. It would remain disbanded for more than two decades, when it would be reorganized in a new place and under a new prophet.

Heritage

As a young girl, Emma Hale Smith could not have imagined the dramatic and difficult course her life would take.

Emma Hale Smith's father, Isaac Hale, a Connecticut-Vermont Yankee, joined the army in the Revolutionary War at age seventeen. Following the war, he decided not to farm the Vermont property he inherited from his grandfather and instead moved to the frontiers of Pennsylvania along the Susquehanna River. He returned to Vermont briefly to find a wife, and in 1790, he courted and married Elizabeth

Lewis, whose family had settled in Wells, Vermont. She was both strong and educated, qualities that suited her well for frontier life.

Isaac and Elizabeth, her brother Nathaniel, and his wife, Sarah, were among the first settlers in the Susquehanna Valley and bought adjoining tracts of land. A good hunter and farmer, Isaac provided well for his and Elizabeth's family, which eventually included nine children: Jesse, David, Alva, Isaac, Phoebe, Elizabeth, Emma, Tryal, and Reuben. Emma, the seventh child and third daughter, was born July 10, 1804.

Early Life

From her older brothers, Emma learned to ride horses expertly and to maneuver a canoe skillfully. Elizabeth taught her daughters to sew and cook, and the girls practiced their culinary talents by helping Elizabeth feed the boarders she took in to add to the family income. The children were taught at home until 1813, when enough people had settled in the valley to build a community schoolhouse. Emma was nine years old when the school opened. Several years later, her father sent her to a girls' school.

The Hales belonged to the Methodist Episcopal Church, of which Elizabeth remained a faithful member all her life. Isaac left the Methodist fold for a time until he heard his young daughter Emma pray for his return.

Emmeline B. Wells, who knew Emma as an adult, described the five-feet nine-inch Emma as "large and well proportioned, of splendid physique, dark complexion, with piercing eyes that seemingly looked one through; noble in appearance and bearing."[18] She also had a lyrical soprano voice, a spirited attitude, and a quick wit that reflected her natural intellect. A granddaughter described her as "a brilliant conversationalist," articulate in both writing and speech, adding that "Emma never used slang and was very particular about her grammar and her choice of words."[19]

Courtship, Marriage, and Family

At twenty-one years of age, she was teaching school when she met Joseph Smith, Jr.

Five years earlier, in 1820, Joseph had received a vision that was the beginning of the restoration of the kingdom of God to the earth—a work for which Joseph's name would be "had for good and evil among all nations, kindreds, and tongues."[20] He also received a series of visitations from an angel named Moroni, who revealed to him the location of an ancient record inscribed on gold plates and prepared him for the time when he would receive the plates for translation.

In October 1825, Joseph left his home near Palmyra, New York, and went with his father, Joseph Smith, Sr., to Harmony, Pennsylvania, to work for a farmer named Josiah Stowell. Stowell hired the Smiths and several other men to help him dig for a silver mine he believed existed near Harmony. Having heard of Joseph's vision, Stowell thought he would be able to divine precious metals. The workers boarded at the Hale home, near the site of the supposed mine, and there Joseph met Emma. A month later, when the project was abandoned and his father returned home, Joseph stayed on with Josiah Stowell and worked on his farm.

Isaac Hale did not like the Stowell crew in general, and Joseph Smith in particular—especially since Emma was attracted to the handsome young man, who was over six feet tall and had light brown hair and blue eyes. Besides objecting to Joseph's religious claims, Isaac thought he was uneducated and without a reputable occupation and was, therefore, not a suitable match for his daughter. Emma said that her father not only bitterly opposed their marriage, but twice refused to give Joseph permission to marry her.

On January 18, 1827, Joseph and Emma eloped. Emma recalled in her later years that she had no intention of marrying when she left home that winter morning but "preferring to marry him to any other man,"[21] she rode with Joseph to South Bainbridge, where Squire Zachariah Tarbell married them in his home. Joseph was twenty-one years old, and Emma, eighteen months older.

Fearing her father's wrath, Emma did not return home for any of her belongings. Instead, the newlyweds went directly to the home of Joseph's parents in Manchester, New York, near Palmyra. Though she had not previously met her new daughter-in-law, Lucy Mack Smith welcomed Emma, and they soon became dear friends.

By summer, Isaac Hale was willing to make peace with his daughter and agreed to give Emma her clothing and some furniture and cows. When Emma and Joseph visited the Hale home, Isaac's welcome was short-lived, for he was still angry with Joseph for taking his daughter and for not having a decent occupation. Nevertheless, he invited them to live with the Hale family in hopes that he could help Joseph get started in a profitable and worthwhile business. He offered the couple thirteen acres and a small cabin to live in. Emma and Joseph moved to Harmony in December 1827—but for different reasons than Isaac had expected. Three months earlier, on September 22, Joseph had gone to the Hill Cumorah and received the gold plates from Moroni, along with a charge to use all his efforts to protect them. When word reached the community that Joseph had gold plates, persecution and threats multiplied. The greedy and the curious attacked him or broke into his home to try to steal the plates. To protect them, Joseph moved them several times, including placing them in a box under the hearthstone of his parents' home and then in his father's cooper shop in a pile of flags. Finally, Martin Harris, an affluent friend, gave Joseph fifty dollars to help him and Emma move away from the increasing persecution in Palmyra.

In December, Joseph and Emma, now pregnant, began the four-day trip to Harmony, thinking it would provide the peace Joseph needed to concentrate on his translation work. To protect the plates during the move, he hid them in the bottom of a forty-gallon barrel of beans.

The Smiths lived in the cabin on the Hale farm for the next two and a half years, and it was there that Joseph translated the characters on the plates. Emma served as his first scribe. Although she never saw the actual plates, she felt them. "The plates often lay on the table without any attempt at concealment, wrapped in a small linen table-cloth which I had given him [Joseph] to fold them in," she recalled. "I once felt the plates as they lay on the table, tracing their outline and shape. They seemed to be pliable like thick paper, and would rustle with a metallic sound when the edges were moved by the thumb, as one does sometimes thumb the edges of a book."[22]

Martin Harris visited the Smiths in Harmony in February 1828 and returned two months later to take over as Joseph's scribe. His wife, Lucy, accompanied him and stayed for two weeks, disrupting the Smith household. Because Lucy thought Joseph an imposter and feared that Martin would continue to give him financial support, Martin begged

Joseph to let him show her the translation. After repeatedly taking Martin's request to the Lord, Joseph received permission for Martin to take the 116 pages that had been translated to show only to certain family members. Martin left Harmony on June 14, taking the manuscript with him to show Lucy in Palmyra.

The next day, June 15, Emma gave birth to a son, whom she and Joseph named Alvin, after Joseph's deceased brother. The child died a few hours after birth. With Emma critically ill for several weeks, Joseph put aside translating to care for her. As she began to recover, she wondered, as did Joseph, why Martin had not returned the manuscript, so she suggested that Joseph go back to Palmyra to locate Martin and the manuscript. When Martin confessed that he had lost the 116 pages, Joseph despaired: "O, my God! All is lost, is lost! What shall I do? I have sinned. It is I who tempted the wrath of God by asking him for that which I had no right to ask, as I was differently instructed by the angel."[23]

Joseph feared not only the Lord's wrath but also the effect the news would have on Emma's health. She finally recovered, and in February 1829, Joseph resumed translating, with Emma again serving as scribe. Shortly thereafter, in April, Joseph's brother Samuel brought Oliver Cowdery, a teacher who had boarded with the Smith family in Manchester, to meet Joseph. Oliver agreed to serve as scribe for Joseph's translation, and he remained until the translation was completed.

With the translation completed, Joseph now sought a way to get the book published. Much to Lucy Harris's dismay, her husband, Martin, mortgaged his farm to pay for the printing of five thousand copies of the book, which was now known as the Book of Mormon, and on March 26, 1830, the finished books went on sale in Palmyra. Eleven days later, on April 6, Joseph gathered a group of believers together at the Peter Whitmer farm in Fayette, New York, to organize a church, the restored Church of Jesus Christ. Nearly sixty people crowded into the farmhouse. For legal purposes, six of those present— Joseph Smith, Jr., Oliver Cowdery, Hyrum Smith, Peter Whitmer, Jr., Samuel H. Smith, and David Whitmer—were named as the founding six members of the organization.

Emma Smith was not present at that first meeting, but two months later, on June 28, she was baptized in a dammed-up stream near Colesville, New York. The baptism was marred by a jeering mob, and before her confirmation could take place that evening, a constable arrived with a warrant for Joseph's arrest. Emma watched helplessly as her husband was led away to jail. After two hasty trials, Joseph was released from jail, and he and Emma returned to Harmony.

An "Elect Lady"

In July 1830 at Harmony, the Lord gave to Emma through her husband, Joseph, a revelation that is now section 25 of the Doctrine and Covenants. In it Emma was told:

> Behold, thy sins are forgiven thee, and thou art an elect lady, whom I have called. . . . And the office of thy calling shall be for a comfort unto my servant, Joseph Smith, Jun., thy husband, in his afflictions, with consoling words, in the spirit of meekness. . . . And thou shalt be ordained under his hand to expound scriptures, and to exhort the church, according as it shall be given thee by my spirit. . . .

> And verily I say unto thee that thou shalt lay aside the things of this world, and seek for the things of a better. And it shall be given thee, also, to make a selection of sacred hymns, as it shall be given thee, which is pleasing unto me, to be had in my church. For my soul delighteth in the song of the heart; yea, the song of the righteous is a prayer unto me, and it shall be answered with a blessing upon their heads.

> Wherefore, lift up thy heart and rejoice, and cleave unto the covenants which thou hast made. . . . Keep my commandments continually, and a crown of righteousness thou shalt receive.

The couple stayed in Harmony only two months before returning to Fayette. When she left Harmony, Emma bade farewell to her parents for the last time; she would not see them again. During the following winter at Fayette, Joseph received a revelation commanding the Saints to move west to Kirtland, Ohio. Emma was again pregnant, and on April 30, not long after they arrived in Kirtland, she gave birth to twins, a boy and a girl. The babies, who were given the names Thaddeus and Louisa, died the same day. By coincidence, the following day Julia Murdock, a newly baptized member, died while giving birth to healthy twins, a boy and a girl. John Murdock, realizing he could not care for his babies, asked Joseph if he and Emma would adopt them. The Smiths, grateful for this opportunity, agreed, and they named the twins Joseph and Julia.

For the first three years they were in the Kirtland area, Joseph and Emma lived in the homes of others. In the fall of 1831 they moved to the farm of John Johnson near Hiram, Ohio, thirty miles south of Kirtland. Six months later, on March 24, a drunken mob burst through the door at night and dragged the Prophet from his bed into the snow, tore off his clothes, and smeared his body with tar. In the confusion, baby Joseph, who was ill with measles, was exposed to the cold. That night Emma helped peel the tar from her husband, and for the next five days she tried desperately to save the baby, but he died on March 29. Emma and Joseph had now buried four of their five children. At the time, she was in the fourth month of another pregnancy.

Immediately after the baby's burial, on April 1, Joseph left on a journey to Missouri on Church business. Fearing that the mob would return, he advised Emma to take Julia back to Kirtland to stay with the Newel K. Whitneys, with whom they had boarded when they first arrived in Kirtland. But Sister Whitney's aunt was visiting and refused to allow Emma to stay, so she sought shelter with others. Over the next two and a half months, until Joseph returned, she and baby Julia stayed with three different families. Soon after he returned, he secured a small apartment for his family above the Whitney store, and that would be their home for the next two and a half years, as well as the center of Church activity. Their son Joseph III was born while they lived there, and to Joseph and Emma's great joy, he was a healthy baby.

Emma was, in part, responsible for Joseph's receiving the revelation known as the Word of Wisdom. During the winter of 1833, Joseph established the School of the Prophets to teach languages, geography, and doctrine. The school met in the Smith apartment. The men who attended the school smoked pipes and chewed tobacco, and Emma complained to her husband about having to clean up the room after they left. After thinking about the conduct of the men, particularly as it pertained to tobacco, Joseph prayed to the Lord. In response he received a revelation outlining a health code that forbade the use of tobacco and strong drink and urged the use of fruits and grains in season and meat eaten sparingly.

As the Prophet's wife, Emma welcomed many visitors to the small apartment. Guests remembered seeing her often in an apron, the corner of which she would finger as she talked. She also frequently wore a string of gold beads Joseph had given her. Lucy Mack Smith said of her daughter-in-law's hospitality: "How often I have parted every bed in the house for the accommodation of the brethren, and then laid a single blanket on the floor for my husband and myself, while Joseph and Emma slept upon the same floor, with nothing but their cloaks for both bed and bedding."[24] In December 1834, Joseph Smith, Sr., presiding patriarch of the Church, gave blessings to Joseph and Emma. Emma's blessing addressed many of the difficulties of her life, including her father's anger, the persecutions against Joseph, and the loss of her babies; it also made known the role she would play in Relief Society in instructing the women of the Church.[25]

Emma experienced two other important events in 1836. First was the birth of a son, Frederick Granger Williams Smith, on July 20—another healthy boy. The second was Emma's completion of the hymnal she had been instructed to compile. The collection was published in 1836, although the title page had an 1835 date: "A collection of SACRED HYMNS, for the Church of the Latter Day Saints. Selected by Emma Smith, Kirtland, Ohio: Printed by F. G. Williams & Co 1835." Included in the book were well-known Methodist hymns and many new hymns written by Church members such as Eliza R. Snow, W. W. Phelps, Edward Partridge, and Emma herself. She worked on subsequent revisions in 1839 and 1842.

As hostilities against the Saints in Ohio escalated, plans were made to move the Church's headquarters to Jackson County, Missouri, which had been identified by revelation in 1831 as Zion, the "central gathering place" of the Saints. Narrowly escaping mob violence in Ohio, Joseph left for Missouri in January 1838. Emma, again pregnant, left

Kirtland soon afterward and joined him in Far West, Missouri. There a son, Alexander Hale, was born on June 2. In good humor despite her difficult circumstances, Emma noted that at Alexander's birth, a regular "Halestorm" occurred.

In Missouri the Saints received an extremely hostile reception, with mobs again destroying their property and trying to drive them out. As a result, Emma not only lived in poverty, sharing what little she had with those in need, but also suffered persecution. In early November, she watched in terror and in tears, with her children clinging to their father's legs, as a mob dragged him and his brother Hyrum away to jail in Liberty, Missouri. Emma nursed Hyrum's wife, Mary Fielding Smith, who was hovering near death after the birth of her first child. Later that month, Emma visited her husband for several days in the dark, cramped jail. She returned to the jail in December 1838 and again in January 1839 with Mary Fielding Smith.

As the persecutions increased in Missouri, Emma and her children were forced to flee Far West in February 1839 with a group headed by Stephen Markham. They headed east across Missouri and the frozen Mississippi River to Illinois, with Emma carrying her two babies, Alexander and Frederick, while Joseph III and Julia clutched her skirts. Joseph's papers were tied to her waist in cloth bags under her dress. She wrote in a poignant letter to her husband:

> No one but God, knows the reflections of my mind and the feelings of my heart when I left our house and home, and almost all of everything that we possessed excepting our little children, and took my journey out of the State of Missouri, leaving [you] shut up in that lonesome prison. But the reflection is more than human nature ought to bear, and if God does not record our sufferings and avenge our wrongs on them that are guilty, I shall be sadly mistaken.[26]

In April, Joseph escaped from Liberty Jail and appeared at the home of John and Sarah Cleveland, in Quincy, Illinois, where Emma and the children were staying. Emma recognized the pale man in rags and ran into his arms.

Nauvoo, "the Beautiful"

The Saints were offered property at Commerce, Illinois, some fifty miles north of Quincy. Although the site, on the east bank of the Mississippi River, was low-lying and swampy, Joseph saw its potential for becoming a prosperous river port. The Saints purchased the land, and the Smith family, along with other refugee Saints, moved to Commerce, whose name Joseph changed to Nauvoo, which he said meant "the beautiful." Within just five years, Nauvoo became a thriving community, second in size in Illinois only to Chicago.

In Nauvoo, Emma at last had her own home. A two-story log house, which the Smiths named the Homestead, was built for her family. A constant stream of Saints from other parts of the United States and from Europe arrived in Nauvoo, and many were invited to lodge temporarily with Joseph and Emma. By 1842, more space was needed to house the arrivals, so a larger home, the Mansion House, was built on a corner lot across from the Homestead. Eventually, the Mansion House had twenty-two rooms; the Prophet's family occupied three, and the rest served as hotel rooms. W. W. Phelps once remarked to Emma, as she struggled to feed the many visitors, that Joseph should have a smaller table in order to limit the number of guests, as did Napoleon. Her reply was, "Joseph is a bigger man than Napoleon; he could never eat without his friends."[27]

Establishing their new headquarters in Nauvoo and surrounding environs wasn't without difficulties and sorrows for the Saints, however. The swampy marshlands bred mosquitoes that carried malaria, and hundreds of the Saints became ill with the disease, or swamp fever, as it was called. Many died in the epidemic, including Don Carlos, Emma and Joseph's son who had been born in Nauvoo on June 14, 1840. Despite the threat to their own lives, Joseph and Emma opened their home to the sick. And when there was no more room in the house, Joseph and Emma gave up their own bed and slept in a tent in the yard. Emma's nursing skills and her kindness in sharing her store of herbs and medicines endeared her to the Saints.

Five months after the death of Don Carlos, Emma anxiously awaited the birth of another baby to fill her empty arms. A son was born but died at birth, unnamed. Emma was so heartbroken that Joseph made arrangements with the MacIntires, who had recently had twin girls, to allow Emma to care for one of the twins during the day. Joseph returned the baby girl to her parents every evening. When this child died two years later, Joseph and Emma grieved as if she were their own. Emma mothered a number of children whose own mothers had died or who, for whatever reason, needed a home.

Although Emma constantly faced heartache, hard work, and worry about her husband's safety, she nevertheless found relief and pleasure in hostessing parties, leading a parade on horseback dressed in her black velvet riding habit, attending plays, singing, and teaching and delighting in her children. In one letter to Joseph, who was often away from home, she wrote: "Little Alexander who is now in my arms is one of the finest little fellows, you ever saw in your life. He is so strong that with the assistance of a chair he will run all round the room."[28]

Emma also found joy and comfort in the love and support she received from her husband, the Prophet. On one occasion, when he was forced to leave Nauvoo to avoid arrest, she managed to join him after dark at an island on the Mississippi River between Nauvoo and Montrose, Iowa. He wrote of that meeting:

> With what unspeakable delight, and transports of joy swelled my bosom, when I took by the hand, on that night, my beloved Emma—she that was my wife, even the wife of my youth, the choice of my heart. Many were the reverberations of my mind when I contemplated for a moment the many scenes we had been called to pass through, the fatigues and the toils, the sorrows and sufferings, and the joys and consolations, from time to time, which had strewed our paths and crowned our board. Oh what a commingling of thought filled my mind for the moment, again she is here, even in the seventh trouble—undaunted, firm, and unwavering—unchangeable, affectionate Emma.[29]

The Nauvoo Temple was not yet completed when Hyrum Smith performed the sealing ceremony for Joseph and Emma on May 28, 1843, at the Old Homestead. In September of that year Emma was the first woman to receive the temple endowment, which was given to her in the upstairs room of the Mansion House. She then presided over the administration of the temple ordinances for the women.

Although Joseph and Emma often signed their letters to each other "forever" and "eternally yours," only through the power of the priesthood could they be sealed for all eternity in the new and everlasting covenant of marriage. Earlier the Prophet had received a revelation that instituted among the Saints the practice of plural marriage. Emma struggled with this doctrine, and in what would become section 132 of the Doctrine and Covenants, the Lord instructed her to "receive all those that have been given unto my servant Joseph" (v. 52). Although at one point she apparently accepted it, she never fully embraced the principle, and in her later years she publicly denied that Joseph had ever practiced the doctrine.

Polygamy was one of the key issues that fired anti-Mormon feelings against the Saints in Illinois, and Joseph, the primary target of that hatred, had a price put upon his head. All during the month of June 1844, tension in Nauvoo mounted, climaxing with the city council's order to destroy the anti-Mormon newspaper, the *Nauvoo Expositor*. Joseph and several others were charged and tried for instigating a riot. Their acquittal outraged many Illinois citizens, who threatened to march on Nauvoo if the new governor, Thomas Ford, did not cooperate with their demands. Convinced that the Mormons were guilty of various crimes, Governor Ford tried to schedule another trial. But Joseph, realizing that the mobs wanted him and Hyrum, decided to go across the river to Iowa and then head west. Emma, who was again pregnant, sent a letter to him through Porter Rockwell and begged him to return to Nauvoo. Joseph came back and spent his last night with Emma and the children. Accompanied by about twenty men, he left the next day for Carthage, some twenty miles southeast of Nauvoo, to answer the charges in the *Expositor* incident, though he knew he was going "as a lamb to the slaughter."

Emma wanted Joseph to give her a blessing before he left, but since there wasn't time, he suggested that she write out the blessing she desired and he would sign it upon his return. After his departure, Emma composed what she termed "the desires of my heart":

> First of all that I would crave as the richest of heaven's
> blessings would be wisdom from my Heavenly Father
> bestowed daily, so that whatever I might do or say, I

could not look back at the close of the day with regret, nor neglect the performance of any act that would bring a blessing. I desire the Spirit of God to know and understand myself, that I desire a fruitful, active mind, that I may be able to comprehend the designs of God, when revealed through his servants without doubting. I desire a spirit of discernment, which is one of the promised blessings of the Holy Ghost.

I particularly desire wisdom to bring up all the children that are, or may be committed to my charge, in such a manner that they will be useful ornaments in the Kingdom of God, and in a coming day arise up and call me blessed.

I desire prudence that I may not through ambition abuse my body and cause it to become prematurely old and care-worn, but that I may wear a cheerful countenance, live to perform all the work that I covenanted to perform in the spirit-world and be a blessing to all who may in any wise need aught at my hands.

I desire with all my heart to honor and respect my husband as my head, ever to live in his confidence and by acting in unison with him retain the place which God has given me by his side, and I ask my Heavenly Father that through humility, I may be enabled to overcome that curse which was pronounced upon the daughters of Eve. I desire to see that I may rejoice with them in the blessings which God has in store for all who are willing to be obedient to his requirements. Finally, I desire that whatever may be my lot through life I may be enabled to acknowledge the hand of God in all things.[30]

Joseph, Hyrum, Willard Richards, and John Taylor were locked in the upper room of the jail in Carthage. Late in the afternoon of June 27, a mob with blackened faces overpowered the guards, rushed up the stairs of the jail, and fired shots through the closed door, killing Hyrum. Shots were also fired through the window from the outside. John Taylor was wounded, and one bullet struck his pocket watch, stopping it at 5:16. The mob then broke through the door and fired at Joseph, while others outside the jail continued to shoot through the window. Crying "O Lord my God!" Joseph, mortally wounded, fell through the window to the ground.

Lorenzo Wasson, a nephew, broke the news to Emma that Joseph and Hyrum were dead; others went to tell Lucy Mack Smith, the brothers' mother, and Hyrum's wife, Mary. The women, in shock, were overcome with grief. When a friend tried to console Emma, telling her that her sorrow would be the crown of her life, she responded, "Joseph was my crown."[31]

Eliza R. Snow wrote of Emma after Joseph's death:

> I knew her ere she had been left
> In her heart's loneliness—
> Before her prospects were bereft
> Of all its happiness.
> I've seen the willow bending low,
> And 'tis unbroken still.[32]

Emma and Joseph's last child, David Hyrum, was born November 17, 1844, five months after the Prophet died. One of the greatest sorrows of Emma's life was the fact that out of eleven Smith children (including two who were adopted), just five lived beyond childhood. Frederick died at age twenty-six, and only Julia, Joseph III, Alexander, and David Hyrum lived through adulthood.

Emma's Last Years

Emma elected not to go west with Brigham Young and the majority of Saints in the exodus from Nauvoo that began in February 1846, choosing instead to remain in Illinois with about a thousand other Mormons. Perhaps the years of poverty and homelessness she had endured contributed to her decision, for she reportedly said in her own defense, "You may think I was not a very good Saint not to go West, but I had a home here and did not go because I did not know what I should have there."[33] Contention between Emma and Brigham over the disposition of properties and possessions in Joseph's name may also have influenced her decision.

Although she wanted to remain in Nauvoo, Emma feared the continued anti-Mormon sentiment in the area, so she took her family to Fulton, Illinois, for six months. When she returned to Nauvoo and reopened the Mansion House, she took in boarders for income, as she had done many times before.

In the next few years Emma had several suitors, but it was Lewis Bidamon who won her hand. She was then forty-three and he was forty-five. Handsome and charming, he was nicknamed "the Major" because he occasionally wore military attire. Twice married, Lewis was not religious and imbibed liquor, but Emma and her children admired his sense of humor and his generosity. She welcomed Lewis's two daughters into the family, and Lewis, in turn, helped raise her children. While he did not believe that Joseph Smith was a prophet of God, he would not allow anyone to criticize him.

Lucy Mack Smith went to live with Emma and Lewis in 1851. Lucy regarded Emma highly, writing in her history:

> I have never seen a woman in my life, who could endure every species of fatigue and hardship, from month to month, and from year to year, with that unflinching courage, zeal, and patience, which she has ever done; for I know that which she had had to endure: She has been tossed upon the ocean of uncertainty; she has breasted the storms of persecution, and buffeted the rage of men and devils, which would have borne down almost any other woman.[34]

When Lucy became too crippled with arthritis to walk or to feed herself, Lewis built her a wheelchair and Emma tended to her every need. Lucy's death on May 14, 1856, ended her thirty-year relationship as mother-in-law and close friend of Emma.

As Mrs. Bidamon, Emma continued as she had always done, caring for the sick and taking people into her home. She welcomed her grown children, as well as Lewis's, to live with them at various times. She raised Charles, Lewis's illegitimate son, then hired his mother,

Nancy Abercrombie, as a housekeeper so Nancy could be with her son. Weeks before her death, Emma asked Lewis to marry Nancy. A year later they married.

Although Emma no longer affiliated with the main body of the Saints and her sons later led the Reorganized Church of Jesus Christ of Latter Day Saints, she continued to testify that Joseph was a prophet and that the work he was instrumental in restoring was divine. A few years before her death, she was quoted by her son Alexander Hale Smith as declaring, "I know Mormonism to be the truth; and believe the church to have been established by divine direction."[35] To Parley P. Pratt she reportedly said: "I believe [Joseph] was everything he professed to be."[36] In her last recorded testimony she said, "My belief is that the Book of Mormon is of divine authenticity. I have not the slightest doubt of it. . . . Though I was an active participant in the scenes that transpired, and was present during the translation of the plates . . . and had cognizance of things as they transpired, it is marvelous to me, 'a marvel and a wonder,' as much so as to anyone else."[37]

In the early morning hours of April 30, 1879, Emma lay weak and dying in her Nauvoo home. Suddenly she called, "Joseph, Joseph, Joseph." Her husband, Lewis, and her children, Julia, Joseph III, and Alexander, witnessed her passing as she murmured, "Joseph! Yes, yes, I'm coming."[38]

Two days later, the family held a funeral service for Emma in the Mansion House. Speakers remembered her "loving hand, her consoling and comforting words, her unswerving integrity, fidelity, and devotion, her wise counsel."[39] On a bank overlooking the Mississippi River, in the yard of the Homestead, she was buried beside Joseph, whose unmarked grave she showed to her sons before her death.

Emma Hale Smith was an elect lady. As first president of the Relief Society, she filled a role different from that of her successors, serving at a younger age and for a shorter time than any of the other Relief Society presidents. Circumstances and personal struggles kept her from moving to Utah with the rest of the Church. But although she no longer affiliated with the restored Church or the reinstated Relief Society, she continued throughout her life to act in the spirit of her office, which, as she told the sisters in 1842, was to "seek out and relieve the distressed . . . [to] be ambitious to do good."[40]

Notes

1. Minutes of the Female Relief Society of Nauvoo, March 17, 1842, Archives, The Church of Jesus Christ of Latter-day Saints [hereafter cited as LDS Church Archives]. This source is hereafter cited as Minutes.

2. Edward W. Tullidge, *The Women of Mormondom* (New York, 1877), p. 76.

3. "Story of the Organization of the Relief Society," *The Relief Society Magazine* 6 (March 1919): 129.

4. Minutes, March 17, 1842.

5. Minutes, June 9, 1842; also Joseph Smith, *History of the Church [HC]* 5:25.

6. Minutes, March 17, 1842; also "Story of the Organization of the Relief Society," p. 133.

7. Ibid., pp. 134–35.

8. Minutes, March 17, 1842.

9. Minutes, March 24, 1842.

10. *History of the Relief Society, 1842–1966* (Salt Lake City: General Board of the Relief Society, 1966), p. 21.

11. Ibid.

12. *HC* 4:605.

13. Minutes, April 28, 1842.

14. *History of the Relief Society,* p. 22.

15. "LDS Women of the Past: Personal Impressions," *Woman's Exponent* 36 (February 1908): 1.

16. *History of the Relief Society,* p. 22.

17. Ibid., p. 22.

18. "LDS Women of the Past: Personal Impressions," p. 1.

19. Quoted in Raymond T. Bailey, "Emma Hale Smith: Wife of the Prophet Joseph Smith" (master's thesis, Brigham Young University, 1952), p. 13.

20. Joseph Smith—History 1:33.

21. Joseph Smith III, "Last Testimony of Sister Emma," February 1879, in possession of the archives of the Community of Christ, Independence, Missouri.

22. Ibid.

23. Lucy Mack Smith, *The Revised and Enhanced History of Joseph Smith by His Mother,* ed. Scot Facer Proctor and Maurine Jensen Proctor (Salt Lake City: Bookcraft, 1996), pp. 165–66.

24. Lucy Mack Smith, *Biographical Sketches of Joseph Smith the Prophet and His Progenitors* (Liverpool, 1853), p. 250.

25. Emma Hale Smith, Patriarchal Blessing, given December 9, 1834, Kirtland, Ohio, Patriarchal Blessing Book No. 1, LDS Church Archives.

26. Emma Smith to Joseph Smith, March 9, 1839, Joseph Smith letterbooks, LDS Church Archives.

27. *HC* 5:107.

28. *HC* 6:165–66; also Gracia N. Jones, *Emma's Glory and Sacrifice: A Testimony* (Hurricane, Utah: Joseph Smith, Jr., Family Organization, 1987), p. 138.

29. Emma Smith to Joseph Smith, March 7, 1839, Joseph Smith letterbooks, LDS Church Archives.

30. Copy of blessing in LDS Church Archives; copy of blessing also in possession of Gracia N. Jones.

31. B.W. Richmond, as quoted in E. Cecil McGavin, *Nauvoo the Beautiful* (Salt Lake City: Stevens and Wallis, 1946), p. 144.

32. Eliza R. Snow, "The Bereaved Wife," *Poems: Religious, Historical, and Political,* 2 vols. (Liverpool, 1856, and Salt Lake City, 1877), 1:149–50.

33. Statement of Nels Madsen, November 27, 1931, LDS Church Archives.

34. *The Revised and Enhanced History of Joseph Smith by His Mother,* p. 249.

35. Alexander Hale Smith, sermon delivered July 1, 1903, at Bottineau, North Dakota, as reported by L. A. Gould, *Zion's Ensign,* December 31, 1903, p. 76.

36. Parley P. Pratt, Jr., and Nels Madsen, interview with Emma Smith Bidamon; statement of Nels Madsen, November 27, 1931, LDS Church Archives.

37. "Last Testimony of Sister Emma."

38. "The Memoirs of President Joseph Smith III (1832–1914)," *Saints Herald,* November 26, 1935, p. 186.

39. *History of the Reorganized Church of Jesus Christ of Latter-day Saints* (Independence: Herald House, 1973), pp. 268–70.

40. Minutes, March 17, 1842.

2

ELIZA R. SNOW
1866-1887

On a summer day in 1887, Stake President Angus Cannon drove his carriage up Salt Lake City's South Temple Street to the Lion House, where eighty-three-year-old Eliza R. Snow waited. Slight and frail, Eliza had to be lifted in President Cannon's arms to the waiting carriage. This was not the first time he had taken Eliza for an afternoon carriage ride, and it would not be the last, but today the ride would be different. As Eliza enjoyed the warm sunshine, she made her funeral requests known to President Cannon.[1] She had already written her own eulogy:

'Tis not the tribute of a sigh . . .
From sorrow's heaving bosom drawn,
Nor tears that flow from pity's eye,
To weep for me when I am gone . . .

In friendship's mem'ry let me live. . . .
For friendship holds a secret cord,
That with the fibres of my heart,
Entwines so deep, so close; 'tis hard
For death's dissecting hand to part!

I feel the low responses roll,
Like the far echo of the night,
And whisper, softly through my soul,
"I would not be forgotten quite."[2]

An organizer of rare ability, Eliza tended to the details of her funeral with the same energy and strength of purpose as she had tended to countless Relief Society projects during her twenty-one years as president. At her funeral, she said, the choir was to sing the opening hymn—her masterpiece, "O My Father," which spoke of returning to live with heavenly parents. She suggested another detail of importance: the Assembly Hall was to be draped in white and filled with white flowers. She wanted no black, only white, the symbol of hope.

New England Childhood

Priestess, prophetess, and presidentess.[3] These are titles by which Eliza Roxey Snow was known through the fourscore and three years of her life. She was born on January 21, 1804, in Becket, Massachusetts, the second child of Oliver and Rosetta Pettibone Snow. When her older sister, Leonora, was four and Eliza two, the family moved to Mantua, Ohio, then a heavily wooded frontier. There, five more children were born: Percy, Melissa, Lorenzo, Lucius, and Samuel. Eliza was especially close to her brother Lorenzo. Though he was ten years her junior, the two had much in common, including their love of books and intellectual pursuits. They both loved history and felt pride in their Revolutionary War heritage.

Eliza and her brothers and sisters worked hard and learned self-discipline as their parents maintained New England values in their home on the Western Reserve of Ohio. Rosetta Snow taught her daughters how to keep a clean and orderly home, and during these early years she taught Leonora and Eliza how to sew. Both became skilled seamstresses and called upon their sewing skills many times throughout their lives. Eliza also learned to weave straw and won first prize two years in a row at the county fair for her leghorn hats.

Oliver Snow held various public offices, and Eliza often helped him with clerical duties. This early working experience, which also brought her into association with community leaders, may have helped her to develop her organizational and verbal skills and to explore new ideas.

Throughout her life, Eliza often expressed her feelings and ideas in writing, especially poetry. Once, as a child, she even wrote a school assignment in verse. As a young poet, she used pseudonyms to avoid drawing attention to herself, but her talents were soon recognized. When two former United States presidents, John Adams and Thomas

Jefferson, died on July 4, 1826, she was asked to write a requiem,[4] and with the publication of this poem she received national recognition. However, she did not write the requiem for fame; she wrote it out of a deeply instilled sense of patriotism. "I was born a patriot," she said. "Narratives of revolutionary sufferings recounted by my grand-parents, so deeply impressed my mind, that as I grew up to womanhood I fondly cherished a pride for the flag which so proudly waved over the graves of my brave and valiant ancestors."[5]

Despite Eliza's patriotic sentiments, she opposed Lorenzo's decision as a young man to join the military. However, she agreed to sew his military uniform. "It was beautiful, magnificent," she wrote, "and my brother donned it with as much, if not of military pride, of self-satisfaction as ever Napoleon won a battle."[6]

The Snows were a religious family. They regularly attended the Baptist Church in Mantua, where Oliver served as a deacon. But, Eliza wrote, their home "was a welcome resort for the honorable of all denominations."[7] At one meeting in their home, they heard the preaching of Sidney Rigdon, then a follower of Alexander Campbell. For a time the Snows affiliated with the Campbellites, but when Sidney Rigdon left the Campbellites and joined The Church of Jesus Christ of Latter-day Saints, the Snows, too, learned of the restored gospel. "It was what my soul hungered for," wrote Eliza, "but . . . I considered it a hoax—too good to be true."[8]

Mantua was not far from Kirtland, Ohio, where the new Church established its headquarters in early 1831. One evening that year Joseph Smith came to the Snows' home, and as he sat near the fire and told the family about his vision of the Father and the Son in a grove near his parents' home in upstate New York, Eliza studied his face. "I decided that his was an honest face," she later wrote.[9]

Rosetta Snow and her daughter Leonora joined the Church soon after Joseph's visit, but Eliza was not baptized until four years later, in the spring of 1835. "I had to battle very strongly with the powers of darkness," she explained. "The evil one brought forth many strong arguments against my joining the Church, and it was with difficulty that I overcame them. I finally commanded Satan to depart from me. Then my mind was again enlightened and filled with the spirit of God, and I had firmness sufficient to ask for baptism."[10]

Eliza wrote of her feelings following baptism:

> I realized the baptism of the Spirit as sensibly as I did that of the water in the stream. I had retired to my bed and as I was reflecting on the wonderful events transpiring around me, I felt an indescribable, tangible sensation, if I may so call it, commencing at my head and enveloping my person and passing off at my feet, producing inexpressible happiness. Immediately following, I saw a beautiful candle with an unusual long, bright blaze directly over my feet. I sought to know the interpretation, and received the following, "The lamp of intelligence shall be lifted over your path."[11]

"Zion's Poetess" and Schoolteacher

Eliza's creative work went in a different direction after she joined the Church. "For thy approval, Lord, shall prompt my pen," she wrote.[12] National recognition as a poet was no longer her goal; she now saw her poetry serving two purposes: as a means to cheer the Saints and teach them the doctrine of the gospel, and as a vehicle for personal expression, "when there's nobody here but Eliza and I."[13] Within the Church, her talents became highly esteemed. Joseph Smith referred to her as "Zion's poetess," a title that was hers for life and has endured to this day.

Eliza's meticulous and precise approach to everything she did carried over into her appearance. She loved elegant yet feminine clothes. She put extra yards of material into her dresses and trimmed them elaborately, which complemented her slender build and above-average height and added to her graceful, lofty carriage. A high forehead and large, deep-set eyes gave her a regal countenance.[14] Her speech was eloquent and dynamic.

Shortly after Eliza's baptism, Joseph Smith asked her to leave Mantua and go to Kirtland to teach his daughter and nieces in the Smith home. Eliza accepted and, as one of the first school-teachers in the Church, taught in that "select school for young ladies."[15]

During the next three years, as Eliza boarded with the Smiths and continued to teach school in their home, she developed a great love and respect for the Prophet. She wrote of him:

> Again I had ample opportunity of judging of his daily walk and conversation, and the more I made his acquaintance, the more cause I found to appreciate him in his divine calling. His lips ever flowed with instruction and kindness. . . . His expansive mind grasped the great plan of salvation. . . . Three times a day he had family worship; and these precious seasons of sacred household service truly seemed a foretaste of celestial happiness.[16]

When Eliza was asked for a contribution for the construction of the Kirtland Temple, she willingly gave all the money she had. Although Joseph offered her a note in return, she refused to take it, accepting instead a lot near the temple with a two-family home on it. She remained with the Prophet's family and let her sister Leonora and two children live in half the house. She likened the acquiring of this two-family home to "many other trivial events in human life, [which] proved to be one of the little hinges on which events of immense weight occasionally turn."[17]

Not long after Eliza acquired the home, her brother Lorenzo, who had been attending a college of religion, became disillusioned with his studies. He wrote to her, "If [they] have nothing better to offer than this, then good-bye to all religions."[18] Eliza seized this opportunity to invite him to Kirtland, where he could live in the vacant half of her home and study Hebrew at the School of the Prophets. He accepted. Once in Kirtland, he was impressed with Joseph Smith and the other leaders of the Church. He studied Hebrew and also learned of the principles of the gospel, and in June 1836 he was baptized in the Chagrin River, the last member of the Snow family to join the Church.

While living in Kirtland, Eliza became friends with Zina D. Huntington, and a lasting friendship was begun. Both Eliza and Zina would later serve as presidents of the Relief Society, and in their later years would travel together to visit the sisters of the Church.

To Missouri and Nauvoo

As persecution against the Church intensified in Ohio, many of the Saints fled to Missouri, which the Saints called "Zion." Eliza, her parents, two sisters, three brothers, and Leonora's two daughters left Kirtland in the spring of 1838, planning to go to Adam-ondi-Ahman, Missouri, where they hoped to establish a new home. Lorenzo became very ill during the journey, and Eliza held his head in her arms to absorb the shocks as the wagon jolted over the rough roads. When they arrived at Far West, Lorenzo was still very ill, so Eliza volunteered to remain there with him while the rest of the family continued on to Adam-ondi-Ahman. They stayed in Far West with Sidney Rigdon for two weeks, until Lorenzo was well enough to travel.

Though the Saints had hoped to find refuge in western Missouri, anti-Mormon persecution was intensifying. Finally, in 1839, Missouri Governor Lilburn W. Boggs gave the Saints just ten days to leave the state or face extermination. Eliza's father helped widows and others in need, while Eliza directed her family's preparations.

The Snows were among the last to leave the area. The family began their trek back across Missouri on a bitterly cold day, with snow covering the ground. Eliza walked alongside the wagon in order to stay warm and to keep her feet from freezing. Soon the militia overtook them. One of the men shouted at Eliza, "Well, I think this will cure you of your faith!" Eliza stared at him and replied, "No, sir. It will take more than this to cure me of my faith."

Surprised at her response, the man meekly commented, "I must confess, you are a better soldier than I am." She later wrote: "I passed on, thinking that, unless he was above the average of his fellows in that section, I was not highly complimented by his confession."[19] She viewed the expulsion from Missouri and the bitter persecution of the Saints as "a dark, foul stain on the Eagle's crest."[20]

When they left Missouri, the Snows lost many of their possessions, including two homes. Soon after they arrived at Quincy, Illinois, forty miles south of Nauvoo, Eliza and Leonora went to the town of Lima to find work as seamstresses. There they rented an upstairs room from a local family. One evening their landlord loudly criticized the Mormons. Then, after considerable shouting, he changed his tone and praised the "two noble women" who lived upstairs. "No better women ever lived," he proclaimed quietly.[21] Fearing persecution, the sisters had not told the landlord that they were Mormons.

Eventually, members of the Snow family were reunited in Nauvoo. Their peace was short-lived, however, for the spring of 1842 brought unrest to both the Church and the Snows. Some of the family were becoming somewhat disenchanted with the Church, and that year they moved to Walnut Grove, Illinois, seventy-five miles from Nauvoo. Oliver wrote to his son Lorenzo: "Eliza cannot leave our Prophet. Mother [Rosetta] did not like to. For my part I am very glad, at present, to be away. Turmoil and confusion, these stalk abroad at noon day."[22]

This turn of events was upsetting to Eliza. She wondered in her journal why her parents "did not in their trials draw out from the springs of consolation which the gospel presents that support which was their privilege, and which would have enabled them to rejoice in the midst of tribulation and disappointment."[23]

Eliza remained deeply committed to the Church, as did her brother Lorenzo. In about May 1840, an incident took place between brother and sister that reveals their trust in each other. One day as Lorenzo was studying the scriptures, "the eyes of my understanding were opened," as he would later describe the experience, and he formed in his mind the following couplet:

> As man now is, God once was:
> As God now is, man may be.

Lorenzo felt this to be a sacred communication, and he related it only to Eliza at the time. Three years later he recited the couplet to the Prophet Joseph Smith, and Joseph replied that it was "a true gospel doctrine, and a revelation from God."[24]

Despite her personal heartache over her parents' diminishing faith, Eliza's seven years in Nauvoo were a time of wonderful flowering in her life. Again she taught school in the home of the Prophet, and when the Relief Society was organized on March 17, 1842, she was called to be secretary. Among her duties were maintaining orderly minute books and seeing that the meetings began and ended on time. She did not own a watch, so the Prophet laid his own gold watch on the table for her to use. Later, he gave it to her as a gift.[25]

This gift possibly represented more to Joseph than simply a means of accurate timekeeping. "I was sealed to the prophet, Joseph Smith, for time and eternity," Eliza wrote in her journal in the early summer of 1842, "in accordance with the celestial law of marriage which God had revealed. . . . This, one of the most important events of my life, I have never had cause to regret."[26] The sealing took place on June 29. Eliza retained her maiden name, possibly to avoid calling unnecessary attention to Joseph's plural marriages, but throughout her life she referred to Joseph Smith as "her first and only love . . . the choice of her heart and the crown of her life."[27]

When Joseph and his brother Hyrum were martyred on June 27, 1844, Eliza was overcome with grief, unable to eat or to sleep, and even pleaded with the Lord to let her die also. One night as she lay in bed still sorrowing, Joseph appeared to her and told her she must not desire to die. Though his mission was complete, he said, hers was not—the Lord desired her to live and to help build up His kingdom. She was to be of good cheer and help lighten the burdens of others.[28]

This vision served as a motivation for Eliza for the rest of her life. From that time forward, she put her grief to work for her and dedicated her talents to the Church. "The mob in the vicinity of Nauvoo, knowing that I wielded the pen, had threatened my life, lest, as they said, I should write about the tragic scene at Carthage," she wrote. "Although I had neither fear nor dread of death, I felt as I expressed in the following":

> Let us go—let us go to the wilds for a home
> Where the wolf and the roe and the buffalo roam—
> Where beneath our own vines, we in peace may enjoy
> The fruits of our labors, with none to annoy.
>
> Let us go—let us go where our Rights are secure—
> Where the waters are clear and the atmosphere pure—
> Where the hand of oppression has never been felt
> Where the blood of the prophets has never been spilt.

Let us go—let us go where the Kingdom of God
Will be seen in its Order extending abroad—
Where the Priesthood of heaven, unopposed will go forth
In the regeneration of man and of earth.[29]

In October 1844, Eliza R. Snow became a plural wife of Brigham Young. Though this was primarily a marriage of respect and convenience, it provided Eliza with security.

During the following year, 1845, Eliza lived in an attic room at the home of Stephen Markham. It had been a year since the death of the Prophet. The mother of her dear friend Zina Huntington had also died. Contemplating these events, Eliza took up a small gold pencil given to her by Joseph Smith and wrote of eternal life:

O my Father, thou that dwellest
In the high and glorious place!
When shall I regain thy presence,
And again behold thy face?
In thy holy habitation,
Did my spirit once reside;
In my first primeval childhood,
Was I nurtured near thy side?

For a wise and glorious purpose
Thou hast placed me here on earth
And withheld the recollection
Of my former friends and birth;
Yet ofttimes a secret something
Whispered, "You're a stranger here,"
And I felt that I had wandered
From a more exalted sphere.

I had learned to call thee Father,
Thru thy Spirit from on high,
But, until the key of knowledge
Was restored, I knew not why.
In the heav'ns are parents single?

No, the thought makes reason stare!
Truth is reason; truth eternal
Tells me I've a mother there.

When I leave this frail existence,
When I lay this mortal by,
Father, Mother, may I meet you
In your royal courts on high?
Then, at length, when I've completed
All you sent me forth to do,
With your mutual approbation
Let me come and dwell with you.[30]

In February 1846, Nauvoo, "the city beautiful," was in chaos as once again the Mormons were driven from their homes. Eliza went with the Markham family across the frozen Mississippi River and began the long journey westward with the Saints. On the journey she learned to drive a team of oxen. She wrote about the experience: "Had it been a horse-team I should have been amply qualified, but driving oxen was entirely a new business; however, I took the whip and very soon learned to 'haw and gee,' driving most of the way to Winter Quarters."[31]

At Winter Quarters, a temporary stopping place built by the Saints on the west bank of the Missouri River opposite Council Bluffs, Iowa, Eliza became ill with "a slow fever that terminated in chills and fever." She wrote: "Sometimes wet nearly from head to foot, I realized that I was near the gate of death; but my trust was in God, and his power preserved me."[32]

Keeper of the Flame

When she recovered, both her practical and spiritual skills were put to use. With her abilities as a seamstress, she helped the women to prepare wagon covers, clothing, and camping equipment. And, as the sisters gathered in tents or cabins in the evenings, Eliza and other leaders, including Zina D. H. Young, bore their testimonies and shared their spiritual gifts. Entries such as "spent the eve[ning] at Sarah Ann's—had a pow'rful time—deep things were brought forth which were not to be spoken,"[33] and "truly a glorious time with the mothers

& daughters of Zion,"[34] filled Eliza's diary. "I then blest the girls in a song," she wrote on one occasion, "singing to each in rotation."[35] Spiritually invigorated, Eliza even left a meeting on Tuesday, June 8, after a heavy rain, "with Loisa & Zina in the mud rejoicing."[36]

In many ways, these meetings were an extension of the spirit of the Relief Society, which had been disbanded in Nauvoo in March 1844. With nearly half of the households headed by women (for many a temporary situation),[37] it is not surprising that the women would reach out to one another for support. One woman's account lists 217 out of 556 days filled with visits or meetings of women.[38] Eliza's natural leadership skills kept her at the forefront of such activities, and many sisters looked to her for spiritual strength and direction.

For Eliza, these gatherings filled a need for companionship. Now forty-two years old, she had lived most of her life without a husband or children. As a plural wife of Brigham Young, while she was part of a large polygamous family, she had few close family ties. Most of the Snow family remained in Illinois when the Saints left Nauvoo.

Sometime in the winter of 1846–47, Eliza received word of her mother's death in Walnut Grove, Illinois, on December 22, 1846. Leonora left Winter Quarters and returned to Walnut Grove to help care for the family. Eliza wrote that she felt "a sweet consolation inasmuch as she [Rosetta] is freed from the ills of the present life."[39] Eliza's father, Oliver, had died in October 1845, four months before Eliza left in the exodus from Nauvoo. Of the Snow family, only Leonora, Lorenzo, and Eliza traveled west with the Saints.

As the winter of 1846–47 passed, preparations began to be made for the trek west. Gathering her belongings together, Eliza noticed that an indispensable item was missing, and with her last remaining dime she purchased a bottle of ink.[40] From this ink bottle and her pen came remarkable songs, letters, and journal entries written as she traveled to the Salt Lake Valley.

With the coming of summer, Eliza joined the second company that departed Winter Quarters, traveling with the Robert Pierce family. She had packed the minute books from the Relief Society in Nauvoo and now brought them west with the same careful concern for their preservation that she had exhibited in writing them. By day on the trail, she intermittently drove the horses or visited with other women as they walked beside the wagons. At night, she climbed into her wagon box and took up her pen and ink and wrote. Though the trek was strenuous, Eliza's heart overflowed with song. The Saints rejoiced in fervently singing all seven verses of her composition "Camp of Israel, Number One." Upon crossing the Mississippi River she wrote "Camp of Israel, Number Two." And on the banks of the Platte River, she penned "Song of the Desert":

> Beneath the cloud-topp'd mountain—
> Beside the craggy bluff,
> Where every dint of nature
> Is wild and rude enough:
> Upon the verdant meadow—
> Upon the sun-burnt plain—
> Upon the sandy hillock,
> We waken music's strain.
> Beneath the pine-tree branches
> Which have for ages stood—
> Beneath the humble cedar,
> And the green cotton-wood:
> Beside the broad smooth river—
> Beside the flowing spring—
> Beside the limpid streamlet,
> We often sit and sing.
> Beneath the sparkling concave,
> When stars in millions come
> To cheer the weary strangers
> And bid us feel at home.
> Amid the cheering moon-light,
> Fair Cynthia's mellow rays
> In social groups we gather,
> And join in songs of praise.
> Cheer'd by the blaze of fire-light,
> When evening shadows fall,
> And when the darkness deepens
> Around our spacious hall;
> With true and warm emotion

To saintly bosoms given,
In strains of pure devotion
We praise the God of heaven.[41]

In the Valley of the Mountains

When the company arrived in the Salt Lake Valley in August 1847, Brigham Young arranged for Eliza to live with Clara Decker, another of his wives, in one of the eighteen-foot square log houses that lined the walls of the Old Fort. It was not long before a spirit of sisterhood, similar to that in Winter Quarters, found its way into meetings held in these log dwellings. The women found many of the same spiritual experiences and the same leaders surrounding them, in the absence of a formal organization, that they had experienced in Nauvoo and Winter Quarters. The nucleus of the Relief Society was still intact; the flame still burned brightly.

A humorous incident that occurred after one of these meetings exemplifies Eliza's optimism:

> The roof of our dwelling was covered deeper with earth than the adjoining ones. Consequently it did not leak so soon and some of my neighbors huddled in for shelter; but one evening, when several were socially sitting around, the water commenced dripping in one place, and then in another; they dodged it for awhile, but it increased so rapidly that they finally concluded they might as well go to their own wet houses. After they had gone I spread my umbrella over my head and shoulders as I ensconced myself in bed . . . . During the night, despite all the discomfort, I laughed involuntarily while alone in the darkness of the night I lay reflecting on the ludicrous scene. . . . The storm was much worse indoors than out, and as the water . . . pattered on the floor, [it] washed stones from the earth above, and they went clink, clink, while numerous mice . . . ran squealing back and forth.[42]

In 1856, Eliza moved into the Lion House, which Brigham Young had built to house many of his wives and children. President Young respected Eliza's intellect and valued her opinion. She always sat on his right at the dinner table and at family prayers. Clarissa Young Spencer, a daughter of Brigham Young, described Eliza: "She was slight and fragile and always immaculate in dress. I see her now in her full-skirted, lace-trimmed caps and a gold chain around her neck, looking for all the world like a piece of Dresden china."[43]

After the Saints arrived in the Salt Lake Valley, Eliza suffered from ill health. In May 1855, when the Endowment House was dedicated, President Young asked her to preside over the ordinance work of the sisters. He coupled his request with a blessing that her health would improve if she accepted the call. Eliza accepted. After all, she had once written, "To be able to do Father's will is what I wish to live for."[44] She chose to serve, and good health returned.

Eliza's service in helping to prepare the sisters for the sacred temple ordinances undoubtedly gave her a special aura. Historian Maureen Ursenbach Beecher has written, "It is understandable that Eliza's image would take on a special holiness in the eyes of the women of the church, that the aura of the sacred mystery that surrounds the ordinances of the temple should somehow cling to Eliza. It did indeed become a part of the legend, an addition to the sanctity that already clothed her in the eyes of her contemporaries."[45] Eliza apparently had special gifts of the spirit, and many individuals recorded blessings she had given them that resulted in healings and prophecies concerning future potential.

As the Church grew in the arid environs of the Great Basin, Eliza's poetry and songs continued to inspire hope in the Savior and in the future just as they had done on the trek west. "How Great the Wisdom and the Love," "In Our Lovely Deseret," "Behold the Great Redeemer Die," "Truth Reflects upon Our Senses," and "Though Deepening Trials" were some of her hymns sung in the boweries of town squares, in newly built meetinghouses, and in the Saints' homes. The lyrics of these hymns endeared the sometimes aloof Eliza to the people in a way that would have been unlikely on a one-to-one basis.

Called as Relief Society President

Finally, by 1866, Brigham Young called upon the bishops to organize a Relief Society in each ward. Eliza, who had helped keep the spirit of Relief Society burning over all those years, was given "a mission to assist them in organizing, and to take with her Sister Zina D. Young."[46]

"We recommend these Female Relief Societies to be organized immediately," Brigham Young said on December 18, 1867, as he again advised the bishops to organize Relief Societies in every ward. "We have many talented women among us, and we wish their help in the matter. . . . You will find that the sisters will be the mainspring of the movement. . . . Let a sister appeal for the relief of the suffering and poverty, and she is almost sure to be successful. If you take this course you will relieve the wants of the poor."[47]

Eliza's first important job as president was to rekindle the spirit of the Relief Society, which she had loved and nurtured for twenty-three years, and to reestablish its place in the Church. Her primary goal continued to be to establish the organization after the pattern set in Nauvoo by the Prophet Joseph Smith. As she traveled to the various wards, she told the Saints about that original Relief Society and bore her testimony of Joseph as a prophet of God.

As Relief Society president, Eliza also echoed the priorities that her mother had taught her in her childhood. "Let your first business be to perform your duties at home," she said. "Inasmuch as you are wise stewards, you will find time for social duties, because these are incumbent upon us as daughters and mothers in Zion. By seeking to perform every duty, you will find that your capacity will increase, and you will be astonished at what you can accomplish."[48] However, she was quick to see spiritual aspects in everything temporal, encouraging the sisters not to "let go [of the] Golden Harp and take up the Wooden Whistle."[49]

Eliza also exhibited a sense of mercy toward and understanding of the women of the Church, declaring: "There are many of the sisters whose labors are not known beyond their own dwellings and perhaps not appreciated there, but what difference does that make? If your labors are acceptable to God, however simple the duties, if faithfully performed, you should never be discouraged."[50]

When Eliza was asked to collect handmade items from the sisters of the Church to display in Philadelphia at an exposition celebrating the U.S. Centennial in 1876, she was overwhelmed with articles. Since there was not enough money to ship all of the items to the exposition, she organized a territorial exhibition to be held in the Constitution

Building on Main Street in Salt Lake City. This fair opened on July 4, 1876, and ran for two months. As the exhibition drew to a close, Eliza realized that this was an opportunity for women to sell their items. With Brigham Young's approval, she started the Women's Commission Store, which prospered.[51]

Paradoxically, while Eliza was supportive of the women's suffrage movement and a leader of Mormon women, she was not a leader in the suffrage movement. A conference for women held January 13, 1870, in Salt Lake City was one of the few occasions on which she spoke out on the subject. She told the more than six thousand women in attendance:

> Our enemies pretend that, in Utah, woman is held in a state of vassalage—that she does not act from choice, but by coercion. What nonsense!
>
> I will now ask of this assemblage of intelligent ladies, Do you know of any place on the face of the earth, where woman has more liberty and where she enjoys such high and glorious privileges as she does here as a Latter-day Saint? No! the very idea of a woman here in a state of slavery is a burlesque on good common sense. . . . As women of God, filling high and responsible positions, performing sacred duties—women who stand not as dictators, but as counselors to their husbands, and who, in the purest, noblest sense of refined womanhood, are truly their helpmates—we not only speak because we have the right, but justice and humanity demands we should![52]

A Natural Leader

Eliza R. Snow's role in the programs of the Church in early Salt Lake City was distinctive. Brigham Young respected her intelligence and leadership abilities and entrusted her with major responsibilities. Few women possessed as much power and independence as she did; yet it was her dauntless loyalty, obedience, and submission to the Church's leaders that provided her with that power and independence and made it possible for her to serve as a link between the women and the priesthood.

With minor exceptions, Eliza and President Young saw eye to eye on things. One exception is illustrated in the following story: "On one occasion he [Brigham Young] gave his older daughters colorful sashes. When Phoebe Young laid her sash out on the bed while dressing for a dance, the ribbon disappeared. Confronted by President Young, Eliza replied, 'I felt that you wouldn't approve of anything so frivolous for your girls so I put it away.'

"'Sister Eliza,' said her husband, 'I gave the girls those ribbons, and I am judge of what is right and wrong for my girls to wear. Phoebe is to have her sash.'"[53]

Eliza relented, but her true feelings on the subject again became evident in many of the standards established for the Young Ladies Retrenchment Association (now the Young Women organization), which Eliza helped to organize in 1869.

This was not the only organization Eliza R. Snow had a hand in founding. Concurrent with her position as Relief Society president, she aided Louisa L. Greene with the creation of the *Woman's Exponent* in 1872 and helped Aurelia S. Rogers in establishing the Primary Association in 1878.

On June 19, 1880, the leaders of the women's organizations were gathered together for the purpose of firmly establishing their leadership. Eliza R. Snow, as president of the Relief Society, was officially given counselors: Zina D. H. Young as first counselor and Elizabeth Ann Whitney as second counselor. "Mother Whitney," as Elizabeth was affectionately referred to, had had the distinction of having served as second counselor to Emma Smith, first president of the Relief Society. The presidencies of the Primary and of the Young Ladies' Mutual Improvement Association were also established.

Eliza and Zina traveled throughout the territory as they served together in the Relief Society presidency. One of the homes they visited in Pleasant Grove was that of Margaret Zimmerman Brown, mother of Amy Brown Lyman. Amy, who would become the eighth president of the Relief Society, described Eliza as "dignified, reserved, and rather cold, so much so that one would hesitate to approach her or to assume any familiarity whatever. She was so powerful and able, however, that she impressed people, even children, with her superior intelligence, wisdom, vision, and leadership, and won their admiration and confidence. 'Aunt Zina' as we knew her, was a gentle, kind, honey-hearted woman, beloved for her graciousness and the warmth of her soul, for her generous and tender service to the sick, needy, unfortunate, and discouraged. . . . No hand was ever held out to her but that succor was forthcoming."[54]

One of the highlights of Eliza's years as president took place in 1872–73 when she went to the Holy Land with her beloved brother Lorenzo and a group of other Church leaders. Eliza was especially grateful to the women who took up a collection to pay her fare. While there, President George A. Smith rededicated the land for the return of the Jews. Eliza and Lorenzo basked in the spirit of the Savior as they visited many of the places where He had lived, had ministered to the people, and had taught them His Father's plan.[55]

The need for women to serve as nurses, midwives, and even doctors was an early priority for Eliza. Classes in home nursing and midwifery were organized, and many young women—including Ellis Shipp Reynolds and Romania Penrose Pratt—were encouraged to go east to study medicine. As these women returned to practice medicine in the Salt Lake Valley, Brigham Young established the Deseret Hospital Association. Eliza served as president of the association's board of directors in 1881, and on July 17, 1882, she became the first president of the new Deseret Hospital.

Eliza R. Snow devoted much of her life to the women of the Church, nurturing the sisters for more than four decades and serving for twenty-one years as general president of the Relief Society. Through all these experiences her spirit remained strong and vibrant, though her physical health declined. She died at the Lion House on December 5, 1887, just a month before her eighty-fourth birthday. "She seemed to be one of those perfect women that was prepared for the age," said President Jacob Gates of the First Council of the Seventy at her funeral, "and [she] represent[ed] her sex in this great Latter-day work, and nobly filled the mission for which she was appointed."[56] She was buried on a hillside near the Lion House in President Brigham Young's private cemetery.

Eliza R. Snow indeed became a legend during her own lifetime. Women, now as then, honor her as a great woman, but to practical Eliza, "greatness" was simply "usefulness."[57] "I will go forward," she wrote in a summary of her beliefs and goals. "I will smile at the rage of the tempest, and ride fearlessly and triumphantly across the boisterous ocean of circumstance . . . and 'the testimony of Jesus' will light up a lamp that will guide my vision through the portals of immortality, and communicate to my understanding the glories of the Celestial kingdom."[58]

Notes

1. Maureen Ursenbach Beecher, "Eliza: A Woman and a Sister," *New Era,* October 1974, p. 16.

2. Eliza R. Snow, "My Epitaph," *Times and Seasons* 4 (April 15, 1843): 176.

3. Maureen Ursenbach Beecher, "Eliza R. Snow," in *Sister Saints,* ed. Vicky Burgess-Olsen (Provo: Brigham Young University Press, 1978), p. 3.

4. *Western Courier,* August 5, 1826, in *Sister Saints,* p. 5, footnote.

5. Edward W. Tullidge, *The Women of Mormondom* (New York, 1877) pp. 30–31.

6. Eliza R. Snow Smith, *Biography and Family Record of Lorenzo Snow* (Salt Lake City, 1884), p. 4.

7. *Eliza R. Snow: An Immortal* (Salt Lake City: Nicolas G. Morgan Sr. Foundation, 1957), p. 4. A holograph of the original manuscript, Eliza R. Snow, "Sketch of My Life," is in the Bancroft Library, Berkeley, California.

8. *Eliza R. Snow: An Immortal,* p. 6.

9. Ibid.

10. Minutes of the Senior and Junior Cooperative Retrenchment Association, June 22, 1872, LDS Church Archives.

11. *Eliza R. Snow: An Immortal,* p. 6

12. Eliza R. Snow, "Two Chapters of the Life of President Joseph

Smith," *Poems, Religious, Historical, and Political,* 2 vols. (Liverpool, 1856, and Salt Lake City, 1877), 1:15.

13. Ibid., 1:3–6.

14. Jaynann M. Payne, "Eliza R. Snow, First Lady of the Pioneers," *Ensign,* September 1973, p. 62.

15. *Eliza R. Snow: An Immortal,* p. 7.

16. Ibid.

17. Ibid., pp. 7–8.

18. Ibid., p. 8.

19. Ibid., p. 10.

20. Eliza R. Snow, "Appeal to Americans," *Poems, Religious, Historical, and Political,* 1:60.

21. Beecher, "Eliza: A Woman and a Sister," p. 15.

22. Maureen Ursenbach Beecher, "Leonora, Eliza, and Lorenzo: An Affectionate Portrait of the Snow Family," *Ensign,* June 1980, p. 67.

23. LeRoi C. Snow, "Devotion to a Divine Inspiration," *Improvement Era,* June 1919, p. 656.

24. Eliza R. Snow, Diary, December 22, 1846, LDS Church Archives; also, Beecher, "Leonora, Eliza, and Lorenzo," p. 67.

25. Ivan J. Barrett, *Heroines of the Church* (Provo: Brigham Young University Press, 1966), p. 59.

26. Tullidge, *The Women of Mormondom,* pp. 295–96.

27. *Woman's Exponent* 15 (August 1, 1886): 37.

28. Andrew Jensen, *Biographical Encyclopedia* 1:695.

29. *Eliza R. Snow: An Immortal,* pp. 17–18.

30. *Hymns,* 1985, no. 292.

31. *Eliza R. Snow: An Immortal,* p. 21.

32. Ibid., p. ii.

33. Eliza R. Snow, Diary, June 3, 1847, LDS Church Archives; also *Sister Saints,* p. 10.

34. Snow, Diary, June 1, 1847.

35. Snow, Diary, June 6, 1847; also *Sister Saints,* p. 10.

36. Snow, Diary, June 8, 1847.

37. Maureen Ursenbach Beecher, "Women at Winter Quarters," *Sunstone* 8 (July–August 1983): 12.

38. Ibid., p. 13.

39. Snow, Diary, December 22, 1846.

40. *Church News,* November 23, 1963, p. 16.

41. *Eliza R. Snow: An Immortal,* p. 28.

42. Ibid., pp. 350–51.

43. Clarissa Young Spencer and Mabel Harmer, *Brigham Young at Home* (Salt Lake City: Deseret Book, 1963), pp. 82–83.

44. Eliza R. Snow address, "Salt Lake Stake Relief Society Conference," September 15, 1887, *Woman's Exponent* 16 (October 1, 1887): 70.

45. *Sister Saints,* p. 12.

46. Kate B. Carter, *History of the Relief Society* (Salt Lake City: Daughters of Utah Pioneers, 1970), pp. 11–12.

47. Brigham Young, *Journal of Discourses* 12 (December 8, 1867): 115.

48. Jill Mulvay Derr and Susan Oman, "The Nauvoo Generation," *Ensign,* December 1977, p. 38.

49. Maureen Ursenbach Beecher, "Eliza Roxey Snow's Way to Sainthood," *Woman's Exponent II,* Winter 1984, p. 12.

50. "Speech by Eliza R. Snow," July 29, 1868, *Woman's Exponent* 19

(May 1, 1891): 167; also *Ensign,* December 1977, p. 38.

51. Maureen Ursenbach Beecher, "U.S. Centennial," *Church News,* July 5, 1976, p. 16.

52. Maureen Ursenbach Beecher, "Eliza R. Snow," in *Mormon Sisters,* Claudia L. Bushman, ed. (Cambridge, Massachusetts: Emmeline Press, 1976), p. 32.

53. Clarissa Young Spencer, *One Who Was Valiant* (Caldwell, Idaho: Caxton Printers, 1940), p. 76; also Beecher, "Eliza R. Snow," in *Mormon Sisters,* pp. 28–29.

54. Amy Brown Lyman, *In Retrospect* (Salt Lake City: General Board of the Relief Society, 1945), p. 38.

55. Eliza R. Snow Smith, *Biography and Family Record of Lorenzo Snow,* Letters I–XV.

56. *Life and Labors of Eliza R. Snow* (Salt Lake City: Juvenile Instructor Office, 1888), p. 21.

57. *Woman's Exponent II,* Winter 1984, pp. 11–12.

58. *Eliza R. Snow: An Immortal,* frontispiece; also in Eliza R. Snow, *Poems, Religious, Historical, and Political,* pp. 147–48.

3

ZINA D. H. YOUNG
1888–1901

"In my earliest reading of history, Confucius, Columbus, and William Wallace, I used to muse while watching the consuming back log in our old fashion fireplaces why I could not have been born in a day when something was going on in the nations of the Earth, not that I wished to see distress, but some enterprise."[1]

So wrote Zina Diantha Huntington, who, as the daughter of a prosperous New York farmer, enjoyed a comfortable childhood—although to her thinking an uneventful one.

Unbeknownst to Zina at the time, however, something was "going on," an "enterprise" in its beginning stages that would alter the course of her life, her family's, and that of the entire world. In 1820, one year prior to her birth, Joseph Smith had received the First Vision. The subsequent translation and publication of the Book of Mormon and the organization of The Church of Jesus Christ of Latter-day Saints in 1830 set in motion "the stone . . . cut out of the mountain" (Daniel 2:45), the restoration of the gospel—the enterprise she desired. Zina herself would assume a major role in the dramatic unfolding of the restored Church as the third general president of the Relief Society and as a wife of the first two presidents of the Church.

Zina's mother, Zina Baker Huntington, seemed to have a presentiment of this great drama. She had written to her own mother, Dorcas Dimick Baker, in 1817: "I think sometimes I am fitting for the approach of some great event, but hope I shall ever be prepared for all that awaits me, and ever feel reconciled to God's will and rejoice in his government."[2]

Heritage

Zina Huntington's ancestors participated in significant events in American history. Simon Huntington, an English Puritan, sailed for America in 1633 but died at sea, leaving a widow and three sons to join the Massachusetts colony. Samuel Huntington, Zina's great-uncle and a signer of the Declaration of Independence, was, according to family tradition, the source of the Uncle Sam symbol of the United States. As governor of Connecticut and president of the Continental Congress, Samuel was frequently consulted by the colonists for his expertise on a wide variety of subjects, and was known to many as "Uncle Sam."[3] William Huntington, Zina's paternal grandfather, enlisted in the Revolutionary army and was one of the first settlers in the Black River Valley in northern New York. Zina's father, also named William, fought in the War of 1812.

Zina Diantha was born January 31, 1821, in Watertown, Jefferson County, New York, the seventh of nine children of William and Zina Baker Huntington. The first two children, Chauncey and Nancy, were twins; Nancy died as an infant. Another daughter, Adaline, also died in childhood. The other children were Dimick, William, Oliver, John, and Presendia.

William cleared three hundred acres of land for farming and built a comfortable story-and-a-half stone house in Watertown for his sizable family. Before morning prayers each day, the family read aloud a chapter from the Bible. After supper and evening chores, they often gathered around the fireplace and enjoyed folk tunes and hymns, with Father Huntington playing the bass viol; Zina, the cello; William, Jr., the cornet; and Dimick, the drum.

William and his family were strict Presbyterians until a controversy developed between the Presbyterians and the Congregationalists over the method of appointing the clergy. The Presbyterians believed that clergymen should be chosen and appointed by the clergymen themselves, while the Congregationalists believed that the clergy should be chosen by the people. William Huntington decided to join the sect that followed the proper form of worship, and to determine this, he studied his Bible to see what it said.

Zina later recalled her impressions of her father's quest:

I can remember my father sitting quietly perusing the Bible, determined to find the right way, his firm lips closed with the determination to succeed if success was possible. After many hours of study and reading, aided no doubt with hours of anxious prayer, father one day declared that none of the churches were right according to the way he read the Bible, for none of them had the organization peculiar to the primitive church. There were no prophets, no apostles, no spiritual gifts as were possessed by the ancient saints. Nothing could shake him from this belief, and the more he thought and conversed upon the matter, the plainer and simpler it seemed to be presented to his understanding.[4]

A "New and Golden Bible"

At that time a rumor began circulating that a prophet in a "distant country" had found a "new and golden Bible." That "distant country" was actually not far off, Watertown being only a hundred miles from the Hill Cumorah. William Huntington had spent many hours discussing religion with a neighbor, Joseph Wakefield. Both were anxious to meet this so-called prophet, and they decided that one of them should go. Joseph seemed the best candidate because as a cooper, or barrelmaker, he was not working in the winter, while William, a farmer, had animals to feed. Joseph Wakefield left at once. He met Joseph Smith, gained a testimony of the truthfulness of the restored gospel, and returned with a copy of the Book of Mormon and a heart full of zeal for this new book of scripture.

Zina recorded that she knew of the divinity of the Book of Mormon even before she read it: "One day on my return from school I saw the Book of Mormon, that strange, new book, lying on the window sill of our sitting-room. I went up to the window, picked it up, and the sweet influence of the Holy Spirit accompanied it to such an extent that I pressed it to my bosom in a rapture of delight, murmuring as I did so, 'This is the truth, truth, truth!'"[5]

Zina's parents were baptized in April 1835, but she did not join the Church until August, when Hyrum Smith and David Whitmer visited the Huntington home. One morning at prayers, she felt the time had come for her baptism. "I had presented to me a heavenly vision of a man going down into the water and baptizing someone," she wrote. "So when this message came I felt it was a testimony that the time had come for me to receive baptism."[6] She was baptized by Hyrum Smith that very day, August 1, 1835, along with her brother Dimick and his wife, Fanny. Zina was fourteen years old.

Zina wrote:

> Soon after this, the gift of tongues rested upon me with overwhelming force. I was somewhat alarmed at this strange manifestation, and so checked its utterance. What was my alarm, however, to discover that upon this action upon my part, the gift left me entirely, and I felt that I had offended that Holy Spirit by whose influence I had been so richly blessed.
>
> I suffered a great deal in my feelings over this matter, and one day while mother and I were spinning together, I took courage and told her of the gift I had once possessed, and how, by checking it I had lost it entirely.
>
> I walked down to a little spring in one of the meadows, and as I walked along I mused on my blessing and how I had turned away the Spirit of God. When I reached the spring, I knelt down and offered up a prayer to God and told Him if He could forgive my transgression, and give me back the lost gift, I would promise never to check it again, no matter where or when I felt its promptings.
>
> I have kept this vow, but it has been a heavy cross at times, for I know that this gift is the least of all gifts, and it is oftentimes misunderstood and even treated lightly by those who should know better. Yet it is a gift of God.[7]

Zina used this gift throughout her life, often in company with Eliza R. Snow, whose speaking in tongues Zina interpreted. The *Woman's*

Exponent described Zina as having "as perfect a gift of interpretation of tongues as any person in the Church, for although her opportunities for education in language have been limited, and she is not a poet or rhymer, yet she gives the interpretation of hymns, psalms and sacred songs in the most musical and happy manner, without thought or hesitation. There is something divinely beautiful in thus rendering, by the gift of inspiration, words uttered in an unknown tongue."[8] Zina mentioned in her own diary several occasions when she used the gift. One of her diary entries, dated April 1, 1845, reads: "Went to Brother Brewer's to see Mother Brewer, the first time I have been there. Father Huntington came in the evening. He spake in tongues. Henry also sung in tongues. It was very good. I interpreted the talk by the help of the spirit of God. Had an agreeable visit."[9]

Zina was blessed with other spiritual gifts as well. Her patriarchal blessing promised her, for example, that she would witness the ministering of angels; and on one occasion in the Kirtland Temple, she and her sister, Presendia, heard angelic singing. Presendia related: "The whole of the congregation were on their knees, praying vocally, for such was the custom at the close of these meetings. . . . While the congregation was thus praying, we both heard, from one corner of the room above our heads, a choir of angels singing most beautifully. They were invisible to us, but myriads of angelic voices seemed to be united in singing some song of Zion, and their sweet harmony filled the temple of God."[10]

Joining the Saints

The Huntington family moved to Kirtland, Ohio, in 1836 at the advice of Joseph Smith, Sr., who visited Watertown that spring. Chauncey, the eldest son, did not convert to Mormonism, however, and remained in New York.

Zina described her first meeting of the Prophet Joseph at Kirtland:

> On the 10 [November 1836], I saw the Prophet's face for the first time. He was 6 feet, light auburn hair and a heavy nose, blue eyes. . . . When he was filled with the spirit of revelation or inspiration to talk to the saints his countenance would look clear & bright. . . . When

warning the saints of approaching danger if we forsook
the path of truth & right . . . it was truly affecting and
any one that ever heard, I should think, could never
forget.[11]

At Kirtland also, Zina met Eliza R. Snow, a woman seventeen
years her senior, but one to whom Zina would be a very close friend
and an associate in many facets of their lives. Some compared their
friendship to that of Jonathan and David.[12]

Zina encountered other "friends" in Kirtland. Joseph Smith had
purchased four Egyptian mummies, together with hieroglyphic texts
that were eventually translated into the book of Abraham; and on one
occasion when anti-Mormon sentiment posed a threat, the mummies
were removed from the temple and stored in the Huntington home—
under Zina's bed. One evening as she entered her room, she discovered the hidden artifacts. But sleeping in the same room with four
dead bodies did not seem to alarm her, for she reportedly undressed
and went to bed as usual.[13]

Their eighteen months in Kirtland was a joyful time for the
Huntingtons, but they also met with financial reverses in the events
that preceded the exodus of the Church from Ohio. William had sold
his farm willingly, though at a great loss, to make the move from
Watertown. The family's clothing and household goods, shipped by
steamer, never arrived in Kirtland, leaving them with only the few items
they carried with them. William then invested his cash funds in the
Kirtland bank, which failed within a short time. Zina's brother Oliver
good-naturedly recounted, "When the bank went broke we were
broken and as poor as the best of the Mormons; well, we expected to
become poor but not quite so quick."[14] According to Zina, "We were as
bare as a sheared sheep."[15]

The Huntingtons joined the Saints' migration to Far West,
Missouri, arriving at the height of mob persecutions. Zina, who was
seventeen at the time, wrote of the move:

God in his providence saw it best for us to remove to
Missouri in the spring of 1838. We were with the saints
moving with oxteams almost 1000 miles. We were 8

weeks and 3 days on the road, 4 families a pleasant company. The prairie with its sea of flowers, its waving grass was lovely—much more enjoyable than when a wind would strike us in the night with the elements all at war. The rain [fell] in torrents and we had to sit and hold the covers on our wagons or be left without. I need not mention our condition in the morning.[16]

Six weeks later they moved on to Adam-ondi-Ahman.

With the expulsion of the Saints from Missouri a year later, the Huntington family was forced to move again. During their move to Commerce, Illinois (later to be named Nauvoo, "the beautiful"), the entire family—which at that time included Zina, her parents, and her brothers Oliver and John—became ill with cholera. Joseph and Emma Smith took the family into their home to nurse them. But the cholera, combined with the hardships of the Missouri persecutions and the lack of adequate food and shelter, took their toll on Zina's beloved mother. Knowing she would not live, she called Zina to her bedside. "Zina," she said, "my time has come to die. You will live many years; but O, how lonesome father will be. I am not afraid to die. All I dread is the mortal suffering. I shall come forth triumphant when the Saviour comes with the just to meet the saints on the earth."[17] She died July 8, 1839. Only two members of the family were well enough to attend her funeral.

Zina deeply mourned her mother's death, becoming almost inconsolable. But while she was still grieving months later, her mother's words came into her mind one evening: "Zina, any sailor can steer on a smooth sea. When rocks appear, sail around them." Zina, who described this experience many years later, reported that she was consoled and prayed, "O Father in heaven, help me to be a good sailor, that my heart shall not break on the rocks of grief."[18]

In Nauvoo, Zina's life changed dramatically. On March 7, 1841, at age twenty, she married Henry Bailey Jacobs. Like Zina, Henry was born in Jefferson County, New York; he joined the Church in 1832, three years before the Huntingtons were baptized. During the five years he and Zina spent in Nauvoo, Henry served a series of missions, as was common for married men at the time. The Jacobs's first son, Zebulon William, was born January 2, 1842.

Around the time of Zina's marriage to Henry, the Prophet Joseph received a visitation from an angel commanding that Zina become his "celestial wife." The message was so clear that Joseph knew his life, position, and the progress of the Church would be in peril if he disobeyed.[19] Though this was very difficult for both Henry and Zina to accept, they each had unwavering faith in Joseph's prophetic calling and regarded this commandment as a supreme test of their faith and obedience. Zina received heavenly manifestations that this was the Lord's will. Thus, Zina's brother Dimick Huntington performed her sealing to Joseph on October 27, 1841.[20] According to the Saints' belief, the higher law of celestial marriages would take precedence over civil marriages in the eternities, so Zina and Henry's civil marriage did not need to be dissolved. They remained together as husband and wife until they headed west.[21]

On June 27, 1844, Joseph Smith and his brother Hyrum were murdered by a mob at the Carthage Jail. Zina was deeply shocked. "My pen cannot utter my grief nor describe my horror," she wrote in her diary. Nevertheless, "after a while a change came to us to comfort us in the hour of dreadful bereavement. Never can it be told in words what the Saints suffered in our days of trials, but the sweet spirit of the Comforter did not forsake us."[22]

Zina's diary entry the day of the martyrdom indicates her understanding of the purpose of her sealing to Joseph, for she refers to him as the one who "g[a]ve me a seat in thy Celestial Kingdom."[23] When the Nauvoo Temple was completed, both Henry and Zina received their endowments. A few days later, on February 2, 1846, Zina's sealing to Joseph was "confirmed by proxy" as Henry "stood approving."[24] That same day, Zina was married for time to Brigham Young, for Joseph Smith had earlier requested that the Quorum of the Twelve marry his widows.

Leaving Their Homes

In February 1846, eighteen months after the Martyrdom, Zina recorded in her diary:

> 9th Feb. We were informed that we were to leave with
> the first company as the saints were obliged to leave the

State. . . . Clear and cold [—] we left our house [,] all we possessed in a wagon [—] left many things standing in our house unsold for most of our neighbors were as ourselves on the wing. Shall I ever forget standing on Major Russells porch and seeing Tomas Grovers wagon sink on a sandbar, the Brethren taking the little ones from the wagon cover [,] the bows just peeped above the water at the same time the bells were ringing [—] the Temple was on fire and we leaving our homes for the wilderness trusting God like Abraham. . . . After we had crossed the river I sent back . . . to get a little more thread and a few needles [,] not knowing when we should again have the opportunity. . . .

Camped on Sugar Creek and here we found many dear ones [—] some comfortably fixed up for a long journey and others too sad to relate were it not that we knew it to be the work of God we are engaged in and he would bring us off victorious through all our hardships and toils.[25]

Just a few weeks later, on March 22, Zina gave birth to another son. He was named Henry, after his father, and Chariton, after the river beside which he was born. Zina noted the event in her diary:

We reached the Chariton River between 3 and 4 weeks after leaving Nauvoo. I had been told in the Temple that I should acknowledge God even in a miracle in my deliverance in woman's hour of trouble, which hour had now come. We had traveled one [morning] about 5 miles, when I called for a halt in our march. There was but one person with me—Mother Lyman. There on the bank of the Chariton River, I was delivered of a fine son. Occasionally the wagon had to be stopped that I might take breath. Thus I journeyed on. But I did not mind the hardship of my situation, for my life had been preserved, and my babe was so beautiful.[26]

The family went on to Mount Pisgah, Iowa, which served as one of a number of temporary camps on the route westward. Zina's father, William Huntington, who had by then remarried, presided over this camp. Zina described their conditions:

> Sickness was so prevalent, and deaths so frequent, that help enough could not be obtained to make coffins, and many of the dead were wrapped in their grave clothes and buried with split logs at the bottom of the grave and brush at the sides that being all that could be done for them by their mourning friends. Too soon it became my turn to mourn. My father was taken sick, and in eighteen days he died. Like my dear mother, who died in the expulsion from Missouri, he died in the expulsion from Nauvoo. Sad was my heart. I alone of all his children was there to mourn. It was a sad day at Mount Pisgah, when my father was buried. The poor and needy had lost a friend—the kingdom of God a faithful servant. There upon the hillside was his resting place. The graveyard was so near that I could hear the wolves howling as they visited the spot; those hungry monsters, who fain would have unsepulchred those sacred bones![27]

Henry and Zina did not remain together as husband and wife. After Chariton's birth, Henry left on a mission to England, and he later settled in California. He remained interested in and concerned about his sons and occasionally corresponded with Zina. She and her two little sons and her brother Oliver now joined the Young family in the migration first to Winter Quarters and then to Utah in 1848. Zina helped drive the team. Cooking over a campfire, she was apparently "an expert breadmaker, and her salt-rising would come up when all the others were dead and cold."[28]

Arriving at last at the valley of the Great Salt Lake, Zina wrote her impressions, which expressed both relief and dismay: "One log house outside the old fort as it was called, the only sign of civilization. There is no words to describe our feeling. This our future home, to live, raise families and die, as we used to say, 1000 miles from anywhere. I had more to cheer me than many. My only sister Presendia Kimball was with me. My dear Brother Dimick & family that had been in the [Mormon] Battalion had returned."[29]

Oliver converted Zina's wagon box into a home in the Old Fort until log cabins were erected a few months later for Brigham Young's wives. Within a few weeks after arrival in the valley, Zina, seeing children running around with nothing to occupy them, started a school. "This was pleasant to me," she wrote, "and we had 45 scholars."[30] She taught her students more than "book learning"; she also tried to instill in them high values and a desire for improved living.

Zina's only daughter, Zina Presendia Young, was born April 3, 1850, in Salt Lake City in the log home.* When the Lion House was completed in 1856, Zina and her children occupied two rooms at the rear of the house. She also raised four other children—Maria, Willard, Mary, and Phoebe—whose mother, Clarissa Ross Young, died in 1858. Although as a young woman Zina had vowed she could never become a stepmother, she lovingly considered these children her own.

"Angel of Mercy"

In the 1850s, at Brigham Young's suggestion, Zina took a course in obstetrics from a doctor who was visiting in the territory. She subsequently helped deliver the babies of President Young's wives and many other women, a service for which she was not usually paid. "Aunt Zina," as she was affectionately called, combined her medical skills with her great faith. A close friend, Emmeline B. Wells, said of her, "Numberless instances might be cited of her ministrations among the sick, when she seemed to be inspired by some higher power than her own . . . when courage and faith had failed in those around the sick-bed. At such times she seemed an angel of mercy in very deed."[31]

Chariton's wife, Emma, owed not only her own life but also that of her baby to Zina. While in the Salt Lake Temple, Zina heard Emma cry,

---

* This baby was the third in a mother-daughter chain of six Zinas: Zina Baker Huntington, Zina Diantha Huntington Young, Zina Presendia Young Williams Card, Zina Card Brown (wife of President Hugh B. Brown), Zina Lydia Brown, and Zina Elizabeth (Betty) Brown.

"Mother, I need you." She left immediately for Ogden, some forty miles north of Salt Lake, where Emma was in labor and under the care of another midwife. Neither the midwife nor Zina was able to deliver the baby, so Zina insisted that Chariton go for a doctor. When the baby, a girl, was finally delivered, she appeared lifeless. Zina and the midwife breathed life into the baby, who at last began to cry, while the doctor concentrated on saving Emma.[32]

One of Zina's favorite home remedies was an ointment used for treating "caked breasts, strains, lame backs, and rheumatism." She recorded the recipe in her journal: "Good sized live Toads 4[;] put in boiling water—cook very soft[;] take them out[;] boil the water down to 1/2 pint and add 1 lb fresh butter[;] simmer[;] add 2 oz. tincture arnica."

Her treatment for fever sores called for anointing the sore with skunk oil.[33]

With her brief medical education, Zina realized that home remedies and midwives were not adequate to meet the medical needs of the growing population of the area. She was therefore instrumental in establishing the Deseret Hospital, serving on its board of directors for many years. She also started a nursing school and for a time headed a school of obstetrics.

Another critical need of the pioneers was fabric. Although the women carefully patched and mended their clothing, the production of new textiles was urgent. Wool was available, and a woolen mill was built as early as 1852. Also during the 1850s, Church leaders sent groups to Southern Utah to establish the Cotton Mission, but it would be ten years before a successful cotton crop was grown.

Sericulture, the production of raw silk by raising silkworms, appeared to be a promising solution, not only for supplying local needs, but also for producing income through export. Joseph Smith once said that "the time would come when the people would come to Zion to buy the finest of fabrics."[34] Silk seemed to fit that description. Because of the popularity of sericulture in the northeastern United States as well as in Ohio, Indiana, and Illinois during the 1830s and 1840s, many Saints had been exposed to it. A few experienced silkworm raisers brought mulberry seeds to the Salt Lake Valley, and one woman grew silkworms from eggs her husband brought her from England. But sericulture did not get a serious start in the territory until Brigham Young promoted it as a home industry. He charged Zina with the responsibility of establishing silk culture in the early 1870s, and the Deseret Silk Association was formally organized June 15, 1876, with Zina as president.

Zina's first cocoonery occupied an adobe building at the back of Brigham Young's Forest Dale Farm residence, but after several batches of eggs failed to hatch, perhaps due to the dampness of the building, the cocoonery was moved to a larger brick building. Zina and others of Brigham's family raised sixty-four ounces of silkworm eggs and several pounds of cocoons during the first six weeks of operation, indicating that sericulture was suited to the climate and soil of Utah. Wagonloads of rooted mulberry trees and silkworm eggs were then distributed all over the territory along with a printed pamphlet, *Instructions to Silk Growers.* Zina supervised the silk industry, often traveling from Logan in the north to St. George in the south to encourage and advise the growers.

Silkworms were particularly abhorrent to Zina—in her words, a "terror." (Ironically, she had a worm-shaped birthmark on the palm of her hand.) She was plagued with nightmares of feeding the worms, but stalwartly and silently she endured, fed millions of them herself, and watched the silk industry enjoy a quarter-century of success in its primary goal of providing fine fabric, although its secondary goal of providing income was never met.

Zina had not attended the organizational meeting of the Relief Society in Nauvoo on March 17, 1842, but she was voted in as a member at the second meeting. When Brigham Young reorganized the Relief Society in Salt Lake City in 1866, she was chosen as treasurer.

On August 29, 1877, Brigham Young, Zina's third husband and president of the Church, died in Salt Lake City. Brigham and Zina's daughter, Zina, who was at his bedside along with several wives and children, recorded his passing: "When he was placed upon the bed in front of the window, and opening his eyes, he gazed upward, exclaiming: 'Joseph! Joseph! Joseph!,' and the divine look in his face seemed to indicate that he was communicating with his beloved friend, Joseph Smith, the Prophet. This name was the last word he uttered."[35] Following his funeral in the Salt Lake Tabernacle, Zina, her daughter, her stepchildren, the other wives, and four thousand of the Saints formed a cortege to the burial in his private cemetery two blocks away.

The "Heart" of Relief Society

When the general organization of the Relief Society, encompassing all the local Relief Societies, was formed in 1880, Eliza R. Snow, the president, selected Zina as her first counselor. Author Susa Young Gates wrote, "Some spoke of the two as the head and heart of the women's work in Utah. Sister Snow was keenly intellectual, and she led by force of that intelligence. Sister Zina was all love and sympathy, and drew people after her by reason of that tenderness."[36]

Zina and Eliza traveled thousands of miles by wagon and carriage to Relief Societies throughout the territory; their visits were the main line of communication between Church headquarters and the sisters in outlying areas. Frequently on such trips, the two elderly ladies would have to make an unscheduled stop to repair a wagon wheel or fix a broken buggy tongue. When they were unable to make enough mileage between settlements before nightfall, they camped out under the stars.

The Relief Society presidency organized and directed not only the Relief Society but also the Young Ladies' Retrenchment Society and the Primary Association. (Later three separate presidencies and boards were organized.) The *Relief Society Magazine* reported that Zina and Eliza would frequently hold two to four meetings a day, "organizing branches of the Retrenchment, or Mutual Improvement Associations, meeting with the Relief Societies, 'preaching up' silk, or the loyal support of home industry; securing subscribers to the *Woman's Exponent;* urging women and the girls to study well their responsibilities, as mothers, wives and daughters. Then, one meeting dismissed, the same audience would assemble while these two orators and organizers would call a session of the Suffrage Society, or perhaps, a meeting of the children's Primary Association."[37]

In the winter of 1881–82, the First Presidency sent Zina and Ellen Ferguson, a doctor, to New York to advocate women's suffrage and to dispel misinformation about Mormonism. There they met Harriet Beecher Stowe, Susan B. Anthony, and other suffrage leaders and were invited to the Woman's Congress in Buffalo. Both Zina and Ellen were asked to speak to the convention, but when their identity as Mormons was discovered, they were dropped from the program. Ironically, they were the only two women at the meeting who had the right to vote, yet they were denied the opportunity to speak on women's voting rights because of polygamy.

Zina and her daughter, Zina Y. Williams Card, had also attended the National Suffrage Association Convention in New York in 1882. Romania P. Pratt, in the *Woman's Exponent,* reported an encounter Zina had with another woman at the convention. The woman approached Zina, who was dressed in a sealskin sacque and velvet robe. "I believe you are Mrs. Young," she said. Zina replied, "I am." The woman scrutinized Zina from head to toe, stepped back, and with "supreme surprise" declared, "Why you do not look very degraded!"[38]

Called to Lead

Upon the death of Eliza R. Snow in 1888, Zina, now sixty-seven years of age, was called to be the third general president of the Relief Society. She chose Bathsheba W. Smith as first counselor, Jane S. Richards as second counselor, and Sarah M. Kimball as secretary. Emmeline B. Wells served as corresponding secretary. (Both Bathsheba W. Smith and Emmeline B. Wells would later occupy the position of general president.)

As a young girl, Zina was prepared by her mother for her role in Relief Society. Orson F. Whitney, in his "History of Utah," wrote: "Zina Baker Huntington was a 'voluntary relief society in herself.' At Kirtland it was her custom, without direction or prompting from any one, to take her daughter Zina in her buggy and hunt out the distressed and needy in and about that place. Whatever was found necessary beyond her own means to supply, they would travel among the people, in and out of the Church, and secure. Thus early was 'Little Zina' inducted into the spirit and mission of the Relief Society, although it then had no existence."[39]

When President Wilford Woodruff set Zina apart as the president of the Relief Society, he blessed her that she would continue to have her heart "drawn out towards . . . [the] sisters" and that she would "do much good and relieve the suffering of those who are sick and afflicted."[40] Serving as general president enabled Zina to broaden her sphere of service. She continued visiting Relief Societies in the widely spread Mormon settlements in the West, encouraging local units to establish nursing classes and to improve medical care. Before Utah gained statehood in 1896, she also campaigned for the restoration of women's voting rights. (The Edmunds-Tucker Act of 1887 had rescinded the voting priv-ileges granted to women by the territorial legislature.)

At the Chicago World's Fair held in 1893, Zina, at age seventy-two, represented the women of the Territory of Utah and sat on the platform with other territory and state representatives. When Utah became a state in 1896, it was the second state, following Wyoming, to give women suffrage.

During Zina's administration, the Relief Society also became a charter member of the National Council of Women. Zina, who was elected as one of the vice presidents of the council, attended a number of its conferences.

As the Church became too large for the general leaders of Relief Society to continue giving personal instructions to local units, repre-sentatives from each stake were invited to attend the first general conference of the Relief Society. Zina presided at this meeting, held in the Assembly Hall on Temple Square, April 6, 1889.

During Zina's years of service in Relief Society, the program began to spread beyond the Intermountain West area. She traveled as far as New York, Canada, and Hawaii to encourage and instruct sisters in their duties. In New York she visited relatives in Watertown. Of her trip to the Sandwich Islands (Hawaii) in 1879 she wrote, "Friday met with the relief society. They brought gifts for Susa [Young Gates] and I, vegetables of all kinds as much as a wheel barrow load. . . . I thought it was a donation for the poor but they ware [were] tokens of friendship for us."[41] As her gift to the islanders, Zina obtained an organ for their church meetings.

Friendliness was as natural as breathing to Zina. She loved people and they loved her. She addressed letters to her family, "My dear sister Presendia," "My loving son Zebulon," and "My precious son Chariton"— often adding, "Give my love to those dear, dear children." When she stayed at the homes of Relief Society leaders, their families felt she was their "Aunt Zina." Many baby girls were named Zina out of regard for her. On one occasion when Zina was told that a certain woman did not like her, she replied, "Well, I love her, and she can't help herself."[42]

Zina was an effective and powerful speaker, yet one who motivated people through love rather than exhortation. She bore strong testimony to the divinity of the work in which she was engaged. "From the day I received the sweet testimony of the Spirit, when grasping the precious

Book of Mormon in my hands to my breast, I have never doubted nor faltered in my faith," she said. "I know this is the Church and Kingdom of God, and I rejoice in putting my testimony before the daughters of Zion, that their faith may be strengthened, and that the good work may roll on. Seek for a testimony, as you would, my dear sisters, for a diamond concealed. If someone told you by digging long enough in a certain spot you would find a diamond of unmeasured wealth, do you think you would begrudge time or strength, or means spent to obtain that treasure? Then I will tell you that if you will dig in the depths of your own hearts you will find, with the aid of the Spirit of the Lord, the pearl of great price, the testimony of the truth of this work."[43]

When the Salt Lake Temple was dedicated in 1893, the First Presidency called Zina to be president of the sisters' department, or temple matron. She fulfilled that assignment, in addition to her duties as general Relief Society president, until her death. While visiting her daughter in Cardston, Alberta, Canada, Zina suffered a stroke on August 22, 1901, and never regained consciousness. She died August 28, 1901, in Salt Lake City, having served as Relief Society president for thirteen years.

Though she experienced many years of hardship in her adult life, Zina Diantha Huntington Young never looked back on the comfortable life she had led before missionaries brought the message of the restored gospel of Jesus Christ to her as a young girl. For sixty-six years she was one of the leading figures in the Church and took on many roles—as a wife of Joseph Smith, Henry Jacobs, and then Brigham Young, as mother to three and stepmother to four children, as general Relief Society president, and as a close friend of many prominent women in the Church, including Eliza R. Snow, Emmeline B. Wells, and Bathsheba W. Smith.

Whatever her roles, "Aunt Zina" was beloved by all who knew her, for "in her tongue was the law of kindness" (Proverbs 31:26). The *Relief Society Magazine* said of her: "She was thus for [thirteen] years, elect lady of the Church and no more beautiful soul ever occupied that exalted position."[44] At Zina's funeral, Emmeline B. Wells remarked, "No woman was ever greater loved than she," and Elder Anthon H. Lund of the Council of the Twelve added, "She was 'Aunt' Zina to all Israel."[45] Fittingly inscribed on her gravestone is the Relief Society motto, "Charity never faileth."

Notes

1. Autobiography of Zina D. H. Young, LDS Church Archives, p. 2. Hereafter cited as Autobiography.

2. Zina Baker Huntington, letter dated March 5, 1817, LDS Church Archives.

3. Mary Firmage [Woodward], personal letter to Janet Peterson, April 13, 1988.

4. Zina D. H. Young, "How I Gained My Testimony of the Truth," *Young Woman's Journal* 4 (April 1892): 317.

5. Ibid., p. 318.

6. Ibid.

7. Ibid., p. 319.

8. "A Distinguished Woman," *Woman's Exponent* 10 (December 15, 1881): 107.

9. Zina D. H. Young, Diary, April 1, 1845, holograph, LDS Church Archives. Hereafter cited as Diary.

10. Edward W. Tullidge, *Women of Mormondom* (New York, 1877), pp. 207–8.

11. Autobiography, p. 4.

12. David H. Jacobs, "Zina Diantha Huntington Jacobs Smith Young," Church Educational System Church History Symposium, Brigham Young University, August 19, 1977, p. 55.

13. "'Aunt Zina' D. Young Sought after as 'Angel of Mercy,'" *Church News,* November 30, 1963, p. 16.

14. History of Oliver Boardman Huntington, 1842–1900, typescript, LDS Church Archives, p. 27.

15. Mary Brown Firmage Woodward, "Great-Grandmother Zina: A More Personal Portrait," *Ensign,* March 1984, p. 38.

16. Autobiography, p. 2.

17. Tullidge, *Women of Mormondom,* p. 213.

18. "Mother," *The Young Woman's Journal* 22 (January 1911): 45.

19. Zina D. H. Young, "Joseph, the Prophet His Life and Mission as Viewed by Intimate Acquaintances," *Salt Lake Herald and Farm Supplement,* 12 January 1895, p. 212; as quoted in and Martha Sonntag Bradley and Mary Brown Firmage Woodward *4 Zina's: A Story of Mothers and Daughters on the Mormon Frontier* (Salt Lake City: Signature Books, 2000), p. 113.

20. Ibid., p. 114.

21. For further discussion of Zina D. H. Young's complex marital situation, see Richard L. Bushman, *Joseph Smith; Rough Stone Rolling* (New York: Alfred A. Knopf, 2005) and Martha Sonntag Bradley and Mary Brown Firmage Woodward *4 Zina's: A Story of Mothers and Daughters on the Mormon Frontier* (Salt Lake City: Signature Books, 2000).

22. Oa Jacobs Cannon, "Zina Diantha Huntington Young," Relief Society Legacy Lecture, 1982.

23. Diary, June 27, 1844, holograph.

24. Maureen Ursenbach Beecher, ed., "'All Things Move in Order in the City': The Nauvoo Diary of Zina Diantha Huntington Jacobs," *BYU Studies* 19 (Spring 1979): 288.

25. Diary, typescript in possession of Mary Firmage Woodward, p. 1.

26. History of Zina D. H. Young, typescript in possession of Oa Jacobs Cannon, p. 2.

27. Diary, typescript, p. 3.

28. Susa Young Gates, *History of the Young Ladies' Mutual Improvement Association* (Salt Lake City, 1911), p. 23.

29. Diary, typescript.

30. Ibid., p. 34.

31. Emmeline B. Wells, "Zina D. H. Young—A Character Sketch," *Improvement Era* 5 (November 1, 1901): 45.

32. Claire Noall, *Guardians of the Hearth: Pioneer Midwives and Women Doctors* (Bountiful, Utah: Horizon Publishers, 1974), pp. 54–55.

33. Diary, typescript, p. 6.

34. Chris Rigby Arrington, "The Finest of Fabrics: Mormon Women and the Silk Industry in Early Utah," *Utah Historical Quarterly* 46 (Fall 1978): 378.

35. Leonard J. Arrington, *Brigham Young: American Moses* (New York: Alfred A. Knopf, 1985), p. 199.

36. *History of the Young Ladies' Mutual Improvement Association,* p. 21.

37. "Centennial of President Zina D. Huntington Young," *Relief Society Magazine* 8 (March 1921): 134.

38. Romania P. Pratt, "Woman's Suffrage Convention," *Woman's Exponent* 10 (March 1, 1882): 146.

39. Orson F. Whitney, "History of Utah," *Utah Historical Quarterly* 4 (October 1904): 577.

40. Wilford Woodruff, "Blessing of Zina D. H. Young," Salt Lake City, October 11, 1888, copy in possession of Mary Firmage Woodward.

41. Diary, July 25, 1879, holograph.

42. "Centennial of President Zina D. Huntington Young," p. 131.

43. "How I Gained My Testimony of the Truth," p. 319.

44. "Centennial of President Zina D. Huntington Young," p. 133.

45. "Aunt Zina D. H. Young," *Young Woman's Journal* 12 (October 1901): 473.

4

BATHSHEBA W. SMITH
1901–1910

On a cold February morning in 1846, Bathsheba Smith watered her potted flowers for the last time and moved them out of the draft. She looked around the room. Only a few months before, she and her sister Melissa had spent happy afternoons there sewing curtains and making flower pots for their homes. But more recently, as part of the Saints' preparation to leave Nauvoo, Bathsheba had willingly cleared her parlor of its furniture and heirlooms so it could be used as a paint shop for the wagons. And now, pregnant with her third child, she was getting ready to leave Nauvoo with her husband, George A. Smith; their four-year-old son, George A., Jr., and their two-year-old daughter, Bathsheba. With hundreds of other families, they crossed the frozen Mississippi River that day, leaving their homes and many of their possessions behind. Their destination was a temporary refuge called Winter Quarters.

The exodus of the Saints from Nauvoo, Illinois, was just one of many instances in which Bathsheba gave up her home because of her testimony of the gospel, a pattern of sacrifice that characterized the eighty-eight years of her life. Her strongest talents lay in her abilities at the loom and with the needle; her strongest character traits lay in her devotion to husband and family and her diligence in lovingly arranging her surroundings to match the love she felt for them.

Bathsheba had the privilege of witnessing many remarkable events in the early history of the Church, as well as enduring the day-by-day trials weathered by the majority of the early Saints. For example, in the fall of 1838, the company she was traveling with to Far West, Missouri, met up with the group of Saints who were massacred the next day by a mob at Haun's Mill. Their company narrowly escaped being part of the massacre themselves.

Not long after Bathsheba's arrival at Far West, a battle occurred at nearby Crooked River, and David W. Patten, one of the Twelve Apostles, was wounded. He was brought to the house where her family had stopped. She witnessed his death a few days later.

At age eighteen, in Nauvoo, Bathsheba earned the distinction of being the youngest woman present at the organization of the Relief Society in 1842. She also attended the laying of the cornerstone of the Nauvoo Temple. In Nauvoo, too, Bathsheba and her husband, George A. Smith, were among the first to receive their temple endowments and to be taught the principle of plural marriage by the Prophet Joseph Smith. After Joseph's martyrdom, Bathsheba was a witness when the mantle of the presidency fell upon Brigham Young. Having experienced these and so many other landmark events in Church history, she lived, appropriately enough, in the Historian's Office after the Church moved west to Utah, and her husband became Church historian.

Joys and Persecutions

Bathsheba's conversion to the gospel was the pivotal point between the stability of her refined Southern childhood and the sacrifices required of her as a Latter-day Saint. Born May 3, 1822, near Shinnston, West Virginia, she was the eighth of nine children of Mark and Susannah Ogden Bigler: Matilda, Hannah (who died shortly after birth), Nancy, Jacob, Jonathan (stillborn), Maria, Sarah, Bathsheba, and Melissa.[1] A cheerful child, Bathsheba loved to spin, weave, and embroider with her mother and to go horseback riding with her father over their 300–acre plantation. There were occasional opportunities for schooling, too, when her father and neighboring landowners hired a teacher to teach a few months out of the year in a vacant house on the Bigler farm. As a young girl, she and a girlfriend traded names as a symbol of their friendship, and throughout her life Bathsheba kept her childhood commitment and used her friend's surname, *Wilson,* or the initial *W* in place of her own maiden name. Religiously inclined, Bathsheba was careful to say her "secret prayers," as she called them. When Latter-day Saint missionaries knocked on the Biglers' door, they found Bathsheba and her entire family spiritually ready for the message of the restored gospel. Bathsheba wrote of her conversion:

> When I was in my sixteenth year, some Latter-day Saint Elders visited our neighborhood. I heard them preach and believed what they taught. I believed the Book of Mormon to be a divine record, and that Joseph Smith was a Prophet of God. I knew by the spirit of the Lord which I received in answer to prayer, that these things were true. On the 21st of August 1837, I was baptized into the church of Jesus Christ of Latter day Saints. . . . The Spirit of the Lord rested upon me, and I knew that He accepted of me as a member in His kingdom.[2]

One of those missionaries was George A. Smith, a son of John Smith, the Prophet's uncle who would later serve as patriarch to the Church. The missionaries converted and baptized Bathsheba's entire immediate family and her uncle and his family.

Bathsheba and George were attracted to each other. Six months after her baptism they mutually agreed that "with the blessings of the Almighty in preserving us, in three years from this time, we will be married."[3] Soon after this, George was called on a mission to England.

When the Biglers were ridiculed and harshly criticized by neighbors for joining the Church, they decided to leave their home in West Virginia and join the Saints in Far West, Missouri. Bathsheba's married sister Nancy and her family planned to leave immediately, and Bathsheba was disappointed that she couldn't go with them. While pondering this disappointment, she heard a voice say, "Weep not. You will go this fall." The next morning her sister Sarah noticed a change in Bathsheba's attitude and said, "You have got over feeling badly about not going to Zion this fall, have you?" Bathsheba quietly but firmly replied, "I am going, you will see."[4]

She was right. In the fall of 1837, Bathsheba and the rest of the Bigler family left for Far West. She wrote of the experience in her autobiography: "On our journey the young folk of our party had much enjoyment. It seemed so novel and romantic to travel in wagons over hill and dale, through dense forests and over extensive prairies, and occasionally passing through towns and cities sometimes traveling on macadamized roads and camping in tents at night."[5]

Though the journey seemed exciting to young Bathsheba, the Biglers soon found that the closer they got to their destination, the more hostile the Missourians were. Bands of men frequently stopped them and gathered around their wagons asking who they were, where they were from, and where they were going. Bathsheba reported, "Their consultation would result generally in a statement to the effect of, 'as you are Virginians we will let you go on, but we believe you soon will return for you will quickly become convinced of your folly.'"[6]

But Bathsheba and her family never thought of the new life they had chosen as folly, and such experiences only strengthened her conviction of the truthfulness of the gospel. She said: "In these distressing times, the spirit of the Lord was with us to comfort and sustain us, and we had a sure testimony that we were being persecuted for the Gospel's sake, and that the Lord was angry with none save those who acknowledge not his hand in all things."[7]

The Biglers stayed only a short time in Missouri because of intense persecution against the members of the Church. In February 1839, in cold winter weather, they again left their home and farm behind and departed with thousands of other Saints for Illinois. Bathsheba gave up her seat on the wagon to those who were sick and walked most of the way. Despite the cold, illnesses, and death, she reported that at night the exiled Saints gathered around the campfire and sang the songs of Zion, trusting in the Lord that "all would yet be well." Bathsheba and her father both became ill with ague and fever. She recovered, but to her great sorrow, her father died.

The Bigler family stayed in Quincy, Illinois, until 1840, when they were able to move on to Nauvoo. The following year, Bathsheba looked forward to the return of George A. Smith from his mission to England. A cousin of the Prophet Joseph Smith, he now served as the youngest member of the Quorum of the Twelve Apostles. He and Bathsheba were married July 25, 1841, just fourteen days after he returned from England.

A Devoted Homemaker

A meticulous housekeeper, Bathsheba Smith took pride in the appearance of her home as well as of herself. She had grown up in a beautiful home in West Virginia, where she learned the art of Southern hospitality from her mother, who had come from an aristocratic and well-to-do family in Maryland. After her marriage Bathsheba no doubt longed for a nice home but instead set up housekeeping five different times in one year, in dwellings that were shabby at best, compared to her childhood home.

Bathsheba wrote of her attempts to make her first home, located on the Iowa side of the Mississippi River, habitable. Unfortunately, she said, "the house leaked and smoked and was otherwise uncomfortable." Four weeks later, the newlyweds moved to Nauvoo. With new hope that first night, they knelt by their bed and dedicated themselves to God. They thanked him for his mercy in bringing them together after being separated so long, and prayed that he would bless them that prosperity might crown their labors. Their love was warm; however, the house "smoked and was open and cold."[8]

Next, they rented an unfurnished log home from Bishop Vinson Knight. The windows did not have glass, so Bathsheba hung blankets to keep out the cold. George A. built a brick chimney but discovered that it smoked. Although the home was unsatisfactory, that move enabled Bathsheba to become good friends with Bishop Knight's wife, Martha.

Joseph Smith recognized his cousin's housing dilemma and gave George A. a small log house. Bathsheba wrote, "My husband fixed up the house the best he could, but after all it was the worst looking house we had yet lived in; I was ashamed to have any of my acquaintances see me in such a looking place." Then her optimistic nature surfaced and she added, "It had, however, the desirable qualities of neither smoking nor leaking."[9]

Soon George A. obtained another lot, which he fenced and drained, and built a more comfortable, two-story home with two rooms on each floor. He and Bathsheba were so anxious to move in to this new home before the birth of their first child that they set up their bed in one of the unfinished rooms. Twelve days later, on July 7, 1842, a son was born. They named him George Albert Smith, Jr.

Only two months after George Jr.'s birth, George A. was called on a mission to the eastern states, leaving Bathsheba with a new baby and an unfinished home. Many times during their married life, she would see George A., who was an outstanding leader, dynamic speaker, and willing servant, leave on missions and Church assignments. Her letters to him reflected her love for him, her reliance on him for counsel, and her strong testimony of the gospel. A letter dated February 14, 1851, was typical:

> I look at your portrait which I never forget. It hangs back of my bed and is the last thing I see and the first in the morning. Oh, it is such a comfort to me. It always looks pleasant and kind as you do and seems to say when I feel bad, "Cheer up, all is well" and you will return and we will be more happy than if we had been together. . . . When the shades of night fall upon it, it does look so much like you that it makes the tears fall fast.[10]

During George A.'s absences, Bathsheba relied on her mother, sisters, and friends for companionship. Because George A. was related to Joseph Smith, Bathsheba also had many opportunities to associate with Emma Smith, Eliza R. Snow, Zina D. H. Young, and other female leaders.[11] One of her "priceless visual mementos" was her memory of Emma Smith riding on her white horse beside Joseph through the streets of Nauvoo.[12] Eliza asked Bathsheba to read the first manuscript of her poem "O My Father," and the experience made such an impression on Bathsheba that for years afterward she was able to describe in minute detail the room in which Eliza had written it.[13]

Bathsheba was one of the first persons to receive the temple endowment in Nauvoo and to hear the Prophet Joseph Smith teach of the celestial order of marriage. In January 1844, a month after Bathsheba and George A. received their endowments, Joseph performed the sealing ceremony for them. She wrote of the effect of the revelation on celestial marriage on her life:

> Being thoroughly convinced . . . that the doctrine of plurality of wives was from God; and having a fixed determination to attain celestial glory, I felt to embrace

the whole gospel. . . . Like Sarah of old, I gave to my husband five wives, good, virtuous, honorable young women. This gave them all homes, with us; being proud of my husband and loving him very much . . . and believing he would not love them less because he loved me more. I had joy in having a testimony that what I had done was acceptable to my Father in Heaven.[14]

Over the next two years Lucy Meserve, Zilpha Stark, Sarah Ann Libby, Hannah Maria Libby (Sarah's sister), and Nancy Clement were married to George A. Smith, and Bathsheba accepted these women as sisters.

At a Relief Society meeting in Nauvoo, Bathsheba heard Joseph Smith express a presentiment of his. "He opened the meeting by prayer," she later wrote. "His voice trembled very much, after which he addressed us. He said: 'According to my prayer I will not be with you long to teach and instruct you, and the world will not be troubled with me much longer.'"[15] When the Prophet and his brother Hyrum were martyred in Carthage Jail on June 27, 1844, George A. Smith was on a mission in Illinois. Bathsheba wrote to him on July 6, 1844:

We have had strange times since you left. You will no doubt hear, before this reaches you, of the death of our beloved brethren Joseph and Hyrum Smith. They were killed at Carthage on the 27 of June and on the 28 they were brought home and such a day of mourning never was seen. It pains me to write such a painful tale, but the Lord has comforted our hearts in a measure. . . . Brother John Taylor was wounded but is getting better, is quite weak but quite cheerful. Brother Willard Richards was not hurt. They were both in jail at the time of the massacre. I will not write anymore on that subject as I expect you will hear all the particulars before this reaches you.[16]

On August 1, 1844, two weeks after George A. returned from his mission, Bathsheba gave birth to a daughter, whom they named

Bathsheba. An uneasy calm returned to Nauvoo as the Twelve Apostles returned from their various missions. George A. persuaded Bathsheba to take art lessons and to sing in the choir, while Bathsheba persuaded George A. to attend dances, which he did not like in the least.

From December 1845 to February 1846, Bathsheba took part in the temple work as thousands of Saints received their endowments. Here she learned to love the work, a love that dominated her later life in Salt Lake City. On January 25, 1846, George A. and Bathsheba's two children were sealed to them in the Nauvoo Temple.

Moving West

Of the family's exodus from Nauvoo on February 9, 1846, Bathsheba wrote:

> In company with many others, my husband took me and my two little children, and some of the other members of our family, the remainder to follow as soon as the weather would permit, and we crossed the Mississippi River to seek a home in the wilderness. Thus we left a comfortable home, the accumulations and labor of four years, taking with us but a few things such as clothing, bedding and provisions, leaving everything else for our enemies. We were obliged to stay in camp for a few weeks on Sugar Creek because of the weather being so very cold. The Mississippi froze over so that hundreds of families crossed over on the ice.[17]

She also wrote about their journey across the state of Iowa to Winter Quarters, a temporary camp on the banks of the Missouri River:

> I will not try to describe how we traveled through storms of snow wind and rain, how roads had to be made bridges built and rafts constructed; how our poor animals had to drag on day after day with scanty food; how our camps suffered from poverty, sickness and death. We were consoled in the midst of these

hardships by having our public and private meetings in peace, praying and singing the songs of Zion, and rejoicing that we were leaving our persecutors far behind. . . . The Lord was with us, and his power was made manifest daily in our journey.[18]

At Winter Quarters Bathsheba again established a home—this time in a sod-roofed cabin. "In our travels the winds had literally blown our tents to pieces, so that we were glad to get into our cabin," she wrote.[19]

Because the Saints had few vegetables, except corn, to eat, many of those camped at Winter Quarters got scurvy. One of Bathsheba's sister wives, Nancy Clement, and her daughter, Nancy Adelia, died from it. George A. took a personal interest in finding a way to prevent scurvy and discovered that potatoes were effective. He planted potatoes at Winter Quarters in the spring of 1846 and thereafter wherever he lived, earning him the affectionate title of the "Potato Saint."[20]

Death continued to strike at Bathsheba's family. On March 11, 1847, her mother died. Three weeks later, on April 4, Bathsheba gave birth to a son after three days' labor. The little boy, whom they named John, lived only four hours. Bathsheba did not recover from the birth for some months, suffering again with ague and fever. She was never able to bear any more children.[21]

In June 1847, many Saints left Winter Quarters for the Salt Lake Valley. Among them were Bathsheba's sisters, her in-laws, and her husband, George A. Bathsheba longed to go with them, but she decided to remain at Winter Quarters with the rest of George's wives and children, feeling it her duty to care for them. Even though she wondered later if she should have gone, she did what she thought would be her husband's wish.[22] In all, she spent three years at Winter Quarters while George A. traveled back and forth to and from the Salt Lake Valley helping other Saints to migrate west.

By late June 1849, George A. secured enough supplies and a wagon for each of his five families to move west. Bathsheba applied her homemaking skills to her wagon, which she described in her journal:

On this journey my wagon was provided with projections, of about eight inches wide, on each side of the top of the box. The cover, which was high enough for us to stand erect, was widened by these projections. A frame was laid across the back part of our wagon, and was corded as a bedstead; this made our sleeping very comfortable. Under our beds we stowed our heaviest articles. We had a door in one side of the wagon cover, and on the opposite side a window. A step-ladder was used to ascend to our door, which was between the wheels. . . . I had, hanging up on the inside a looking-glass, candlestick, pincushion, etc. In the center of our wagon we had room for four chairs, in which we and our two children sat and rode when we chose. The floor of our traveling house was carpeted, and we made ourselves as comfortable as we could under the circumstances.[23]

Once, while fording a stream, Bathsheba's awkward wagon threatened to wash downstream. Unruffled, she yelled, "Behold, Noah's Ark!"[24]

After months of ferrying streams, fording others, traveling over sterile plains, high mountains, and through deep canyons, and enduring a thirty-six-hour snowstorm as well as a cattle stampede, George A.'s wagons arrived in the Salt Lake Valley. For a while, the families lived in their wagon beds. George A. began building an adobe house for Bathsheba, but before finishing it he was called to colonize Parowan, 250 miles south of Salt Lake City. Before he left for Parowan with his wife Zilpha, Bathsheba hid in his wagon a package containing a small sugar loaf, a bunch of English currants, and a poem that read, in part, "Now I give it unto thee, / That comfort you may in this, / My great large sugar kiss." George A. wrote of Bathsheba's gift in his journal, "For surely, I remember my first love."[25]

Family Life in the Valley

Bathsheba and her children lived with her in-laws until her house was finished. At last she had a home with a shingled roof, plastered walls, glass windows, two fireplaces, and a bake oven. After moving into the new house, the family became ill with whooping cough, or "chin cough," as some called it. But in spite of sickness, Bathsheba industriously set about making her home comfortable. She wrote to George A. on April 13, 1851:

> Now my dear, I do not want you to think I cannot work yet, so I believe I will tell you what I have been doing this winter. I did nearly all Father's folks house-work nine in the family most of the time with the exception of washing, made father two fine shirts, mother two dresses, three caps, made her some pillow cases, made John two fine bosoms, helped quilt two quilts, wrote thirty-odd [patriarchal] blessings, recorded several. Father gave me about seven dollars and a half in money. I made my carpet, made George a pair of pants and coat and siss some clothing, sewed some for Melissa (two dollars and a half worth) made me a nice hearth rug, made some nice soap, made a cushion for my rocking chair, sewed some for myself also knit for the children. . . . I have made my window curtains have three white ones in the best room . . . made my valances, sewed and fitted down my carpet, made some pillowcases and sheets, quilted two comforters . . . made me a dress and bonnet, Bathsheba an apron and various other things besides cooking, washing, mending, churning, feeding my cow, pigs, chicks and visiting the sick as well.[26]

In June 1851, George A.'s wife Sarah died. Her sister Hannah (another of George A.'s wives) did not get along well with Bathsheba and, after Sarah's funeral, argued with Bathsheba over who would raise Sarah's three-year-old son. As first wife, it was Bathsheba's responsibility to handle the situation. Far more comfortable working with her hands than dealing with challenges such as these, she wrote of the conflict to George A.:

> What Hannah will do now I don't know. . . . I could take her home if she would be kind to me, but she will not. I was not very well and my mind was troubled

knowing the feelings that existed in our family and Sarah just being dead and everybody looking on, one saying one thing and another thing for every mean thing that could be said had been said. . . . I will try to do the best I hope I can and if I do not write I hope you will tell me how and I will try to do it as I always have.[27]

By August, Bathsheba could write to her husband of resolving the conflict: "I saw Hannah today at meeting, she was as friendly as I have seen her since you left. I hope she will continue to be friendly for I do hate to have anyone cross with me."[28]

George A. returned briefly the next month. The following year, in August 1852, Church leaders asked him to preside over the Saints in the Provo area, some forty miles south of Salt Lake City. He took wives Hannah and Lucy with him, leaving only Bathsheba in Salt Lake City. Her sister Melissa lived nearby, and Melissa's daughter Julina spent many hours with her aunt Bathsheba. Bathsheba's daughter delighted in making dolls and doll clothes for Julina to play with. Since Melissa had several small children and her husband was on a mission, Bathsheba's caring for Julina was a great help to her. By the time Julina was seven, in 1855, she lived with her aunt but went daily to see her mother.

In October 1857, George A. Smith took another plural wife, Susan Elizabeth West, and brought her to live with Bathsheba. Bathsheba later wrote of the common interest in home industry she shared with Susan:

> Sister Susan and myself for about ten or twelve years have spun, colored and wove full cloth, flannel, linsey janes, kerseys, blankets, coverlids, shawls, wove fringe, wool carpets, stair carpets, rag carpets, and have spun flax and tow, and wove table linen towels, bed ticks, and made sewing thread. We also carded, spun, and wove cotton, made cotton cloth for diapers, dresses, bedspreads, bed ticks, bags, spun candle wicking, spun and wove table cloths, towels, we knit our own stockings, socks, hoods neckwraps mittens, made netting,

embroidery . . . and have done all to encourage home manufactory. We have exhibited many of our home-made goods at our territorial fairs and they always received favorable attention.[29]

Some of their handiwork decorated the Historian's Office, which their families occupied after George A. was called to be Church historian in 1854. (The Historian's Office was built as a duplex, with half serving as an office and the other half as a residence.) In the evenings, the family members enjoyed entertaining visitors, reading, singing, playing musical instruments, and dancing. George Jr. played the flutena, flute, and fife, and he and his sister Bathsheba played the drums. Bathsheba wrote, "They made our home joyous with song and just their pleasure was mine. I was proud of them and so happy with them."[30]

In 1858, U.S. President James Buchanan sent an army, commanded by General Albert Sidney Johnston, to the territory with orders to "put down the Mormons." It took several months for the army to traverse the plains and the Rocky Mountains, giving the Saints time to prepare to evacuate the Salt Lake Valley if necessary. Finally, Brigham Young instructed them to move south; only a few men and boys would remain to tend to crops and livestock and to set fire to buildings if it appeared the army planned to take possession. Before she left, Bathsheba stopped to sweep the floors of her home; then she loaded her trunks into her wagon and took her family to Provo.

The army entered the valley on June 26, and by June 30, Church and government leaders worked out a settlement. On July 3, Bathsheba and her children returned to Salt Lake City, traveling through the too-quiet streets near sunset. As far as she could tell, every door was shut and every window in the city was boarded up. At her home, she found weeds nearly as high as her head all around the house, choking out her flowers.

In 1860, Bathsheba's pleasant home life was shattered when she received news that Indians had killed her only son, George. While serving a mission to the Indians in Southern Utah, he was killed on November 2 in retaliation for a massacre of Navajos by other whites. His companion, Jacob Hamblin, could find only three bones and a lock of George Jr.'s hair to bring home for burial.

Two months later, her daughter, Bathsheba, married Clarence Merrill. Still deeply grieving over her son's death, Bathsheba experienced a profound sense of loss when her daughter left home. But she was not alone. Julina still lived with her, and she was close to the children of Susan, George A.'s seventh wife. She took a particular interest in Susan's oldest daughter, Clarissa.

In time, Bathsheba's daughter had fourteen children, and Julina, who married in 1866, had ten. Bathsheba enjoyed these grandchildren immensely. She made mittens, comforters, hoods, linsey dresses, coats, and petticoats for them, carrying the handiwork in a flower-covered carpetbag. When Grandma Bathsheba came to visit, the grandchildren would run to her, shouting "Hurrah!" and eagerly wait to see what gifts she had brought for them.

As she and George A. traveled to various branches of the Church throughout the territory, they were frequently met by bands playing and children carrying banners and flags and singing songs of welcome. A friend, Julia P. M. Farnsworth, described Bathsheba on one of these trips:

> She was then a tall, stately woman, with an abundance of beautiful brown hair, dark eyes smooth fair complexion, and was traveling in the company of her husband in President Young's party . . . to St. George. . . . I noted her superiority, her dignity of carriage, yet, with all that, she was easy to approach, lovable in manner, for she ever gave a sweet smile and a word of encouragement to little children and young people, also care and tenderness to the sick or aged. She was artistic in temperament, loved the beautiful, appreciated refinement, and always dressed in good taste.[31]

Traveling together was a sweet culmination of Bathsheba and George A.'s thirty-four-year marriage, of which Bathsheba wrote, "I love my husband dearly. I believe but few in this wide world have been as happy as we have been. We have no differences, always agree on all points, our religion and our future hopes and expectations are the same."[32]

George A. Smith died in September 1875 from complications resulting from an old injury, a lung punctured while he was serving on a mission. Bathsheba wrote of his death: "His head lay . . . against my bosom. Good angels had come to receive his precious spirit, perhaps our sons, prophets, patriarchs . . . but he was gone my light, my sun, my life, my joy, my Lord, yea almost my God. . . . I must not mourn but prepare myself to meet him but O my heart sinks within my bosom nearly."[33]

Called to Serve

Bathsheba's remaining years without her husband were filled with grandmothering and with renewed service in Relief Society. In 1866, when Brigham Young reorganized the Relief Society as a Churchwide organization, Bathsheba had been one of several women called to serve with President Eliza R. Snow. When the Relief Society of the Salt Lake Stake was organized in December 1877, Bathsheba became treasurer. Eleven years later, in October 1888, Zina D. H. Young was sustained as general Relief Society president and selected Bathsheba as her second counselor. When the beloved "Aunt Zina" died in August 1901, President Joseph F. Smith called Bathsheba to be the fourth general president of the Relief Society. She selected Annie Taylor Hyde and Ida Smoot Dusenberry as her counselors, Emmeline B. Wells as general secretary, and Clarissa S. Williams as treasurer.

This presidency served together nine years, until 1910. They continued the nursing classes that Zina Young had established, and, building on Bathsheba's interest in home industry, they introduced mothers' classes in which lessons were taught on marriage, prenatal care, child rearing, industry, obedience, honesty, and reverence. Bathsheba strongly believed that women in the Church should learn to be self-sufficient.

Bathsheba, along with many other Mormon women, supported the efforts of the National Woman's Suffrage Association for women's suffrage. While she was not a leader in this movement, she showed her support locally in talks and in articles published in the *Woman's Exponent*.

For much of the time Bathsheba served as general Relief Society president, the organization had no central office. At the Relief Society conference in the Assembly Hall on October 3, 1896, President Zina Young had called for a vote to build an office building, but nothing was done at that time. Three years later the Young Ladies' Mutual Improvement Association and the Primary Association joined with the Relief Society in working toward construction of a building to serve the three organizations. During Bathsheba's administration, the project moved forward, but slowly. In 1908 the plans of the building were changed to include the offices of the Presiding Bishop. The structure, subsequently known as the Bishop's Building, was completed in 1909 in the block on the east side of Main Street, across from Temple Square. It housed offices of the three auxiliaries, the Presiding Bishopric, Church magazines, and some other organizations, and was headquarters for the Relief Society until 1956, when the present Relief Society Building was built.

Bathsheba believed that one of the most important things she could do as president of the Relief Society was to serve in the temple. When the Endowment House was completed in Salt Lake City in 1855, she resumed doing temple work as she had done in Nauvoo. She also worked in the Manti and Logan temples, and after the Salt Lake Temple was dedicated in 1893, she coordinated the women's work there. Until her death in 1910, Bathsheba faithfully attended the temple.

In a portrait painted in the last year of Bathsheba's life, artist Lee Greene Richards portrayed her draped in white lace, probably of her own making. Susa Young Gates, a daughter of Brigham Young, described Bathsheba as she served in the temple: "It is a lovely and an inspiring sight to see this high priestess of righteousness arrayed in her simple white gown of home-made silk, her dark eyes still bright, her fair, delicate face crowned with lustrous bands of shining white hair, her finely-shaped head, with its rich, white lace draping, held erect, as her stately figure moves down the long aisle. The sweet smile of welcome greets all alike in its impartial graciousness. She is indeed the Elect Lady, and wisdom and peace crown her days."[34]

The last of the original twenty members of the Relief Society, Bathsheba Bigler Wilson Smith died September 20, 1910, at the age of eighty-eight.

"When I heard the Gospel I knew it was true," Bathsheba once wrote. "When I first read the Book of Mormon, I knew it was inspired of God; when I first beheld Joseph Smith I knew I stood face to face with a prophet of the living God, and I had no doubt in my mind about his authority."[35] Her testimony remained strong throughout her life. Her gentle, unfailing devotion to her husband, her family, and her home served as an example to others; her skills in spinning, weaving, sewing, and homemaking sustained her in the various moves she made and homes she established; and her singular opportunities made her an influential witness to the unfolding history of the Church.

Notes

1. Family Group Sheet of Mark Bigler, LDS Family History Library.

2. Bathsheba W. Smith, Autobiography, typescript, LDS Church Archives, p. 2. Hereafter cited as Autobiography.

3. George Albert Smith, Journal, July 25, 1841, LDS Church Archives.

4. Autobiography, p. 2.

5. Ibid., p. 3.

6. Ibid.

7. Ibid., p. 5.

8. George Albert Smith, Journal, August 25, 1841, LDS Church Archives.

9. Autobiography, p. 6.

10. Bathsheba W. Smith to George A. Smith, February 14, 1851, holograph, George A. Smith Collection, LDS Church Archives.

11. Autobiography, p. 12.

12. Susa Young Gates, ed., *History of the Young Ladies' Mutual Improvement Association* (Salt Lake City, 1911), p. 26.

13. Julia P. M. Farnsworth, "A Tribute to Bathsheba W. Smith," *Young Woman's Journal* 21 (November 1910): 608.

14. Autobiography, p. 7.

15. Preston Nibley, "She Knew the Prophet Joseph Smith: Part III— Bathsheba W. Smith," *Relief Society Magazine* 49 (June 1962): 410–11.

16. Bathsheba W. Smith to George A. Smith, July 6, 1844, holograph, George A. Smith Collection, LDS Church Archives.

17. Autobiography, p. 9.

18. Ibid., p. 9.

19. Ibid.

20. Richard S. Van Wagoner and Steven C. Walker, *A Book of Mormons* (Salt Lake City, 1982), p. 271.

21. Autobiography, pp. 10–11.

22. Bathsheba W. Smith to George A. Smith, June 7, 1846, George A. Smith Collection, LDS Church Archives.

23. Autobiography, p. 15; also Edward W. Tullidge, *Women of Mormondom* (New York, 1877), pp. 342–43.

24. Mary Isabella Horne, "Migration and Settlement of the Latter-day Saints," dictated memoir, microfilm of holograph, LDS Church Archives.

25. George A. Smith, Journal, March 1851, LDS Church Archives; also *Church News,* May 24, 1975, p. 16.

26. Bathsheba W. Smith to George A. Smith, April 13, 1851, holograph, George A. Smith Collection, LDS Church Archives.

27. Bathsheba W. Smith to George A. Smith, June 12, 1851, and July 12, 1851, holograph, George A. Smith Collection, LDS Church Archives.

28. Bathsheba W. Smith to George A. Smith, August 1851, holograph, George A. Smith Collection, LDS Church Archives.

29. Autobiography, pp. 29–30.

30. Ibid., pp. 23–24.

31. Julia P. M. Farnsworth, "A Tribute to Bathsheba W. Smith," *Young Woman's Journal* 21 (November 1910): 609.

32. Autobiography, p. 24.

33. Ibid., pp. 31–32.

34. *History of the Young Ladies' Mutual Improvement Association,* pp. 26–28.

35. "Past Three Score Years and Ten," *Young Woman's Journal* 12 (October 1901): 440.

5

EMMELINE B. WELLS
1910–1921

At the age of eighty-two, Emmeline B. Wells was called to serve as the fifth president of the Relief Society, the oldest woman chosen for that position. Her life spanned two centuries and two different eras of Relief Society. She had personally known each of the first four Relief Society presidents—Emma Smith, Eliza R. Snow, Zina D. H. Young, and Bathsheba W. Smith; yet she served as president in the twentieth century.

A dainty woman, Emmeline stood barely five feet tall and weighed only a hundred pounds. She refused to wear black dresses or a veil over her face, preferring instead pastel colors and soft, flowing scarves at her neck. Delicate earrings dangled from her pierced ears, layers of slender chains hung around her neck, and rings adorned her fingers, including one on her index finger (then the engagement finger).[1] But her dynamic personality provided a distinct contrast to her small size. "The dominant characteristic of Mrs. Wells' life was her supreme will," wrote her friend Susa Young Gates. "That she turned the current of this forceful will into peaceful channels of the gospel of Jesus Christ made for righteousness and the upbuilding of many good causes."[2] Describing Emmeline at age ninety, Susa called her "our little, delicate, great-minded President of the Relief Society, walking softly, yet with fierce independence into the room."[3]

"I believe in women," said Emmeline, summing up the theme of her own life. "I desire to do all in my power to help elevate the condition of my people, especially women . . . to do those things that would advance women in moral and spiritual, as well as educational work and tend to the rolling on of the work of God upon the earth."[4] The sisterhood of women and their causes filled her ninety-three years. Her life revolved around her five daughters, her sister wives and female friends, the women's suffrage movement, the *Woman's Exponent,* and the Relief Society.

Childhood

Emmeline Blanche Woodward was born in Petersham, Massachusetts, on leap year day, February 29, 1828—an unusual day for an unusual life. She was the seventh of nine children born to David and Diadama Hare Woodward: Lucy, Pallas, Eliza, Manson, James, Cordelia, Emmeline, Adaline, and Ellen.[5]

A precocious child, Emmeline started school when she was only three years old, walking with her older brothers and sisters and spending part of each day napping underneath the teacher's desk.[6] As she grew older, she spent many hours reading old letters, papers, and books stored in boxes in the attic of her home. She knew early in her life that she wanted to be a writer. "Under the hemlock boughs," she once wrote, "I sat on a summer's day with proud ambition burning in my soul, ambition to be great and known to fame, when a gentle whisper came . . . 'There is no excellence without labor.'"[7]

Her mother wanted her to become a teacher; writing did not seem practical. So Emmeline learned to do both, teaching when it was necessary to support herself but writing daily, laboring throughout her life for excellence.

Conversion and Marriage

While Emmeline was away earning her teaching certificate at a select school for girls in New Salem, Massachusetts, her mother and three youngest sisters joined The Church of Jesus Christ of Latter-day Saints. Although Diadama Woodward was not able to convert her older children, who were all married by the time she joined the Church, she found Emmeline to be more receptive to the new religion. Emmeline was baptized at age fourteen, on March 1, 1842, in a nearby brook. It was so cold that the ice had to be cut away, and hecklers—including ministers, judges, and some of her friends from the girls' school—jeered while the ordinance was performed. She withstood both the cold water and the taunts and told her mother that she would dedicate her life to the work of the Church.[8] Unbeknown to Emmeline at the time, sixteen days after her baptism an event took place in faraway Nauvoo, Illinois, that would have significance in her life: the organization of the Female Relief Society of Nauvoo on March 17.

Not long after she joined the Church, Emmeline began teaching school in the nearby town of Orange, Massachusetts, for a dollar and a half a week, and she soon found new friends among the small group of Latter-day Saints in the area. Her mother encouraged a relationship between her daughter and the branch president's son, James Harvey Harris, because she wanted Emmeline to remain secure in the Church. The two—who were just fifteen years of age—were married on July 29, 1843.

In March 1844, James and Emmeline left for Nauvoo with his parents. Emmeline filled her diary account of the monthlong trip with the optimism of a young newlywed. She later described their arrival in Nauvoo aboard a steamboat:

> At last the boat reached the upper landing, and a crowd of people were coming toward the bank of the river. As we stepped ashore the crowd advanced, and I could see one person who towered away and above all the others around him. . . . His majestic bearing, so entirely different from anyone I had ever seen was more than a surprise. . . . When he took my hand, I was simply electrified. . . . The one thought that filled my soul was, I have seen the prophet of God, he has taken my hand.[9]

Just two months later, this man, the Prophet Joseph Smith, and his brother Hyrum were martyred in the Carthage Jail. The dark days that followed the Martyrdom were momentarily brightened for Emmeline when, on September 1, 1844, she gave birth to a son, Eugene Henri Harris. But five weeks later, her baby became ill with chills and fever and died.

Dissension among some of the Saints and increasing persecution from anti-Mormon factions caused a number of people to leave Nauvoo, including James's parents. They encouraged James and Emmeline to return with them to New England, but the young couple chose to stay in Nauvoo with the main body of the Church. Shortly after the baby's death, however, James left to look for work elsewhere, and he never returned. Emmeline received only two letters from him. Heartbroken and lonely, she wrote in her diary on February 2, 1845:

> Last night there came a steamboat up the river. Oh, how my youthful heart fluttered with hope, with anxiety. My limbs were affected to that degree. I was obliged to lay aside my work. I rely upon the promises he has made me and not all that has been said can shake my confidence in the only man I ever loved, but hope returned and was renewed in my bosom. I watched the boat and looked out at the door. I walked a few steps out of the yard . . . I saw a person approaching. My heart beat with fond antic-ipation. It walked like James. He came nearer and just as I was about to speak his name he spoke and I found I was deceived by the darkness. Last night I thought he had come home. I thought it was a reality, a Heavenly Gathering, bringing us together. Today I am alone and I have time for reflection."[10]

Throughout Emmeline's life, in her diary entries she lamented her loss of James and expressed her love for him. For example, in 1874 she wrote, "How dreadful when I remember my agony at that time, my utter loneliness, my inexperience—Oh what heartrending scenes we are called to pass through.[11] Decades later, Emmeline learned that James Harris never remarried and that he died in 1859 in Bombay, India, while working on a whaling vessel. He had written many letters to her but made the mistake of mailing them to his mother, who did not forward them. On a trip to New England after the death of James's mother in 1888, Emmeline visited his childhood home. While rummaging through the attic she came across the letters James had written her. She insisted that her daughter and granddaughter, who were with her, take her to the cemetery. Her granddaughter wrote of the event, "There that tiny but mighty old lady stood with her arms raised over the grave and called down a curse upon her mother-in-law that made Mother tremble—and no doubt caused the wicked one to writhe in her shroud!"[12]

At age seventeen, alone in Nauvoo and grieving over the death of her infant son and the loss of her young husband, Emmeline turned to the only work she knew: teaching. Bishop Newel K. Whitney and his wife, Elizabeth Ann, hired her to teach their children. The Whitneys, thirty years Emmeline's senior, gave her protection and security. On February 17, 1845, Emmeline became a plural wife of Bishop Whitney, and that day he gave her a blessing in which he promised that her abilities would have "tremendous influence in the building of the 'kingdom' in the west."[13] The blessing reassured Emmeline of the sense of destiny she already felt about her life, though she continued to weep over James.

Emmeline joined the exodus of the Saints from Nauvoo in February 1846 and lived for two years at Winter Quarters before beginning the trek west to the Salt Lake Valley. On November 2, 1848, one month after arriving in the valley, she gave birth to a daughter, Isabel (Belle) M. Whitney. Another daughter, Melvina (Mellie), was born on August 18, 1850. Only a few weeks later, Bishop Newel K. Whitney suddenly died.

In the Valley

A widow with two baby daughters, Emmeline wrote that she had lost "as good a man as ever lived, a father to all within his reach and more than father to me."[14] She was not entirely alone, however, for she had the sustaining love and lifelong friendship of Newel's first wife, Elizabeth Ann Whitney, who had served as a counselor to Emma Smith in the first Relief Society presidency.

Emmeline again turned to teaching school to support herself and her two children. She later recalled her teaching experience in Salt Lake City:

> I taught 65 children in a log house without desks, charts, blackboards, or scarcely two books of the same kind. The remuneration was likewise trying, [one] bringing a piece of salt pork, another a bucket of flour, a third perhaps a skein of yarn; to repay the ever toiling task of school teaching; the work was unceasing; the day spent in the school room and the night in planning and working for

the morrow, whole nights being spent in cutting fancy patterns and writing verses in blue ink and working on bits of cardboard mottoes in various colored silks for rewards, to urge the children to diligence and good behavior.[15]

About this time, two events occurred that significantly affected Emmeline's life. First, the *Deseret News,* which was established in 1850, began publishing news of the suffrage movement for women. As she learned more about the movement over the next twenty years, Emmeline became not only a sympathetic reader but also a suffrage leader. Second, in 1852, Brigham Young publicly announced plural marriage as a doctrine and practice of the Church.

Only twenty-four years old and with daughters to support, Emmeline knew she would benefit from the security that marriage offered. Therefore, following the public announcement of plural marriage, she sent a letter to Daniel H. Wells, a close friend of her late husband, Newel K. Whitney, asking him to "consider the lonely state of his friend's widow." She wrote that she hoped to be "united with a being noble as thyself," and asked him to "return to her a description of his feelings for her."[16] In response to her gentle proposal, Daniel married Emmeline, his seventh wife, on October 10, 1852.

As a member of Daniel Wells's family, Emmeline at last had financial security. Both prosperous and prominent, Daniel would later serve as a member of the First Presidency of the Church for twenty-three years, superintendent of public works, mayor of Salt Lake City for ten years, and chancellor of the University of Deseret (which later became the University of Utah). A daughter, Emmeline (Emmie) Whitney Wells, was born to Emmeline and Daniel on September 10, 1853.

Emmeline's diaries reveal, however, that her marriage with Daniel was frustrating at times, and she often felt lonely and neglected. She also felt that she had little in common with his other wives, her relationship with them being amicable but not close. Preferring time for her own projects to the busyness of the large Wells household, Emmeline moved into a small adobe house on South Temple with her three daughters in 1856. Two more daughters were born to Emmeline and Daniel: Elizabeth Ann (Annie) on December 7, 1859, and Louisa Martha (Louie) on August

27, 1862. The adobe home was not far from "the Big House" where most of the Wells family lived, and the families frequently visited each other. Emmeline and her daughters went there every day for family prayers. Nevertheless, she appreciated the independence her new home gave her, and she especially loved her large garden, making it the theme of one of her favorite poems, "The Dear Old Garden."

Emmeline had a close relationship with each of her five daughters—Belle, Mellie, Emmie, Annie, and Louie—mentioning them in nearly every diary entry. As they grew up, she not only gave them every motherly attention but also showed them by example how to assume responsibilities in the world outside their home. In 1875 she expressed her strong feelings about combining motherhood and other duties:

> It is the opinion of many who are wise and learned that woman's mission upon the earth is maternity, with its minor details, its accompanying cares and anxieties, and needful exigencies; that these fill the measure of her creation; and when this is done, she should with becoming matronly dignity, retire from the sphere of active life and gracefully welcome old age. . . . That motherhood brings into a woman's life a richness, zest and tone that nothing else ever can I gladly grant you, but that her usefulness ends there, or that she has no other individual interests to serve I cannot so readily concede.[17]

Emmeline herself certainly did not "retire from the sphere of active life and gracefully welcome old age." Her usefulness began rather than ended with motherhood, and for the next several decades, she juggled family and personal challenges with her responsibilities with the *Woman's Exponent*, the women's suffrage movement, and the Relief Society.

A Woman's Woman

When the Relief Society was reorganized by President Brigham Young in 1866, Emmeline was one of ten women called to lead it, beginning a career of service to the women of the Church that would span the next fifty-four years. It was during the late 1860s, too, as political action increased against plural marriage, that the women of Utah became more actively involved in the national women's movement as a means of stopping legislation against them. Emmeline was at the forefront. In January 1870, she spoke to two thousand women at a meeting in Provo to protest the Cullom Bill, which would have outlawed polygamy. Women's suffrage was also an issue, and Emmeline rejoiced the following month when women in the Utah Territory were given the right to vote.

The movement for women's rights, which had begun in America as early as 1848, rapidly gathered momentum after 1869, when Susan B. Anthony and Elizabeth Cady Stanton organized the National Woman's Suffrage Association in response to the passage of the Fourteenth Amendment, which guaranteed the right to vote only to men. At first glance, it may seem peculiar that two groups of women as different as Mormon plural wives from Utah and feminist leaders from the East should become part of the same women's movement. But the fact is that each group had something the other group was working toward, and they realized that they could help each other. Utah women already had the right to vote, which is what the feminists were fighting for; and feminists believed that legislation should not limit women's rights, which is what the women from Utah were fighting for. So although the feminists involved in the women's movement did not understand or condone plural marriage, they believed in a woman's right to live her life as she chose.

Over the years, Emmeline became dearly loved by leaders of the women's movement. She wore a gold ring Susan B. Anthony gave to her and said of the gift, "It is a symbol of the sympathy of two great women for one great cause."[18] Emmeline sent a black brocaded dress made from Utah silk to Susan B. Anthony on her eightieth birthday. In a large part it was this friendship that encouraged women involved in the national suffrage movement to accept Emmeline and the women of Utah.

While Emmeline gained prominence in the suffrage movement, she continued to serve in the Relief Society. In September 1876, Brigham Young asked her to direct a project for women to gather and store wheat. She accepted the responsibility and asked women throughout the territory to gather wheat scattered along the fences and ditch banks after the harvest. In an article for the *Woman's Exponent* pleading for support of the project, she wrote, "Who is there that can feel these things as deeply as a mother can; think what it would be to hear your little one cry for bread."[19] The sisters gleaned from the fields, private granaries donated storage, and ward Relief Societies planned to build their own granaries as soon as they could raise the money. Emmeline was delighted with the results: 10,465 bushels of wheat were stored the first season, with the hope of 50,000 bushels the next year. The Relief Society donated wheat to the poor and loaned or sold several thousand bushels to farmers for spring planting.

The wheat project, which continued to grow over the years, became one of the most successful long-term Relief Society projects. As a result, Utah grain eased the effects of the drought that ravaged the southern part of the state in 1898–99; it helped survivors of the San Francisco earthquake and fire in 1906; and it fed thousands during World War I, when the Relief Society sold 100,000 bushels to the United States government for $412,000. President Woodrow Wilson personally thanked Emmeline in 1919 for the wheat.

Emmeline's abilities and confidence grew as a result of her experiences in the women's movement and the grain project. Once she had written that she felt "timid" and "trembled like a frightened bird,"[20] but as she continued to accept responsibilities, she became more confident. She also became more eloquent, which was plainly evident as she labored in the women's movement, for she believed that "a good Mormon was not silent; silence meant consent."[21] She said she did not want "just the crumbs, but the whole loaf of bread for women."[22]

In 1877, when Emmeline was forty-nine years old, she became editor of the *Woman's Exponent,* the first women's magazine published in the West and only the second published in the United States. With her two oldest daughters, Belle and Mellie, married, and her three other daughters twenty-four, eighteen, and fifteen, Emmeline had time to pursue her writing interests. She began her writing career with the magazine in 1873, using a pseudonym, Blanche Beechwood, to write forty-two articles on women's issues. After she became editor, articles signed by the liberal-thinking Blanche were replaced by writings of the increasingly conservative "Aunt Em."

For the next thirty-seven years, Emmeline remained passionately devoted to the *Woman's Exponent.* She developed the format and content of the magazine, which was published twice a month and contained as many as twenty pages with three columns each. Sometimes her children and grandchildren helped to set the type and fold the printed sheets. She was so committed to the success of the paper that she often spent her own money to publish it.

Under Emmeline's direction, the magazine became a powerful voice not only for Mormon women but also for the suffrage movement. Emmeline felt that Mormon women "should be the best informed of any women on the face of the earth, not only upon our own principles and doctrines but on all general subjects."[23] Therefore, the magazine contained local, territorial, and worldwide news pertaining to women.

Emmeline believed that another purpose of the *Woman's Exponent* was to change the widely held perception that Mormon women were degraded and repressed. The publication projected a positive image of intelligence, commitment, self-confidence, and ability. One reader in the East wrote that while she did not support polygamy, she "frequently read the *Exponent,* and truly admir[ed] the bold manner with which [it dealt] with all questions pertaining to public interest."[24] For more than twenty years, the masthead carried the motto "For the Rights of the Women of Zion and All Nations."

Women's Suffrage Leader

Emmeline's continuing involvement in the suffrage movement focused on preventing or repealing antipolygamy legislation. In January 1879, she and Zina Y. Williams Card, the daughter of Zina D. H. Young, represented the Utah Territory at a conference of the National Woman's Suffrage Association in Washington, D.C. Susan B. Anthony introduced Emmeline as a speaker, and her address was well received. Emmeline and Zina also visited President Rutherford B. Hayes at the White House to present a paper defending plural marriage and to urge the repeal of an antipolygamy law. Their efforts brought about no change, but it was evident that as a leader, Emmeline had developed enough confidence to take her case directly to the president of the United States.

Controversy over plural marriage in Utah continued to increase, and in 1886 Emmeline attended another suffrage convention in Washington, D.C., remaining there until May. She fought to prevent the creation of an industrial home for plural wives in Utah. The home was subsequently built, but few plural wives ever used it. Though difficult for others to understand, there were advantages to plural marriage. Many women viewed it as a form of liberation, for when wives lived in the same home, each woman was free to pursue individual interests because child care and housework were shared. Most also enjoyed the companionship of their sister wives. And plural marriage gave more women a greater choice of a worthy husband and an opportunity to have children.

When Emmeline's involvement in Utah's bid for statehood had begun in 1878 with her service as one of seven delegates and as secretary to the Territorial Convention, statehood was not linked to the women's movement. But with the passage of the stridently antipolygamy Edmunds-Tucker Act in 1887, Utah women lost their right to vote. Now the bid for statehood, which would give Utah the opportunity to make its own suffrage laws, became part of the same fight for suffrage that propelled the women's movement. The Utah Woman's Suffrage Association was organized in Utah in 1889, many of its leaders also being leaders in the Relief Society. The next year, 1890, President Wilford Woodruff issued the Manifesto, which officially ended the practice of plural marriage. "After doing and suffering what we have through our adherence to this principle," said President Woodruff, "[we are] to cease the practice and submit to the law" (see Doctrine & Covenants, Official Declaration 1).

The legal battle was over. The power of the Edmunds-Tucker Act of 1887 had nearly broken the back of the Church, and the Saints had little choice but to stop the practice of plural marriage. Daniel H. Wells moved to Manti, Utah, to serve as the temple president in 1890, and Emmeline and his other wives visited him only occasionally. Emmeline continued to earn her livelihood as editor of the *Woman's Exponent* and received some support from her daughters. She also remained active in the Utah Woman's Suffrage Association, though her energies were no longer focused on the defense of plural marriage, but on obtaining statehood for Utah. She became president of the association in 1893 and continued to work in that position until 1896, when Utah became a state and full suffrage was returned.

Among other highlights of Emmeline's work in the women's suffrage movement was the opportunity in July 1899 to speak at the International Council of Women's Quinquennial Convention held at Westminster Hall in London. While in England, she had the opportunity to meet

Queen Victoria. The national movement continued until 1920, when the Susan B. Anthony Federal Suffrage Amendment, which had been placed before Congress in 1917, was finally ratified and became the Nineteenth Amendment to the Constitution. At last, all women in America had the right to vote.

Meeting Other Challenges

Emmeline's personal life presented her with other kinds of challenges. First, her daughter Emmie, at the age of twenty-four, died on April 8, 1878. For the rest of her life, Emmeline noted the anniversary of Emmie's death every year in her diary. Next, Elizabeth Ann Whitney, who had been a dear friend, sister wife, and surrogate mother to Emmeline, died in 1882. Then, in April 1887, Emmeline rushed to San Francisco to care for her daughter Louie, who was seriously ill from complications following the birth of a stillborn son. Louie died on May 16. Heartbroken, Emmeline returned home to discover that Daniel had had to sell her home due to some financial difficulties. She moved into a small adobe house on South Temple.

Against this backdrop of family heartaches and political activity, Emmeline continued to work in other areas. The Relief Society established the Deseret Hospital in 1882, after many of the women who had been encouraged to attend medical school had returned to Utah. Emmeline served as secretary for the hospital for twelve years and treasurer for ten years. Also in 1882, Emmeline helped Eliza R. Snow and Aurelia S. Rogers organize the Primary Association.

Emmeline served as corresponding secretary for the Relief Society general board in 1888—her first position on the general level of the Relief Society. She participated in the first general Relief Society conference in April 1889, when she read Zina D. H. Young's presidential address, and at the following conference in October, Emmeline herself was asked to speak. Her work with the *Woman's Exponent* and with the women's suffrage movement had already established her as a political and intellectual leader among the women in Utah. Her efforts in Relief Society would establish her as a spiritual leader.

In the midst of all of Emmeline's activity in 1891, her husband, Daniel H. Wells, died. Emmeline had gone east to attend a suffrage convention, and when she returned home on March 20, he was ill. The relationship between Daniel and Emmeline had been rekindled two years earlier. She had written, "Such intense love he has manifested towards me of late years. Such a remarkable change from the long ago, when I needed him so much more, how peculiarly the things come about."[25] He died on March 24. Her journal entry for Memorial Day that year reads, "I wanted to go to the graveyard last evening but could not and had no flowers to take up—but tears, tears in abundance, a soft rain came and it grew so dark—this morning the city is lively with music and flags are flying but my heart is more sad than usual. . . . I want to tell you . . . there never was a man like him."[26]

When Emmeline was called to the position of general secretary of the Relief Society in 1892, she discovered that her job required more than clerical skills. She was responsible for a new department that provided burial clothes and a department that supplied food and clothing to needy Church members. Also, under the direction of Relief Society President Zina D. H. Young, Emmeline took charge of the jubilee anniversary of the founding of the Relief Society. Among the most impressive events of the jubilee celebration on March 17, 1892, was a prayer circle, held in Salt Lake City, symbolizing international unity. Women from Canada, Mexico, the Sandwich Islands, Australia, New Zealand, Great Britain, Switzerland, Germany, Holland, Denmark, Sweden, and Norway joined hands in prayer.[27]

Emmeline was also appointed chairman of a churchwide effort to raise funds for a new Relief Society building. She believed that the money should be raised by the sisters through home industry. Relief Society members participated in many varied projects. One group in Ephraim, Utah, headed by Sarah Peterson, donated all the money from the sale of eggs their chickens laid on Sundays. Some wards had sewing or quilting groups. Another group unraveled old cotton stockings, then knitted and crocheted articles from the yarn and sold them. The Relief Society, however, would not have its own building until 1956.

Following the death of Zina D. H. Young in August 1901, Emmeline continued her fundraising efforts as secretary for the new president, Bathsheba W. Smith. Of her workload as general secretary, she wrote on one occasion, "Work is not done by looking on and really I do as much work as seven other women I firmly believe."[28]

The Fifth General President

On October 3, 1910, after twenty-two years of service on the general level of Relief Society, Emmeline was called to be the fifth general president of the organization, with Clarissa Smith Williams and Julina Lambson Smith as her counselors.

During Emmeline's administration, the Relief Society adopted the motto "Charity Never Faileth." The Relief Society owned real estate, storage buildings for grain, dressmaking shops, and cattle and sheep herds; and from these ventures, thousands of dollars were dispensed to help the poor and orphaned. To meet the demands of this expanding program, a social services department was organized in January 1919 under the direction of Amy Brown Lyman.

Emmeline placed a high value on education, and, as a result, the Relief Society established courses in theology, genealogy, art, literature, home science, obstetrics, and nursing. However, she opposed a centralized educational program and encouraged each ward and stake to decide how to shape its own program.

During her years of involvement in Relief Society and the suffrage movement, writing and the *Woman's Exponent* remained high priorities for Emmeline. She filled the magazine's pages with her poetry, editorials, and articles, and even serialized her autobiographical short story "Hephzibah" in its pages in 1889. In 1896, she also published a book of her poetry entitled *Musings and Memories*. She wanted to publish a book of "Aunt Em's Stories" in 1902 and tried to raise money through requests in the *Exponent,* but was unsuccessful.

Bathsheba W. Smith had proposed making the *Woman's Exponent* a publication of the Relief Society in 1910, but Emmeline did not feel ready to give up control and refused the offer. However, as president herself at eighty-six years of age, she found that the *Exponent* was becoming too difficult for her to continue editing, and at last she offered to turn it over to the Relief Society. But the Relief Society was no longer interested, and the board rejected her offer. Shortly afterwards, the Relief Society asked Susa Young Gates to be the editor of a new publication, to be called the *Relief Society Magazine.* In what must have been a difficult decision for Emmeline, the February 1914 issue of the *Woman's Exponent* was its last. Perhaps to ease the pain of the loss of the magazine she so dearly loved, she issued a second edition of her book of poems in 1915.

Throughout her life, Emmeline often fought off depression, which she referred to as "low-spiritedness," or "nervous attacks." She now commented in her diary, "I have been very ill again one of those old nervous attacks which I dread so much, and seem so like death."[29] Similar entries are found throughout her forty-six diaries. The prose of her journal entries reveals private suffering; the poetry of her life reveals public strength.

In 1917, Emmeline moved into the Hotel Utah in downtown Salt Lake City so that she could work into the night in her Relief Society office nearby. Her life had come full circle: sixty-nine years earlier, she had given birth to her first daughter, Isabel, in a wagon bed on the site of the hotel.

Emmeline amusingly attributed her vigor to the fact that she was born on leapyear day and only aged every fourth year. On her eighty-fourth birthday in 1912, which could be observed on its actual date, February 29, she wrote in her diary, "The greatest day when was conferred upon me the degree of Dr. of Literature by President Jos. F. Smith & the Brigham Young College or more properly University."[30] She was only the second person and the first woman to receive an honorary doctorate from Brigham Young University, and one of only a hundred women nationally who had received an honorary degree from any university. More than six hundred people attended a reception in her honor, hosted by the Relief Society general board in the Bishop's Building. Also in celebration of her eighty-fourth birthday, she unveiled a new monument on Temple Square—the Seagull Monument.

When Emmeline turned ninety, a party was given for her at the Hotel Utah. In honor of the occasion, a moving picture was made of her and other pioneers who had been living in Nauvoo at the time the Prophet Joseph Smith was martyred. On her ninety-second birthday, more than a thousand people attended her birthday party, which was also held at the Hotel Utah.

Susa Young Gates described the "Aunt Em" so many had come to know and love:

> Her mind is keen, her intellect sure, and her powers
> unbending. She possesses a rarely beautiful spirit, and is

affectionate, confiding and exquisitely pure. No unclean thing could enter her presence, or remain in her atmosphere. She is an eloquent speaker, a beautiful writer, a true friend, and a wise counsellor. She is beloved by all who dwell in the Church, and by all who know her, and their name is legion.[31]

When President Heber J. Grant went to Emmeline's home on April 2, 1921, and released her as Relief Society president after eleven years of service, she was taken by surprise. Though she was ill at the time of the release, she had assumed that hers was a lifetime calling. After all, she had once fallen down an elevator shaft and was later hit by a streetcar, both while she was president, and on neither occasion had there been talk of a release. After President Grant left, she suffered a stroke on her way upstairs. She lay nearly comatose for the next three weeks and died on April 25, 1921, at the home of her daughter Annie Wells Cannon. Her funeral was one of the largest ever held in the Tabernacle. On April 29, flags flew at half-mast in Utah to commemorate her death—the first time this had been done in honor of a woman.

On the hundredth anniversary of Emmeline's birth, February 29, 1928, the women of Utah commissioned a marble bust of her to be placed in the rotunda of the State Capitol. The inscription reads, "A Fine Soul Who Served Us."

Emmeline B. Wells indeed believed in women and did all in her power to elevate them. Her words, penned in this letter to a sister wife, express her feelings of love, not only for her sister wives, but for women in general:

> Pardon me for my familiarity but even as a sister do I love and esteem you—those who feel for me, who administer to my wants, who always seek to cheer and comfort me—they to me are sisters indeed, and in the truest sense of the word; the kindness, the sympathy and cordiality, with which I have been treated by you, constrains me to love you, as well as the rest of the band of sisters, with which I have (very fortunately) become associated and I would to heaven that the

same benevolent and generous principles which exist in the bosoms of those of whom I now speak also had an existence in every female who helps to form this vast community.[32]

Notes

1. Based on description of Abbie H. Wells to Judith R. Dushku, March 27, 1975, which appears in part in *Sister Saints,* ed. Vicky Burgess-Olsen (Provo: Brigham Young University Press, 1973), p. 468.

2. Susa Young Gates, *Improvement Era* 24 (June 1921): 719.

3. Susa Young Gates, "Our Lovely Human Heritage," *Relief Society Magazine* 4 (February 1917): 74.

4. Emmeline B. Wells, Diary, January 4, 1878, Special Collections, Harold B. Lee Library, Brigham Young University, Provo, Utah, p. 207. Hereafter cited as Diary.

5. Family Group Sheet of David and Diadama Hare Woodward, LDS Family History Archives.

6. *Sister Saints,* p. 461.

7. Carol Cornwall Madsen, "Emmeline B. Wells," in *Supporting Saints,* ed., Donald Q. Cannon and David J. Whittaker (Provo: Brigham Young University, 1985), p. 311.

8. Carol Cornwall Madsen, "Aunt Em—A Leader and Truly Fine Soul Who Served Us," *Church News,* October 30, 1982, p. 10.

9. *Young Woman's Journal* 16 (December 1904): 554–56.

10. *Sister Saints,* p. 462.

11. Diary, October 6, 1874.

12. Carol Cornwall Madsen, *A Mormon Woman in Victorian America,* Ph.D. dissertation, University of Utah, 1985, p. 78. Her source was a letter from Geneva Ramsey Kingkade to Carolyn Chouinard, August 24, 1970, copy in possession of Carol Cornwall Madsen.

13. Augusta Joyce Crocheron, *Representative Women of Deseret* (Salt Lake City, 1884), pp. 65–67.

14. Diary, September 23, 1874.

15. *Woman's Exponent,* 17 (June 1, 1888): 1–2.

16. Emmeline B. Whitney to Daniel Wells, March 4, 1852, LDS Church Archives; also *Supporting Saints,* pp. 309, 459.

17. "Life Lessons," *Woman's Exponent* 4 (October 1, 1875): 70.

18. Phyllis C. Southwick, "Emmeline B. Wells—If She Were Here Today," paper delivered at the Women's Resource Conference, "Perspectives on Women," Salt Lake City, October 1974; also Rebecca Anderson, "Emmeline B. Wells: Her Life and Thought," master's thesis, Utah State University, 1975, p. 33.

19. *Woman's Exponent* 5 (November 1, 1876): 84.

20. *Woman's Exponent* 16 (October 1, 1887): 67.

21. *Woman's Exponent* 10 (March 1, 1882): 148.

22. *Woman's Exponent* 18 (August 15, 1889): 46.

23. Emmeline B. Wells to M. E. Lightner, Salt Lake City, April 7, 1882, in Emmeline B. Wells papers, LDS Church Archives.

24. *Woman's Exponent* 16 (May 1, 1888): 177.

25. Diary, March 26, 1891.

26. Diary, May 30, 1891.

27. *Woman's Exponent* 24 (October 1, 1895): 60.

28. Diary, August 1, 1895.

29. Diary, August 16, 1875.

30. Diary, February 29, 1912.

31. Susa Young Gates, "President Emmeline B. Wells," *Album Book: "Daughters of the Utah Pioneers and Their Mothers,"* ed. Joseph T. Jakeman (Salt Lake City: Daughters of Utah Pioneers, 1911), p. 54.

32. Emmeline B. Wells to Hannah Wells, December 31, 1855, Emmeline B. Wells Papers, LDS Church Archives.

6

CLARISSA SMITH WILLIAMS
1921–1928

Clarissa West Smith Williams, sixth general president of the Relief Society and the first native Utahn to fill the office, enjoyed the benefits of being a third-generation Latter-day Saint. She had a secure home life, educational opportunities, and financial stability not known by her five predecessors in the Relief Society. Yet her pioneer heritage, her unique experiences, and her sympathetic concern for the welfare of others helped Clarissa, as the Relief Society president, to focus her energies on improving the lives of the women she served.

Heritage

Clarissa's mother, Susan Elizabeth West, was born in Chalk Level, Tennessee, in 1833. That same year, two Latter-day Saint missionaries, David W. Patten and Warren Parrish, visited the West home, and Susan's mother, Margaret, was immediately convinced of the truthfulness of their message. She and her husband, Samuel Walker West, were soon baptized. They stayed in Tennessee for several years and gave generously to the missionaries who visited them from time to time.

One of the missionaries who visited the West family in Tennessee was George A. Smith. When the Wests moved to Nauvoo, Illinois, in 1842, Elder Smith helped them get established and introduced them to his cousin, the Prophet Joseph Smith, and also to Brigham Young.

Living in Nauvoo was a difficult adjustment for a family used to gentle Southern winters and modest prosperity. The Wests were cold and uncomfortable in their unfinished house, and for the first time in their married life, Samuel and Margaret were poor. Nevertheless, they did not consider their circumstances a hardship, for, as Margaret said,

"We had learned to eat food we had thought impossible to relish, but who was to be blamed, no one. We felt that we had the priceless jewel worth striving for, which I had seen in my dreams three years before we had heard of the Gospel."[1]

With the main exodus of Saints from Nauvoo in 1846, Samuel and Margaret took their nine children first to Mount Pisgah, Iowa, then to Kanesville, on the Iowa side of the Missouri River across from Winter Quarters. In 1851 they completed their journey to the Salt Lake Valley, arriving in September. Two weeks later at the October general conference, they heard their names read from the pulpit to join the Iron County Mission in Parowan. There they renewed their friendship with George A. Smith, the leader of the mission, who would soon become first counselor to President Brigham Young as well as Church historian.

By 1856, when Susan was twenty-three years old, three of her sisters were married. Her brother John, serving a mission in Hawaii, wrote of his concern about her marital status:

> I would like to ask, if it would not be amiss, when Susan
> is getting married? This is what I have been expecting to
> hear for sometime, but it has not as yet greeted my ears,
> but is yet expected. You should know that in order to
> become perfect in the eternal worlds, you must be
> attached to some good man. . . . I suppose when the one
> comes along that you are looking for, it will all be right
> if your sight should be good enough to perceive him.[2]

Both pretty and intelligent, Susan indeed had sight "good enough to perceive" a "good man" in George A. Smith. She accepted his proposal and married him in October 1857, becoming his seventh wife. He took her to Salt Lake City to live in his home in the Historian's Office with his first wife, Bathsheba Bigler W. Smith. The Historian's Office, built in 1857 and "quite grand by pioneer standards,"[3] had separate wings for the office and for the residences of Bathsheba's and Susan's families.

Home Life

Clarissa West Smith, the first of Susan's five daughters, was born April 21, 1859; she was named after Clarissa Lyman Smith, her paternal grandmother. Her four younger sisters, Margaret, Elizabeth, Priscilla, and Emma Pearl, were also born in the Historian's Office. Clarissa, her sisters, and her mother lived there until 1870, when George A. left on a mission to Palestine. They had two subsequent homes in Salt Lake City, one on Second West and the other on West Temple.

Clarissa, unlike her mother and grandmother, spent her childhood in one city and much of it in one home, unhampered by the anti-Mormon persecution her family had suffered in Nauvoo and the hardship of crossing the plains to Utah. Because of his large family, her father was not prosperous until his later years; yet the Smiths were not poor. Clarissa enjoyed her comfortable home, family, friends, and neighborhood.

The close and harmonious relationship between Clarissa's mother, George A.'s last wife, and Aunt Bathsheba, his first wife, promoted a pleasant home life. Susan was known as a "kindly, gentle, lovable and self-sacrificing" person. Like most polygamous wives, she operated a cottage industry to help support her family. Clarissa remembered a typical Christmas in the Smith home: "A shiny red apple was placed on the mantle shelf for each, and each also had a home-made wooden doll, the head and body hand-turned, the head painted, the arms and legs made of cloth, and dressed in clothes made by [our] mother."[4]

Clarissa and her friends often used nicknames for each other. Clarissa was "Clint" to some of her friends and "Clarissy" to her family. Her best childhood friends were Maimie and Josephine Young, daughters of Brigham Young. One afternoon President Young asked his two daughters to meet him at ZCMI, the Church-owned department store. They invited Clarissa to go with them. President Young asked the store clerk to cut two lengths of brown velvet for cloaks for his daughters, and when he saw Clarissa gazing at the beautiful material, he instructed the clerk to cut off another length for her.[5]

Living literally at the center of Church headquarters afforded the Smith girls many social and educational opportunities. Brigham Young and his family lived across the street; the mayor, Daniel H. Wells, and his family also lived close by. Within a block or so were the Deseret Store, the Tithing Office and yard, offices of the *Deseret News,* and Temple Square. The Council House, which for many years was the civic and educational center, and the Social Hall, also a social, recreational, and educational center, were both within a few blocks, as was the Salt Lake Theater.[6]

As the Smith girls grew older, they took organ, voice, and art lessons and attended the theater. Clarissa learned to card, dye, and reel yarn before it was spun and woven; and she learned hand sewing, patching, knitting, lace making, netting, embroidery, fruit drying, corn drying, and the art of making hair and wax flowers. She also enjoyed cooking and reading. She was particularly adept with words and excelled in correctly pronouncing, defining, and spelling almost any word.

Even as a young girl, Clarissa showed leadership ability. John Henry Smith, her half-brother, affectionately called her "the Little General." She often played the leading lady in school and church dramas, which, according to her friends, she enacted with "queenly dignity." Many times she traveled with her father when she was young. George A. was responsible for setting up post offices between Salt Lake City and St. George, and he also traveled frequently on Church assignments. Clarissa enjoyed the times alone with him that these trips afforded.

Clarissa may not have had her father at home constantly, but she did have a second mother in Bathsheba Smith. Bathsheba's only son, George A. Smith, Jr., had been killed by Indians in 1860 while on a mission with Jacob Hamblin. Two months later, her daughter married and moved away. Thus Aunt Bathsheba, a mother with an empty nest, devoted herself to Susan's five daughters, taking particular interest in the oldest, Clarissa. Bathsheba would have a lasting influence on the direction of Clarissa's life. Not only did she involve the young woman in Relief Society as a block teacher (now called visiting teacher), but she also predicted that Clarissa would one day become general president of the Relief Society.[7] Clarissa later recalled, "I began my Relief Society work when I was sixteen years old, going around the block as an assistant teacher, and I feel that the experience I gained at that time has been most valuable and formed the foundation for much of the work that I have been able to do since."[8]

Although the territorial legislature set up school districts within Utah Territory in 1851, tax-supported education was not available until 1890. Parents thus had the choice of sending their children to either ward schools or private schools. Clarissa attended Miss Cook's School, which was held in the Social Hall. Besides studying reading, spelling, arithmetic, and grammar, she took drama and gymnastic exercises. Mary Cook and her sister, Ida, were genteel women who graduated from normal schools in New York State and came to Utah to open a school in 1870. Because of its reputation for excellence, Miss Cook's School had a large enrollment and thus required several assistants. At age fourteen, Clarissa was hired as a pupil teacher.

Clarissa's next educational venture was at the University of Deseret (later the University of Utah), where she graduated with a teaching certificate with the first class. She taught school while attending the university, and after her graduation in 1875 she established her own private school, first in her parents' home and then in Parowan.

George A. Smith died the same year Clarissa graduated. Although he provided well for his wives at his death and Susan had a large, comfortable home, she decided to board university students and young working people. Her home was also a stopping-off point for the many friends and relatives who came to the city for Church or other business. As the oldest daughter, Clarissa helped her mother in taking care of their guests.

Also in 1875, Clarissa met a handsome, blond Welshman, twenty-four-year-old William Newjent Williams, whose family had immigrated to Utah when he was ten. William's mother, Sarah Jeremy Williams, and her two brothers were among the first converts to the Church in Wales. His father, Evan, was not interested in this new religion and would not allow his children to be baptized. He was, however, willing to leave Wales and move to Utah so his family would not be separated. During the trek to Utah, Sarah became very ill, and after witnessing her miraculous healing, Evan joined the Church.

Courtship and Marriage

During their two-year courtship, William and Clarissa's attraction for each other continued to grow. Then William received a mission call to Wales. Realizing the depth of their commitment to each other, they hurriedly decided to get married before he left and were thus married the following day, July 17, 1877, by her uncle, Judge Elias Smith. The next day, William left for a two-year mission to his native land. A week later, Clarissa wrote to Will, as she called him:

Darling old Will, If you only could imagine how
badly I want to see you would come right straight
back to me. . . .

Oh! Will, when I think that I won't see you again for
two years, it nearly drives me wild, and I don't expect
you back in less than that. . . .

The Sunday after you went away was the most lonesome day I ever spent. . . . On the Twenty Fourth I
went to the jubilee, . . . then Sade came down and said
that John Henry wanted Maggie and I to go to the
party with him. . . . I never realized my darling Will,
how much you contributed to my happiness until that
party. It was worse than eating beefstake without salt.

Do you know Will, this is the first letter I ever wrote
to you? Well it won't be the last for now you are my
hus_____. I can't write the rest it makes me blush.[9]

To keep herself busy and relieve her loneliness, Clarissa taught
school in Parowan in the Old Rock Church. Neither William nor his
parents thought she needed to teach school to support him, but independent Clarissa wrote to William: "You wrote and advised not to
teach any more but my dear . . . I have disobeyed you. I feel as if I
had rather be independent as long as I possibly can."[10]

William served his mission faithfully in Wales and wrote to Clarissa:

Very pleased to say that I have had joy and consolation
in my labors and feel satisfied with them. I realize that
the Lord has been with and has blessed me in various
ways. I have had kind friends to minister to my wants,
and have not suffered for the comforts and necessaries
of life; have continually enjoyed excellent health and
spirits, for which favors and blessings, I ever ascribe the
praise, honor and glory to the Almighty Giver.

I have walked 2227 and rode 924 miles. Preached (or rather attempted to) 177 times, 36 of which was in the open-air. Written 140 letters, 50 of which were to you. . . . Baptized 1; confirmed 6; children blessed 6; ordained 4.[11]

He returned home in July 1879.

Family Life

William and Clarissa's first home was at 37 North West Temple in Salt Lake City, next door to Clarissa's mother and across the street from the west gate of Temple Square. It was in this home that their eleven children were born, eight daughters and three sons: Clarissa, Susan, William Newjent, Sarah, Josephine, Hetty, Eva, Georgia, George Albert, Bathsheba, and Lyman Smith. Three of the children died before they reached adulthood: Susan as an infant; William Jr. of diphtheria at age five, on Christmas Eve; and Hetty of a rheumatic heart at age eighteen.

Aside from these periods of grief, the Williamses' home was a happy one, filled with laughter and good-natured humor. The children affectionately referred to their parents as "Mama" and "Papa." Though Clarissa did not raise her voice to discipline her children, they knew when their behavior disappointed her. At the dinner table she always sat at her husband's right so they could hold hands, characteristic of their devotion to each other. Dinner conversation centered around the children and what they were doing and the day's activities. Alice Merrill Horne, a granddaughter of Bathsheba Smith, often visited the home and remarked on the orderly yet loving atmosphere there:

At noon times, each child curled, clean-bibbed and fresh-aproned, sat up at a table, ready for the father's entrance with his loving kisses at the stroke of 12:00. When the mother finished the weekly ironing of 28 starched dresses—the weekly allowance for the girls adorned the ample clotheshorse. The writer often wondered how the children were up and dressed with such promptness and she one morning witnessed the

method: Uncle Will and Aunt Clarissa chose up sides
and ran races to see which side should be dressed first,
and every child was washed and smiling dressed and
up to the breakfast table almost before I could say
"Jack Robinson."[12]

In 1919, Clarissa and William built a large home at 1401 Sigsbee
Avenue in the Federal Heights area of Salt Lake City, near the University
of Utah. When their children were grown, they gathered every Sunday
evening at their parents' home for supper and visiting with the ever-
expanding family.

The Williamses valued education and urged their children to
attend college. Clarissa especially had strong feelings about education
for women and believed that higher education for girls was a necessity,
not a luxury. She and William gave Eva, their first child to graduate
from the University of Utah, a black graduation gown, which was
worn by all succeeding college graduates in the family.

In 1884, William established Co-op Furniture on West South
Temple in Salt Lake City. A few years later the company moved to
Main Street, next door to ZCMI. William was known as an astute
businessman, but one who was fair and honest. Clarissa occasionally
helped in the store as a bookkeeper. Co-op Furniture provided a good
living for William and Clarissa, who enjoyed their money but were not
ostentatious, although William always had fine horses and owned one
of the first automobiles in Salt Lake City. When they traveled on both
business and pleasure trips, they frequently took the children with
them. During the summers, the entire family, joined by an extended
family of aunts, uncles, and cousins, spent time together in their
mountain summer home.

Clarissa and William supported and complemented each other to
a remarkable degree. In addition to running his furniture business,
William was involved in numerous church and civic commitments,
serving as Red Cross city chairman, state senator, and member of the
Board of Regents of the University of Utah. He was active in several
Welsh organizations as well. He, in turn, supported and encouraged
Clarissa's activities outside the home. She once reminisced:

When I was married and had seven children, I was asked to be secretary of the Seventeenth Ward Relief Society. I felt that I could not do this with all of my little babies. But my husband said, "My dear, you must do it; it is the very thing you need; you need to get away from the babies, and I will help you all I can, either by taking care of the children or making out your reports or copying your minutes, or any other thing I can do."[13]

Clarissa was later called to preside over the Salt Lake Stake Relief Society. She also became involved in community organizations, including the Daughters of the Revolution and the Daughters of the Utah Pioneers. She was president of the Authors' Club and a member of the Friendship Circle, both literary clubs. During World War I, she served as state chairman of the Woman's Committee of the National Council of Defense and on the Red Cross Civilian Committee. Clarissa and the woman who would become her successor as general Relief Society president, Louise Yates Robison, became friends while preparing surgical dressings for the Red Cross.

Clarissa and William were gracious hosts and entertained frequently. Their home on Sigsbee Avenue had a ballroom downstairs and was the scene of many parties. Clarissa was an expert cook, having taken classes from well-known chefs as well as helping to cook for her mother's boarders. She owned thirty-six place settings of fine china, which she used often. But her hospitality extended beyond setting a beautiful table and serving a delicious meal. She made her guests feel genuinely welcome in her home. A generous woman, she often served meals to uninvited guests. Her daughter Eva Williams Darger recalled:

As a little girl I remember the many hobos, vagrants or tramps who would knock at the back door for a "handout." One summer day when three or four men had come to the door for food, Mama asked, "Where are these men coming from?" The hungry hobo said, "Ma'am, there is a mark on the tree in your front yard that tells us that you are generous with your food. We have marks that let our friends know about mad dogs, gun crazy men and good victuals. You ought to be proud, Ma'am, of your generous reputation."[14]

Clarissa's daughters inherited their mother's love of entertaining, for as adults, they and the daughters-in-law took turns hosting weekly Thursday luncheons at which Clarissa was the honored guest. These luncheons, Eva said, were "viewed as productions so the fine china, silver, crystal and linen were always used to set the table (often a card table in a small apartment) and the latest recipe from one of the current women's magazines was tried. All of the Williams girls prided ourselves on being excellent cooks and have always been as interested in the attractive presentation of the food as the taste and nutritional value."[15]

A grandson, William C. VanLaw, described William and Clarissa as the "king and queen." He said:

> Grandmother Williams was absolutely a beautiful woman and she had a stateliness about her that I've seen in very few people in all my life. When she walked into a room, everyone stopped talking and looked at her and admired her. She was always extremely well-groomed. She was a little on the heavy side and was extremely well-dressed. Navy was her favorite color. She had attractive jewelry which Grandfather I'm sure had given her. She was a stately woman. Grandfather, by the same token, was a very fine looking man. He was a little under six feet tall and was broad shouldered, very neat in appearance, wearing basically gray or navy suits.
>
> As I look back, I wonder what caused the charisma that they created with their family and with their friends. And it was just this graciousness about both of them and the stately approach they took. But they were just natural about everything; I don't ever remember either one of them putting on any airs. They were just delightful people to be around.[16]

One of the reasons people liked Clarissa was that she loved people and remembered details about them. Evalyn D. Bennett, a granddaughter, said that with Clarissa's remarkable memory, "she could recall the face and name of just about everyone she ever met. She could come up with the circumstance of the meeting and incidentals about the events that would astound people. And she enjoyed laughing and had a wonderful sense of humor."[17]

In 1901, Bathsheba W. Smith, the general Relief Society president, appointed Clarissa treasurer and member of the general board. When Emmeline B. Wells succeeded Bathsheba as general president in 1911, she selected Clarissa as first counselor.

The "Gracious General"

President Heber J. Grant called Clarissa to serve as the sixth president of the Relief Society in April 1921. She chose Jennie Brimhall Knight as first counselor and Louise Yates Robison as second counselor. Both women served in the presidency until Clarissa's release in 1928. The *Salt Lake Telegram* said of her appointment, "Mrs. Williams is gifted with rare executive ability and is a natural leader of women, being endowed with the highest quality of mind and heart. Her genial and friendly disposition, her pleasant personality and her goodness instinctively draw everyone to her."[18]

During Clarissa's progressive administration, she combined the offices of secretary and treasurer and instituted modern accounting procedures for handling Relief Society funds. One of her major contributions came in her emphasis on social services. Concerned about infant and maternal mortality rates, the high number of child and adolescent deaths, lack of opportunities for the handicapped, and the low standard of living for many women, she expanded the Social Service Department of the Relief Society. The purpose of social service work, as she saw it, was to bring about advancements in "health, opportunity, and a decent standard of living for all those with whom we come in contact. Such an undertaking for general betterment comprehends careful preparation, training, educational work, and actual service."[19]

Amy Brown Lyman, who was serving at that time as secretary-treasurer of the Relief Society, summarized some of the organization's programs: "With a view of improving the humanitarian work of the Society, regular study in the field of social service has been introduced in every ward and branch through the educational department in connection with the other well established courses. This study has included child welfare, poverty, disease, crime, employment and economic conditions, leisure time activities, etc. In addition, social service institutes have been held for the training of local workers and for the purpose of assisting them in solving some of their pressing practical problems. In connection with this work, a laboratory or department for experimental purposes and for training purposes has been established at Relief Society Headquarters."[20]

Clarissa traveled extensively in the United States and abroad, visiting the ever-growing number of stakes. She also represented the Relief Society at two congresses of the National Council of Women, one in New Orleans, Louisiana, and the other in Cleveland, Ohio. In May 1914, she was one of nine United States delegates to the international Council of Women in Rome; and in 1925, when the council met in Washington, D.C., she was again in attendance.

William accompanied her to the Rome conference, and they toured Europe afterwards, making an excursion to Wales in order to visit his family home in Brechfa. They were in England when World War I broke out and returned home immediately.

At the close of World War I, the U.S. government forbade any group or individual to store large quantities of food. The wheat from the grain storage program, which the Relief Society began in 1876, was therefore sold. As a result, wards that previously had large supplies of wheat suddenly had large supplies of cash. The Relief Society recommended that these funds be centralized in the Presiding Bishop's Office and that the accrued interest be used for health, maternity, and child welfare services. Clarissa was especially interested in the needs of handicapped and underprivileged children. One project the fund made possible was youth camps operated during the summers of 1924 to 1928, enabling city children to spend two weeks in the country. Other efforts involved health examinations for preschool children, a free-milk fund, and courses in home hygiene and care of the sick.

Clarissa also proposed the creation of memorial funds to honor the past Relief Society presidents and to further important society projects. The general board approved her recommendation and honored her by establishing the Clarissa S. Williams Loan Fund for Public Health Nurses. Other memorials included the Eliza R. Snow Relief Society Memorial Prize Poem Fund, which provided first and second prizes for publication of poems in the *Relief Society Magazine;* the Zina D. H. Young Relief Society Memorial Nurse Loan Fund, for undergraduate nurses; the Bathsheba W. Smith Relief Society Memorial Temple Grant, which provided a yearly amount for temple work for women; and the Emmeline B. Wells Relief Society Memorial Loan Fund, established at Brigham Young University for upper-division female students.

William and Clarissa celebrated their fiftieth wedding anniversary in July 1927, although William was not well enough to greet guests. That December he died of cancer.

Knowing her own health was failing and not wanting to hinder the work of the Relief Society, Clarissa asked for her release in October 1928, having served as general president for seven and a half years. In her last address as president, she said: "Now I like to feel that I have no regrets, that I have done my work as well as I could, that I have tried to have the spirit of the Lord with me at all times."[21]

In the December 1928 issue of the *Relief Society Magazine,* the editors paid tribute to Clarissa: "President Williams always presided with graciousness and with dignity. She was never more lovable or appreciative than in those last days when she confided to the ward and to the stake officers and to her own Board her decision. . . . If there had ever been a particle of doubt about her generalship, which there had not, her closing hour crowned her as supreme."[22]

Clarissa was a "leader of leaders" and an able administrator, but also "a friend of women," said Lotta Paul Baxter, a Relief Society general board member. "All women of her acquaintance felt her interest in them and her desire to make them happier by making surrounding conditions better. Filled with sympathy and understanding of the difficulties that beset women in remote places, she was thinking constantly of something to benefit them."[23] Not only was she concerned about the physical welfare of women, but she also believed that women should develop their talents and skills and further their education so that they might make an impact on both the home and society.

Clarissa Smith Williams died on March 8, 1930, at the age of seventy-one. She was devoted to the Lord's work and to the women she served, and in all of her relationships with family, friends, coworkers, and associates, she made lives happier and better through her gracious and genuine concern.

Notes

1. John James, Jr., Williams Family Reunion booklet, June 19–26, 1977, p. 15.

2. Letter of John A. West, July 28, 1856, Hoolau, Hawaii, in W. N. Williams Grand Family Reunion booklet, August 7–10, 1970, p. 7.

3. Richard W. James, "Mission to Wales—1877–79" (privately published, 1987), p. vi.

4. Reunion booklet, 1970, p. 9.

5. "Brigham Young," *Friend,* June 1971, pp. 20–21.

6. "Mission to Wales," p. vii.

7. "Sketch of the Home Life of Clarissa S. Williams," Alice Merrill Horne, p. 1; in possession of Richard W. James.

8. "Report of Relief Society Conference," *Relief Society Magazine* 15 (December 1928): 668.

9. Clarissa S. Williams to William N. Williams, July 27, 1877, in "Mission to Wales—1877–79," p. 40.

10. Clarissa S. Williams to William N. Williams, March 19, 1878, in possession of Richard W. James.

11. William N. Williams to Clarissa S. Williams, December 31, 1878, in "Mission to Wales—1877–79."

12. "Sketch of the Home Life of Clarissa S. Williams," p. 3.

13. "Report of Relief Society Conference," p. 668; quoted in Evalyn D. Bennett, Relief Society Legacy Lecture, March 1982.

14. Personal history of Eva W. Darger.

15. Ibid.

16. Oral History of William C. VanLaw, typescript in possession of Richard W. James, pp. 11–12.

17. Relief Society Legacy Lecture.

18. *Salt Lake Telegram,* April 2, 1921, p. 8.

19. Clarissa Smith Williams, quoted in *Deseret News,* September 23, 1926, p. 2.

20. Amy Brown Lyman, "Clarissa Smith Williams," typescript in possession of Evalyn Darger Bennett.

21. Relief Society Legacy Lecture.

22. "Report of Relief Society Conference," p. 651.

23. "Tributes to Clarissa Smith Williams," *Relief Society Magazine* 16 (May 1930): 226.

7

LOUISE YATES ROBISON
1928–1939

Louise Yates Robison, shy, self-effacing, and with minimal formal education, could not have imagined as a young girl or even as a young mother that she would one day serve as general president of the Relief Society. Yet her faithful convert parents, her selfless service to others, her varied leadership experiences, and her understanding of the common women of the Church prepared her well to lead the Relief Society during the Depression years.

Heritage

Louise's parents, Elizabeth Francis and Thomas Yates, were both from England. As a child, Elizabeth was told by her father, "We do not have the gospel the Bible tells about, but someday it will come and when it does, you must not be afraid to accept it."[1] After she was married and had four children, Elizabeth heard about the restored gospel and was converted to The Church of Jesus Christ of Latter-day Saints. Her husband demanded that she abandon her new religion or give up her family, and her mother disowned her. But Elizabeth put her faith in a verse in the Bible that her father had taught her: "He that loveth father or mother more than me is not worthy of me; and he that loveth son or daughter more than me is not worthy of me" (Matthew 10:37).

Elizabeth's husband left her, and she found work at a woolen mill to support her family. When he saw that she was getting along and still very happy with her new religion, he abducted their four little girls. Brokenhearted, Elizabeth spent the next six years and every pence she earned trying to locate her children. Two of the girls died when they were small, and she never saw them again. But many years later, in Utah, she and her remaining two daughters were finally reunited.

During those years of searching, Elizabeth met Elder Thomas Yates. His family were among the early converts in England, and Thomas served a six-and-a-half-year mission there. When Thomas saw how despairing and destitute Elizabeth was, he suggested that she live with his family. The two subsequently decided to join the gathering of Saints to Zion, and they were married in July 1863 on the journey west.

Arriving in Utah in October that year, Thomas and Elizabeth Yates lived in Lehi for a short time; then Church leaders sent them south with six other families to colonize Round Valley in Millard County. Finding only a few cottonwood trees and knee-high grass to greet them, the settlers lived in dugout shelters while they built log houses at the townsite of Scipio. There the Yateses' first child, Elizabeth (Lizzie), was born in 1865. The next year Indians killed three members of the little colony in Scipio and drove off the settlers' cattle and horses. All the men were needed to recover the stolen livestock. Knowing it would not be safe for his wife and fifteen-month-old Lizzie to remain alone in the log house, Thomas hid them in a potato pit and secured the cover. Elizabeth, who was nine months pregnant, slipped on the crude ladder, fell in the pitch-dark pit, and spent a terrifying night injured and afraid the Indians might find her. A few days later Thomas and Elizabeth's second daughter was born in the only log house in town. The family soon moved to the log meetinghouse, where all the families in the settlement "forted up" as a further protection in the uneasy relations with the Indians. Elizabeth and Thomas named their second daughter Sarah Louisa Yates, and she became known as Louise. They had three other children: Emily, born in 1868; Thomas, 1870; and Maud, 1874. Emily and Maud died as children.

Growing-Up Years

Pioneering had its hardships but also its pleasures, and Louise thought of her childhood as happy and her parents as "splendid, . . . refined, spiritual and loving."[2] As a young girl, she learned to wash, dye, and spin wool, knit stockings, and braid straw hats. Louise and her sisters always wore straw hats they fashioned themselves because

Elizabeth would not let her daughters wear sunbonnets to church. She decorated their dresses and underclothing with velvet ribbon and lace she had brought from England. Louise knew the value her mother placed on fine things, for Elizabeth had given up her wagon seat and had walked across the plains rather than throw out her trunks of fabric and Haviland china.

"While candy was unknown," said Louise, "we always had a Christmas tree, decorated with molasses cookies, cut in fascinating shapes, and the ends of homemade tallow candles which had been saved for lighting the tree. Birthdays were never forgotten. There were always gifts under our breakfast plates—a new pinafore, handknit stockings, and often a homemade toy. For spring birthdays, a magic whistle made from the green twig of a tree was always a treasure." On their birthdays, the children were exempted from chores; the other children carried extra firewood and chips and did household duties for the birthday sibling.

A large child for her age, Louise claimed she was the ugly duckling of the family. She related an incident when her clumsiness, however, benefited her:

> One time a neighbor gave my sister and me a real treat; a stalk each of sugar cane. Gentle cows roamed the streets, and they too enjoyed sugar cane. As we passed a cow on the way home, she caught Lizzie's cane in her mouth and easily drew it out of small hands. We were both frightened and ran home; Lizzie, wailing loudly, told of her adventure. Father asked how I had saved mine and I replied, "I fell on it." For years I could not understand my parents laughing over such a serious episode and Mother said, "My poor child," and laughed again.

In later years, Elizabeth acknowledged that Lizzie actually cried herself to sleep because her sister Louise was "so ugly no one would love her." Throughout her life, Louise was reserved and shy.

Louise learned fastidiousness from her mother, who maintained dignity and order in spite of pioneer conditions. Every evening one of the children carried water from the ditch so that Elizabeth and the children could take a sponge bath the next morning. Louise often heard her mother quote Grandfather Francis's words: "A lady does not leave home until her gloves are fastened and her veil adjusted." And Elizabeth seldom went out without her gloves and veil, even in Scipio. Louise followed her mother's example. Belle S. Spafford recalled in her own memoirs, "I never saw [Louise], not once to my memory, that she didn't have a pair of white gloves in her purse."[3] Elizabeth also told her children that since they were gentle-born, their conduct must be good.

Since her mother served as ward Relief Society president for three years and then as president of the Millard Stake Relief Society for twenty-five years, Louise grew up with Relief Society. At her mother's side, she gleaned wheat for the Relief Society grain storage program, gathered "Sunday eggs" (money from eggs gathered on Sunday was donated to the Perpetual Emigration Fund), helped care for the sick, and prepared the dead for burial.

Louise learned lasting lessons on honesty from her father, who served as bishop of the Scipio Ward from 1882 until his death in 1903. He once bought a calf from a man who, several months later, claimed that Thomas had not paid for the animal. Thomas was sure that he had paid, but he did not have a receipt. Although he had saved enough money to attend general conference, he felt that he would not have the spirit to go if he had cheated someone so he paid for the calf a second time. Later, the man's wife remembered that Thomas had paid, and the man apologized.

As a young girl, Louise attended "School M'am Martin's" home school. Ann E. Martin set a high standard for education in the one-room dwelling that housed both her school and her family. Later, Louise attended classes in the Scipio town hall, which served as church, school, and amusement center.

When Lizzie was fifteen and Louise fourteen, they ventured from Scipio to Provo to attend the Brigham Young Academy. Riding to Provo on the train was a new adventure for the girls, and after their father found a home for them to live in, they experienced another first—going to the big city of Salt Lake for a "lark." Before he left Lizzie and Louise in Provo for his return trip to Scipio, Thomas bought the girls a bag of oranges, candy, and nuts, but he would not let them see him off at the train station—he didn't want to cry in front of them. After he left, Louise and Lizzie felt very homesick. Louise recalled, "Even our new dresses and the joy of wearing them for every day, our cambric underwear trimmed with store embroidery instead of the bleached muslin with homemade lace, could not make up to us our loneliness for our home."

The thoroughly English Yateses wanted their children to have not only academic learning but also vocational training. They reared their children on the maxim "knowledge is never a burden; learn all you can." Thus, at the end of the year at Brigham Young Academy, Elizabeth took the girls to Salt Lake City and arranged for Lizzie to take a course in millinery, and Louise, in dressmaking.

Louise and Lyman

In 1882, when Louise turned sixteen, her formal education ended abruptly when Joseph Lyman Robison returned to Millard County from a mission to England and attended stake conference with his father, a member of the stake presidency. This was the first time stake conference had been held in their town hall, and all the Church members in Scipio turned out to give the building a thorough cleaning. They were proud of the spiffed-up hall except for the calcimined ceiling, which no amount of scrubbing could improve. Louise said, "There was nothing to do about it except to pray that the 'city visitors' would not notice the ceiling and upper walls, but we were sensitive over the mottled appearance."

Louise thought the young men in Scipio were "fine, but when this boy [Lyman Robison] came with his dashing sideburns, a derby hat and caned umbrella, latest clothes—well . . ." However, she observed that the first thing he did during the conference was notice the ceiling. "My high estimation dropped immediately," she said, "and I was hopping mad." Their next meeting occurred early one morning after Louise had stayed up all night sewing burial clothes. Her father called her to the kitchen and there she met Lyman face to face, embarrassed that he saw her "in such a mess."

Nonetheless, Lyman and Louise's relationship developed through the spring and summer months, and they were married October 11, 1883. Their first child, Lyman Harold Robison, was born eleven months later, followed over the next several years by the births of Florence, Rulon, Winifred, Gladys, and Dorothy.

The Family Years

For six years, Louise and Lyman and their growing family resided in Fillmore. Then they moved to Provo for a short time before settling in Salt Lake City. Although a hard worker and a devoted family man, Lyman was not a businessman. He was, by nature, a philosopher who read widely and thought deeply. Because his dreams to become a doctor were stifled by his strict New England father, Lyman ended up as a traveling corset salesman, an occupation he neither enjoyed nor prospered in.

Lyman and Louise had a warm, loving relationship throughout their marriage. Whenever Lyman's work took him out of town, he wrote cheerful and tender letters to her and also to his children as they began to leave home. He loved poetry and often included a poem or two in his letters.

Although financially hard-pressed, the Robisons provided a happy home environment for their children, who claimed they never noticed a lack of material goods, due, in part, to Louise's creativity in making holidays festive occasions. She continued the tradition of celebrating birthdays with the birthday child doing no work and choosing the dinner menu and manner of celebration. At Easter time, Louise created elaborate eggs, painting faces on empty egg shells—a baby in a baby bonnet, a Chinese man with a long black pigtail, a Floradora doll with an elegant hat.

Christmas brought its traditional festivities to the Robison household, although they seldom had a Christmas tree because Lyman admired trees so much he thought it a terrible sin to cut one down. He often told his children, "The groves were God's first temples." The children's homemade decorations adorned the house. They traditionally hung their stockings until adulthood, and Louise always set out two kinds of pie for Santa Claus on Christmas Eve. Her daughter Gladys R. Winter recalled, "Oh, those pies! I wonder if all children grow up as we did, with the firm assurance that Mama was the one best cook in the world. Her pies were superlative and generous."

Gladys also recalled the clever ways Louise devised to present the gifts:

> I remember one Christmas morning, there was a myriad of colored ribbons with one end attached to the center light fixture in the dining room. There was a different color for each child, and when we'd follow the ribbon we'd find a gift. They went all over, upstairs, the back porch, under a sofa, until the whole morning was spent in retrieving them. Another time when we were older, every gift had to be accompanied by a bit of poetry or a rhyming jingle. Often, we didn't have the fancy things that most of our friends had, but our home was always full of understanding, happiness, and love.

Louise manifested that love especially when the children were sick. Rulon recalled his mother bending over him when he awakened from one of his illnesses, "with the sweet, warm kindness that was so much a part of her." During Gladys's frequent bouts with tonsillitis, Louise would pick rose petals from the garden and press them against her hot face, then scatter more petals on the pillow to leave a pleasant fragrance. When the fever subsided and Gladys began to feel better, her mother made her comfortable in mounds of pillows, kept her warm with the best quilts, and served her "the daintiest, most appetizing trays with special linen and china." In fact, Gladys wondered how any child ever wanted to get well with Louise's pampering.

Louise was a cheerful person, often singing as she worked, and she had a sense of humor. Her method of discipline was very mild, and her children soon found that a disappointed look or an "I'm grieved to have my little girl [or boy] act like that!" was punishment more effective than a spanking.

She frequently recited poetry to her children. A typical verse was:

> God give me sympathy and sense
> And help to keep my courage high,
> God give me calm and confidence
> And, please, a twinkle in my eye.

Her children also heard her repeat maxims, such as:

> "Never put a nickel so close to your eye that you cannot see a dollar beyond it."
> "Live above petty things; don't descend to their level."
> "Welcome the task that takes you beyond yourself."

One of the philosophies Louise also lived by was to always accept a call in the Church and, even though it might be difficult at times to fulfill, to do her best. Rulon said:

> I remember when we were growing up, [Mother] would leave the younger children in the charge of those who were older, and every week, through rain, snow or sleet, walk the 2 or 3 or miles each way to take care of the Mutual Improvement duties. . . . She was alone and I knew she was afraid crossing the (then) empty fields and streets in the dark, but she never hesitated. . . . With such determination, one would expect a rather harsh, insensitive, uncompromising personality, but this was by no means the case. She was warm and sympathetic, self-forgetful, but thoughtful of others; demanding much from herself, she asked little of others. . . . She had a knack of thawing cold hearts; and those who talked with her, almost always went away with a smile and a lighter heart.

Despite her humble circumstances, Louise continued to appreciate the finer things of life. She loved nature, especially trees and flowers, which she planted in abundance everywhere she lived. Jennie Brimhall Knight, a friend of Louise's, admired the maple trees she planted in Provo. At Louise's suggestion, a Churchwide home beautification campaign was introduced. In the 1940s, a Daughters of the Utah Pioneers post in California honored Louise with a plaque in a eucalyptus grove commemorating her beautification efforts.

Although early marriage interrupted her schooling, Louise never quit learning. As each of her children went to school, she went through school with them, studying their lessons as she helped them with their homework. Rulon explained:

> By the time the youngest child was through school, Mother was better in his studies than any of us. I remember her discussing with us the various points of German, history, grammar, and mathematics. Not content with all this, when her children were grown, she enrolled in university extension courses, and during the time she spent seven or eight hours a day in the Burial Clothes department of the Relief Society, she would arise at 4:00 each morning and work two hours on this extension work, doing her housekeeping and the work she loved in the garden between 6:00 and 7:30 A.M., and again in the evening after work. This program went on, not for a few weeks, but for years. This is surely remarkable for its energy, and desire for improvement, and the ability to hold fast to such a program in spite of difficulties.

While Louise and her family were living in Provo, she noticed a large sore growing on her face, which her doctor diagnosed as cancer. Louise's bishop sent the stake patriarch, who asked if he could give Louise a patriarchal blessing before administering to her. In this blessing, he told her that her voice would be heard in many parts of the world. It was an extraordinary blessing under the circumstances, for until she moved to Provo, Louise had not held a church position, and at the time of the blessing she was secretary of the Mutual in her ward. Her face healed without a scar and without surgery, and through her forthcoming service the patriarchal blessing would be literally fulfilled—despite the fact that she was by nature, according to Gladys, "the shyest and most self-effacing of women, with little education and no wealth nor social position."

Concerning her mother's self-consciousness, Gladys said:

> I have never known a woman who was more eager to avoid the limelight. For instance, I worked in a large

office, and for some time my health was not good, and
when it was possible, Father would come in the car to
pick me up, and often would ask Mother to come into
the office to tell me he was ready. Although all the
workers there were her good friends, it seemed physically impossible for her to face that big expanse of
desks, with eyes looking at her. So I can imagine what
courage and trust in her Father in Heaven it took for
her to preside over and conduct a large conference of
women or meet with the highest officials of the state
and nation and represent them throughout the world.

Opportunities to Serve

The Robisons moved to Logan and then to Salt Lake City. Louise
continued working in the MIA and learned a valuable lesson while
serving as YWMIA president. She wanted two friends for her counselors, but the bishop called two other women instead. As they worked
together in the presidency, Louise found these women to be ideal
counselors, and they became the dearest of friends. She also endeared
herself to the Mutual girls, who enlisted her help when the bishop, a
strict man, objected to young people dancing the new round dances,
including the waltz. At least once during an evening dance, Louise got
the bishop in a corner of the room, with his back to the dance floor,
and earnestly discussed problems so that he would not notice the
young people doing the daring waltz. The bishop thought Louise a
conscientious executive, while the MIA members thought she was an
understanding leader.

Louise saw many opportunities to serve in both the Church and the
community. During World War I, she took a Red Cross training course
and prepared surgical dressings. An expert seamstress, she taught courses
in gauze preparation and headed the Red Cross volunteers who worked
at the Gardo House, the old home of Brigham Young's wife Amelia. She
also volunteered with Travelers' Aid and gathered old clothes for refugees
in the Near East. Gladys remarked about her mother's service:

In later years, I have realized the tremendous amount
of energy and time that Mother used in the various

activities, for she never used a committee for honor or prestige, but she would volunteer for the hardest, grubbiest work, as in assembling and distributing old clothes, or in meeting the earliest and latest trains in serving with the Traveler's Aid. I can still see her in the middle of mounds of old clothes and old shoes, sorting and matching pairs and selecting and packing piles of clothing to be sent to those unfortunate refugees.

Although her children were nearly grown when she was the busiest in these organizations, we were never conscious of her responsibilities and accomplishments because somehow she kept the home running smoothly with very few late meals, and the cake we wanted to take to a party, or a special dress that was needed, was always ready.

Relief Society Service

In 1914, Louise began her service in Relief Society, first as a stake board member and then as first counselor in the presidency in the Granite Stake Relief Society. At the Relief Society general conference in October 1928, President Heber J. Grant released Emmeline B. Wells as president and announced the calling of Clarissa Smith Williams, with whom Louise had become good friends during their World War I Red Cross work. Then President Grant announced Jennie Knight as first counselor and Louise Robison as second counselor. Louise raised her hand in approval, surprised that the second counselor had a name so similar to hers. "I had never heard of her but I voted for her," Louise later said. "When I realized it was myself, I was so upset." She did not think she had the ability or the background to fulfill this calling, and she worried for days. But the words of her good friend Anna Musser gave her comfort and courage: "True, many people have money, but it is the poor and humble people that make up the Church."

Louise enjoyed her association with the other members of the presidency and with the Relief Society sisters they met in their visits to wards and stakes. Public speaking was difficult for her, but it helped her to overcome her inherent shyness. She extended her warmth and wit to everyone she served. "I enjoyed every minute that we spent in visiting the different wards and stakes, and going with the president to visit at conferences," she said. "We had many contraptions to travel in, such as a Ford without any brakes. That made President Williams very nervous."

Seven years later, on October 7, 1928, President Grant extended a call to Louise to serve as the seventh general president of the Relief Society. She chose Amy Brown Lyman as first counselor, Julia A. Child as second counselor, and Julia A. F. Lund as secretary-treasurer. Kate M. Barker succeeded Julia Child in April 1935.

Sustained on the eve of the Depression, Louise was a woman for her time. Acutely aware of her own lack of formal education and of material wealth, she focused her concern on those in similar circumstances. One of her significant accomplishments was the establishment of the Mormon Handicraft Shop in 1937. The economic stresses of the Depression forced many women to work, but Louise felt strongly that wherever possible, mothers should be at home with their children rather than in the workplace. The Mormon Handicraft Shop thus provided an outlet for women to market their home crafts. Such a concept was not entirely new to Louise, for her father had operated a co-op in Scipio for many years. Relief Society co-ops had also existed when a number of Relief Societies had their own halls in the early settlements, but these had gradually been discontinued. The Mormon Handicraft Shop located near Relief Society headquarters was the most successful of these cooperative ventures. The shop would continue to be operated by the Relief Society until 1986, when, because it no longer fit the needs of the worldwide Church, it was turned over to Deseret Book Company.

Another of Louise's programs was the Singing Mothers Chorus. In 1934, the Relief Society sought a name for the choruses that sang at Relief Society general conferences and in the wards and stakes. One of Louise's favorite quotations, "A singing mother makes a happy home," inspired the selection of the name Singing Mothers. Always keeping women of modest means in mind, Louise insisted on a uniform of dark skirts and white blouses because she believed that most women would own a skirt and blouse and thus would not have to spend money on new outfits.

Although Louise held a position of influence and prestige, she never lost the common touch, according to Dorothy R. Bosquet, her youngest daughter. Dorothy and her sisters used to joke that they could never walk down Main Street if they were in a hurry because their mother would always stop and talk with everyone they met. Louise, warm and sympathetic in spite of her shyness, reached out to people, endearing herself to them by remembering the details of their lives. She remembered people's names as well as the names of their children and spouses. Rulon believed that such warmth and consideration made her "one of the most widely beloved women in the Church."

Once a young woman, away from home, pregnant, and unmarried, came to Louise's office—her door was never closed. While Louise listened to the woman's problems, she mended and cleaned her visitor's jacket, then arranged for interviews with several businesses and gave her money to buy a new dress and to have her hair done.

Louise also suggested that the general board adopt blue and gold as the official Relief Society colors. As early as 1896, general board minutes referred to Relief Society colors, but they were not made the official colors until Louise's administration.

Just as Louise reprimanded her children gently, when the Relief Society sisters needed a little nudging she did so with good humor and gentleness. Although General Authorities suggested that women remove their fashionably large hats during meetings, many women kept them on rather than disturb their hair or appearance. At the beginning of one Relief Society conference, Louise announced to the congregation, "Sisters, we are going to remain seated while we sing our first song. I'm sure you have books and papers and your hats on your laps, and I'm afraid it would be hard for you to hold all of them if you stand." There were smiles and surprise in the congregation as the embarrassed ladies quickly removed their hats.

As president of the Relief Society, Louise participated in the hundredth anniversary of the founding of The Church of Jesus Christ of Latter-day Saints in April 1930. One of the celebration events was the opening of the Relief Society jubilee box, which contained letters, photographs, and memorabilia that had been gathered five decades earlier by Sarah M. Kimball, general secretary of the Relief Society. President Heber J. Grant, Church Historian Joseph Fielding Smith, the Relief Society presidency, members of the general board, and descendants of Sarah M. Kimball and other early Relief Society leaders opened the box. In it was a letter addressed to the secretary of the Relief Society in 1930:

> Hon. Secretary: This is dedicated to you with the fond hope and firm belief you are enjoying many advantages and blessings that were not enjoyed by your predecessors.
>
> May God abundantly bless you and your labors.
> [Signed] Sarah M. Kimball
> Sec. Relief Society
> Salt Lake City
> April 1st, 1881

In 1933, the First Presidency dedicated a monument at the site of the Joseph Smith store in Nauvoo, Illinois, commemorating the organization of the Relief Society at that site on March 17, 1842. General Authorities, Relief Society board members, descendants of Joseph and Emma Hale Smith, leaders of the Reorganized Church of Jesus Christ of Latter Day Saints, and officials from the state of Illinois and surrounding communities attended the dedicatory ceremonies. Twenty years later, the monument was moved to a new location, the site of the Nauvoo Temple.

Worldwide Influence

Louise fulfilled the promise in her patriarchal blessing that her voice would be heard in many parts of the world. She was the first general Relief Society president to visit branches and districts of the Church in England and Europe. She went to Hawaii, which she described as "paradise." She also attended a national conference of social workers in Toronto and visited Boston, Philadelphia, and Valley Forge.

By virtue of her position as Relief Society president, Louise was a member of the National Council of Women. In that capacity, she traveled to Washington, D.C., for an NCW conference and was entertained at the White House. When the NCW planned an international convention and invited women from all over the world to attend, Louise was asked to take charge of one of the meetings. At first, she felt that she simply could not do it. "Then," she said, "the thought came to my mind to make the best of all opportunities. The names I had to pronounce were terrible, most of them being foreigners. But it was a wonderful experience." She also traveled to Paris for an International Council of Women conference and worked on the Equal Moral Standards Committee.

Louise's husband, Lyman, who cheerfully encouraged his wife to serve in her various capacities, died in October 1935 at the age of seventy-six. On New Year's Eve, 1939, Louise was released after eleven years of service as general Relief Society president. She then moved to California to live with her daughter and son-in-law, Gladys and Stephen Winter. Ill for the last few months of her life, Sarah Louisa Yates Robison died on March 30, 1946, at the age of seventy-nine. Fittingly, the Singing Mothers sang at her funeral, which was held in the Assembly Hall on Temple Square in Salt Lake City.

Louise Y. Robison lived by the motto "Welcome the task that takes you beyond yourself." A "common" woman, she had such strong faith in the Lord that she overcame extreme shyness and fear of public speaking to address audiences throughout the world. Called to the presidency at a stressful economic time, she established programs that helped lift the financial burdens of many Relief Society sisters. Her practical spirituality and refined humility made her an effective president for the era in which she served.

Notes

1. All quotations in this chapter but two (notes 2 and 3) are taken from the family scrapbook compiled by Gladys Robison Winter, LDS Church Archives.

2. Jennie Knight Brimhall, "Louise Yates Robison," *Relief Society Magazine* 16 (January 1929): 3.

3. Oral History of Belle S. Spafford, LDS Church Archives, p. 40.

8

AMY BROWN LYMAN
1940–1945

Amy Brown Lyman, general president of the Relief Society, sat at the honored guests' table in the Lafayette Ballroom of the Hotel Utah. It was the evening of March 20, 1943, and the Salt Lake City Council of Women had prepared a large banquet to honor seven women, including Amy. After dinner, the lights dimmed and a miniature drama opened on the stage. The spotlight focused on a young girl dressed in pale pink chiffon, Amy Kathryn Lyman, granddaughter of Amy Brown Lyman.

Amy Kathryn opened a book representing the autobiography of her grandmother and read, "Our home, a one and one-half story adobe house, was lighted with kerosene lamps and candles—lamps for downstairs and candles for upstairs. The candles were molded by my mother's own hands. As we ascended the stairs each evening, a mark on the candle indicated how long we could study or visit or play before we retired."[1]

As Amy Kathryn read, Amy Brown Lyman's daughter, Margaret Lyman Schreiner, walked onto the stage dressed as Amy's mother and sat in a chair by an old-fashioned table. Four children came in and gathered around Mother Brown, who went through the motions of lighting a candle. In pantomime, she explained the mark on the candle, kissed each child good night, and sent all four up a set of rag-carpeted stairs.

Memories no doubt flooded Amy's mind as she watched the spotlight return to Amy Kathryn, who closed the book and then said to the audience:

The idea intrigued me. I visualized my grandmother as a little girl, in a gray linsey-wool dress, her dark hair combed smoothly from her face. In my mind I could see her eyes fastened on the mark her mother had made on the candle she carried, and I know she was hoping it would burn slowly that she might get as much reading done as possible. Again and again I thought of her letting a brother or sister light a candle from hers, and of the uncountable times she has let others light theirs also. I thought of the dark corners into which she carried her lighted candle. Then suddenly I knew it was because she carried a "candle," because she shared her "light" with thousands of others that she is a great and noble woman.[2]

Picking up a white candle set in an old-fashioned candlestick decorated with fresh, pastel-colored flowers, Amy Kathryn continued, "She is my grandmother and I should be modest, but she lighted my candle too, and I am grateful. So now, dear Grandmother, I return the light to you, the giver, that you may go on sharing it with others!"[3] She carried the candle the full length of the ballroom and presented it to her grandmother. As applause filled the room, tears filled Amy Brown Lyman's eyes.

Amy Brown Lyman's brilliant mind and humanitarian efforts did indeed provide a light during the dark years of World War I, the Great Depression of the 1930s, and World War II. A pioneer in the field of social services, she was also a teacher, a master of organization, and a loving wife, mother, and friend. Her energy was as boundless as her willingness to serve.

A Compassionate Child

Amy Cassandra Brown was born on a cold, brisk morning, February 7, 1872, in Pleasant Grove, Utah. Her father, John Brown, an early Utah pioneer, served as city mayor for twenty years, as ward bishop for twenty-eight years, and as state legislator for nineteen years. To stimulate his love of learning and his fine intellect, he spent a considerable amount of money on books and built up a fine library in his home. He believed that all his children should receive an education, including the girls.

Not only did John's educational philosophy become an integral part of Amy's personality, so did his precepts of self-discipline. A gentle man, he believed that emotional upsets and temper tantrums were infantile reactions that people later regretted and should always avoid. He taught his children to control themselves and master unpleasant situations.

Amy was the twenty-third of John's twenty-five children, a daughter of Margaret Zimmerman, his third wife. Together, they had ten children: Julianna, Harriet, twins Josephine and Joseph, Lydia, Margaret, Susan, Amy, John, and Lawrence. Margaret was proud of her German ancestors, especially her parents, who joined the Church in Pennsylvania and moved to Utah in 1851. And, like her husband, she placed a high value on education, creating in her home an atmosphere of learning where her children's minds could thrive.

Though Pleasant Grove was a small town, Amy thought of it as a delightful, interesting, and even sacred place. She thrilled to the stories of many early Utah pioneers who lived there, stories of the Mormon Battalion, Zion's Camp, the persecutions in Missouri, and the Indian Wars in Utah. Converts from Scandinavia, England, Ireland, Wales, Scotland, and Germany added a touch of the Old World. There was little evidence of wealth or elegance, but high educational, moral, and spiritual standards prevailed. As Amy remarked, "We had plain living, but high thinking."[4]

Amy's intellectual development was balanced by a concern for others, which grew and matured as she followed her mother's example. She reminisced in her autobiography, *In Retrospect,* that although her mother was a partial invalid as the result of improper care during childbirth, she not only directed the affairs of her household but also helped solve the social and economic problems of many of her friends and neighbors. Amy noted that her mother "was forceful, dynamic, and efficient, yet she was tender and sympathetic. A strict disciplinarian, she kept both her children and her house 'in order.' Some might have thought that she dominated the lives of her children and required too much of them, and probably this was the case, but she was so wise and farseeing, and her judgment was so good, that we had more confidence in her ideas than we had in our own, and usually were willing to accept any plan she had for us without much argument."[5]

Margaret's example showed Amy that one person with initiative can make a difference in the community. For example, when contagious diseases threatened, Margaret studied *Doctor Gunn's Medical Book* and learned the various symptoms and treatments, after which she advised and treated the whole neighborhood. During one epidemic of smallpox, she secured a piece of scab from a sore on the arm of a relative in Lehi who had been vaccinated. Following Doctor Gunn's advice, she dipped a needle in alcohol, then on the scab, and proceeded to vaccinate all her children.

Serious disease was a part of daily life in those years. During one outbreak of diphtheria, three of the five children in a neighbor's family died. Amy remembered seeing the black, homemade coffins passed through a bedroom window and placed on the bed of a farm wagon to be taken to the cemetery. In another family, in which five out of eight children contracted diphtheria, Amy watched the frightened parents set fire to their own home. She knew of children who lost their hearing from scarlet fever and others who suffered from the measles. Such experiences struck a responsive chord in young Amy, but the strongest impact came from the death and disease that hovered over her own family.

When Amy was ten, her half-sister Laura and five other women in Pleasant Grove died from childbed fever. A midwife had innocently transmitted the disease, leaving six newborn babies motherless. A woman of action, Margaret Brown secured a teacher and organized a class in obstetrics and nursing for the benefit of young women in Pleasant Grove. Amy learned from her mother's example, and throughout her life she organized many social-service classes and agencies.

Eliza R. Snow and Zina D. H. Young came on several occasions to bless and comfort Amy's semi-invalid mother. Their visits impressed Amy, who wrote:

> On one occasion we children were permitted in the room and were allowed to kneel in prayer with these sisters, and later to hear their fervent appeals for mother's recovery. They placed their hands upon her head and promised that through our united faith she would be spared to her family. This was an impressive spiritual

experience for us, and the fulfillment of this promise was a testimony.[6]

Not only did Margaret Brown live to raise her family, she lived a total of ninety-three years, a generous fulfillment of the blessing.

Education and Marriage

The high expectations of her parents motivated Amy to seek an education. She attended classes first in the old United Order Hall in Pleasant Grove, then in the community schoolhouse. Six teachers, including one of her older sisters, taught her during her school years. Two of these teachers had attended Brigham Young Academy in Provo, and Amy decided to follow their example. More young people attended Brigham Young Academy from Pleasant Grove than from any other town of its size. Amy wrote of her experience there:

> To me the school was a surprise, a marvel, and a delight. It did not matter that the building was a plain, ordinary warehouse, nor that the desks were long, crude, table affairs, with chairs of the kitchen variety. It was the spirit and atmosphere of the institution which were so fascinating and satisfying. I had heard a great deal from my brothers and sisters and other former students about how fine the school was, how the spirit of the gospel permeated every quarter, and how the students regarded religion as the most important subject in the whole curriculum. I had anticipated much, but the reality exceeded my expectations, and I found that the wonders of the school had not half been told. That year seemed to me to be the happiest of my life, and the world such a fascinating place in which to live. It was during this period that I met and fell in love with my future husband, Richard R. Lyman—so why shouldn't it be the happiest time of my life?[7]

Richard came from a prominent pioneer family. His father, Francis M. Lyman, was a member of the Quorum of the Twelve Apostles, and his great-grandfather, Amasa Mason Lyman, served at one time as a counselor to the Prophet Joseph Smith. Tall and handsome, Richard possessed a brilliant mind and high ambitions, and he was pleased to find an intellectual equal in Amy Brown. They enjoyed long, stimulating discussions of ideas and issues and shared deep religious beliefs. Their wedding plans were delayed, however, because Richard had been accepted for admission to the University of Michigan. Since only single students could pursue undergraduate studies, Amy patiently remained behind while Richard moved to Ann Arbor. Marriage would have to wait until after his graduation.

While Richard was away at school, Amy continued her studies at Brigham Young Academy, where Dr. Karl G. Maeser became her mentor. She said of his tutelage: "Next to my own parents, Brother Maeser influenced my life. He stood at the head and was really the soul of the institution. Tall and thin, dressed in a Prince Albert coat, he personified the idea of the old professor, and ruled the school like a general. Trained for his work in Old-World education centers, he was an educator of the first rank, a fine scholar, and a finished teacher."[8]

Amy graduated from the academy's normal school in June 1890, giving a speech at the commencement exercises. A few weeks later, Dr. Maeser asked her to come back to the academy and take charge of the Primary Department. She accepted the position, at a salary of forty dollars a month. During the next three years, she boarded in the Maeser home, where she was treated as a daughter. Though she enjoyed her work, at times she "felt that teaching in a Church school had its handicaps, especially for young women who loved fun, parties, and dancing as I did."[9] On one occasion Brother Maeser advised her not to attend a masquerade ball. She argued the point with him but she gave in and sat on "the bald-headed row" with the older people and watched her friends dance.

In 1894, Amy decided to leave the academy and found a job teaching in the Salt Lake City schools. The end of that school year marked the end of the long wait for Amy and Richard. In the summer of 1895, she traveled with her future father-in-law, Francis M. Lyman, to Ann Arbor for Richard's graduation. A popular student on campus, he had served as president of his class during both his sophomore and senior years. Richard's sense of humor and optimistic outlook won him many friends.

Richard's friends were also impressed by his fiancée. A friend, Alice Louise Reynolds, described Amy at that time: "The beauty of her hair and the exceptional loveliness of her brown eyes typified the unusualness of her intellectual and spiritual qualities. Her charm as a girl made her attractive in all circles. She was the most popular young person I have ever known. Back of her joyousness in life and its unfolding was the character developed in her pioneer home. Whatever she did, she sought to do well, and she succeeded."[10]

On September 9, 1896, Amy and Richard Roswell Lyman were married in the Salt Lake Temple by President Joseph F. Smith. The couple moved to a home near the University of Utah, which was then located in downtown Salt Lake City, where Richard taught in the engineering department. Eventually he surveyed property along Salt Lake City's east bench for the present University of Utah campus. On December 8, 1897, Amy and Richard welcomed their first child, Wendell Brown Lyman.

By the summer of 1901 the Lymans needed a change, and Richard decided to take a leave of absence from the university for graduate studies at Cornell University in Ithaca, New York. While waiting for school to start there, he attended summer school at the University of Chicago.

Living in Chicago proved to be a turning point in Amy's life. A class in sociology opened a new world for her, and before the end of the quarter, she had made a commitment to help raise human life to a higher level through the expanding field of social work. She did volunteer work for various Chicago charities, including the famous social settlement Hull House, where she met its founder, Jane Addams. They became lifelong friends. Amy wrote of these experiences, "While my summer at Chicago University was only incidental to my husband's work there and was therefore of minor concern, it proved to be one of the very valuable periods of my school life."[11] It was with reluctance that she left Chicago for Ithaca.

During their two-and-a-half-year stay at Cornell University, Amy again took classes while Richard earned a master's degree in civil engineering and a doctorate of philosophy. On September 15, 1903, their daughter Margaret was born. Meanwhile, Ithaca struggled with an epidemic of typhoid fever that infected more than a thousand victims within a few weeks and took many lives. Observing such suffering strengthened Amy's resolve to help others. Upon their return to Salt Lake City, the Lymans moved back to their home near the old University of Utah campus, and Richard returned to teaching. Over the years Amy also continued to take university classes.

On the Relief Society Board

In October 1909, Amy received a call to serve on the Relief Society general board. This came as a surprise, because she had previously served in the Young Ladies' Mutual Improvement Association and the Primary, but never Relief Society. Her first board meeting prompted her to write, "As I timidly entered the room I faced what seemed to me the most imposing group of women I had ever seen at such close range. I was well acquainted with only a few of them."[12]

She had reason to feel intimidated. At the head of the table sat Bathsheba W. Smith, the only living member of the original Relief Society in Nauvoo and the fourth general Relief Society president. Emmeline B. Wells, editor of the *Woman's Exponent* and future president of the Relief Society, sat nearby. Among other prominent women gathered around the table were Clarissa S. Williams, also a future Relief Society president; Julina L. Smith, wife of President Joseph F. Smith; and Emma S. Woodruff, widow of President Wilford Woodruff.

That meeting foreshadowed Amy's position as a link between two generations of Relief Society leaders. She personally knew every president of the Relief Society from Eliza R. Snow to Belle S. Spafford. She served only one year with Bathsheba Smith, whom she described as "a large, fine-appearing woman with dignity and charm, balance and poise. She was direct and positive in her speech, however, and fearless in her actions."[13]

When Bathsheba died in 1910, Emmeline B. Wells became president, and a close and cherished association developed between her and Amy that lasted more than a decade. Amy wrote, "Aunt Em was small in stature, dainty in person, very attractive personally, and naturally drew people to her."[14] Amy served as Emmeline's assistant secretary from 1911 to 1913. She then served as general secretary until Emmeline's death in 1921 and throughout the presidency of Clarissa S. Williams. During

Clarissa's administration, President Joseph F. Smith commissioned Amy to modernize the Relief Society offices. He encouraged her to use as many people as necessary and to install the most modern equipment, including typewriters, filing cases, adding machines, and mimeograph equipment. She added secretaries and bookkeepers to the office staff, collected and compiled past records of the Relief Society, and improved reporting procedures by providing uniform record books for ward and stake Relief Societies.

Amy traveled extensively with both Emmeline B. Wells and Clarissa S. Williams. She described Sister Williams as "intelligent, well-read, and well-traveled. She was a large, fine-looking, dignified, motherly woman—cultured, kindly, gentle, and lovable."[15] Amy believed that Sister Williams's attention to detail was her outstanding contribution to Relief Society work and that she was a thorough businesswoman and an able executive.

In 1913, Amy was involved as the Relief Society established a temple and burial clothes department and founded a Relief Society Home for the temporary lodging of women and girls seeking employment in Salt Lake City. In the fall of that year, the general board also began to publish a uniform course of study for the sisters. Susa Young Gates served as editor and Amy as one of the business managers of this monthly periodical, which was titled the *Bulletin*. Two years later the *Bulletin* was expanded and became the *Relief Society Magazine*. Amy worked in the business department of the magazine and served for two years as the editor. She referred to it as her "dearly beloved child."

Dedicated Humanitarian

Despite these many activities, welfare work remained the most interesting and important feature of Relief Society to Amy. She noticed that the Relief Society's early existence coincided with an especially productive period in the history and development of social welfare work. "There has been more progress in this field in this century than in all the centuries which preceded it," she wrote. "Prevention of poverty, disease, and crime is much better and much cheaper than relief or cure. Modern welfare calls for getting at the very roots of the trouble. The suggestive steps in family welfare are relief of existing distress, prevention of new distress, and the raising of human life to its highest level."[16]

Amy contended that the Relief Society functioned as a catalyst for the relief of human suffering, and she was grateful that her positions allowed her to use the knowledge and training she had received. As general secretary, she served as part of a four-woman Utah delegation selected to take a special course in family welfare work at the University of Colorado during the fall and winter of 1917. The purpose of this course was to assist the Church in serving the needs of Latter-day Saint servicemen and their families. All four of the women returned to Utah and eventually became leaders in social work. Amy served as chairman of family consultation for the Salt Lake County chapter of the Red Cross and as supervisor of Red Cross Relief Society family work. In the fall of 1918, she returned to Colorado for additional training.

In January 1919, President Joseph F. Smith established a social welfare department and named Amy as the first director, a position she held until 1934, in addition to serving as general secretary and later as counselor in the Relief Society presidency. To expand the work of the department, she created a training program in which prospective caseworkers received six weeks of training in family welfare work at Brigham Young University. Stake delegates from throughout the Church took this course, then taught similar classes in their local communities. Over the next few years a total of 4,155 women were trained. Not only did they aid their bishops in the charitable work of the Church, but many of them also provided vital assistance to local officials who found themselves confronted with federal relief responsibilities in the midst of the Great Depression of the 1930s.

In 1922, Amy was nominated for a seat in the Utah legislature, an honor she recognized as an opportunity to further her humanitarian desires. Her platform was simple: "Legislative bodies should not be made up entirely of men; there should be enough women to foster and secure the necessary humanitarian social action."[17] She won a seat in the legislature and was appointed chairman of the public health committee. Her responsibilities included gaining Utahns' support for the federal Sheppard-Towner Bill, which provided for maternity and infant care throughout the country. In support of this bill, the general board in 1923 urged local Relief Societies to prepare ready-to-use maternity bundles and layettes. The Relief Society also built two maternity hospitals and authorized the use of interest generated from wheat-storage funds for local clinics in the interest of maternity care and child health.

Amy's concerns also included humane treatment of the mentally ill and developmentally disabled. Through the Relief Society, she helped the women of Utah become instrumental in passing a bill in 1929 providing for an institution for the developmentally disabled. To give women firsthand experience with the conditions of the mentally ill, she rented a bus and regularly took Relief Society presidents to visit the State Mental Hospital in Provo. During the bus ride, she taught the presidents about mental illness and urged them to write letters to their legislators to make them aware of the need for better facilities.

Also in 1929, the governor of Utah selected Amy to work with a newly formed committee whose goal was to select a site for a new training school for the mentally handicapped. The resulting school in American Fork remained one of Amy's favorite projects. She served on the board of trustees for twelve years, from 1930 to 1942.

In all, Amy served on more than twenty-six local, national, and international boards and became acquainted with many prominent and influential people. On three occasions she was a delegate of the National Council of Women at sessions of the International Council of Women—in Washington, D.C., in 1925; in Dubrovnik, Yugoslavia, in 1936; and in Edinburgh, Scotland, in 1938—and for nine years (1925 to 1934) she served as an executive officer of the International Council. She was entertained by royalty in several European countries, and many eminent people honored her for her leadership ability and humanitarian activities. She also represented Utah and the National Council of Women at the 1940 Women's Centennial Congress in New York, an event that celebrated one hundred years of organized women's activities.

Amy managed her personal life with the same flair for organization and high energy that characterized her public service. An excellent homemaker, she bottled some four hundred jars of fruit every year so that her family could have fruit every morning. She was especially proud of her grape jelly. A good cook, she enjoyed formal evening meals in the dining room, not only with her family, but often with friends, important visitors, or perhaps someone in need. The virtually invisible stitches on her hand-hemmed linens and her beautiful tatting attested to her abilities as a seamstress. She cleaned her home in an intense but well-organized week of annual spring cleaning.

To take good care of her health, Amy loved brisk, daily walks and sun baths. Coming home tired from a day's work at the office, she would rejuvenate herself for the evening by taking a bath, then lying on her bed for a while. She often welcomed friends and chatted with them while she rested.

The Lyman household was a hub of activity as Amy and Richard pursued their various interests. Richard, serving as consulting engineer on three great water projects, enjoyed national prominence in hydraulic engineering. He also developed a well-known street-numbering plan, referred to as the Lyman Plan, used in Utah and other western states. His Church service included membership on general boards of the Young Men and the Sunday School, culminating in a call in 1919 to serve as a member of the Quorum of the Twelve Apostles.

New Family Challenges

In late 1925, with their son Wendell married and daughter Margaret in France studying music, Richard and Amy decided to close up their home. Richard was serving as a General Authority and Amy was busy with Relief Society and social work, so they determined that they would spend the winter at the Hotel Utah, on the same block as the Church office buildings. However, their lives changed dramatically on New Year's Eve when Wendell's wife, Rachel, died suddenly, leaving an eight-month-old baby. After Rachel's funeral, Wendell talked to his mother about caring for the child. Amy said, "Wendell, I'm too old to raise a baby." Then she proceeded to move back to their home, taking in Wendell and her granddaughter. Perhaps she remembered the example of her mother, who also raised a grandchild.

Amy Brown Lyman and her granddaughter, Amy Kathryn Lyman, bore similar names, resulting in a confusion that neither minded. Family members called them Big Amy and Little Amy, and the two became best friends. Little Amy always felt that she was at the center of her grandmother's life. Amy read to her granddaughter and taught her to sew, cook, and clean. A housekeeper helped care for the child during the day. After Amy Brown Lyman's call in October 1928 as first counselor to Louise Y. Robison in the Relief Society presidency, her granddaughter went with her to the women's offices in the Bishop's

Building. Young Amy pretended to be at work, sitting at a small desk in her grandmother's office. Soon she became a favorite among all the women, not only in the Relief Society office, but in the YWMIA and Primary offices as well.

When Wendell died tragically in 1933, Amy comforted eight-year-old Amy Kathryn, quoting the philosophy of her own father, John Brown, on the importance of drawing on inner strength. She passed on to Amy Kathryn his belief that one should always be in control and master unpleasant situations.

In 1936, Richard was called to preside over the European Mission and was responsible for all of the Church's missions in Continental Europe and the British Isles. Amy was set apart to take charge of the auxiliaries that served the women and children throughout the mission. They set sail on their fortieth wedding anniversary with Amy Kathryn and their housekeeper, Gladys Jenkins.

Amy enjoyed life in the mission field and developed a deep love for missionary work, for the mission presidents and their wives, for the missionaries, and for Latter-day Saint women in Europe. Through articles and editorials in the *Millennial Star,* she also taught the sisters in the mission. But letters—more in the form of conversations than business letters—served as the main line of communication between Amy and the various female leaders.

The Eighth General President

Impending war brought an early release for the Lymans in September 1938, but Amy's bonds of love and concern for the women she met in Europe only increased, especially when America later became involved in World War II. She carried this empathy for a worldwide sisterhood of Relief Society into her administration as eighth general president of the Relief Society, a calling she received on January 1, 1940, at age sixty-seven. She chose as her counselors Marcia K. Howells and Donna D. Sorensen, and as secretary Vera S. Pohlman. Belle S. Spafford followed Sister Sorensen as second counselor in late 1942.

Amy's immediate goals as president were to increase aid to those suffering from the war and to prepare for the 1942 centennial anniversary of the Relief Society. World War II, however, forced simplification of Relief Society programs. The presidency responded with such measures as discontinuing the Singing Mothers on a general level but encouraging ward and stake groups to continue; shortening the Relief Society educational year from nine months to eight months; limiting the size of stake boards; and eliminating general board travel to stakes and maintaining contact with the field through instructional publications.

The centennial celebrations, too, were scaled down but were nevertheless significant. Hundreds of yards of gold and blue satin were purchased to drape the interior of the Tabernacle and subsequently sold to women who wanted to make centennial quilts. The Relief Society also introduced a new official seal, with its "Charity Never Faileth" motto, and produced a Relief Society pin, a commemorative plate, and a book of selected poems by Relief Society women entitled *Our Legacy*. On March 17, 1942, the presidency planted a hardwood tree on Temple Square and encouraged the wards and stakes to plant trees in their own areas in honor of the centennial. President Heber J. Grant and Amy Brown Lyman broadcast a centennial radio program in the Salt Lake City area on March 17 and March 22 and sent a copy of the recording to every English-speaking Relief Society in North America.

Plans to house the Nauvoo Bell in a campanile on Temple Square as a centennial gift to the Church were also postponed because of the war. Sections of the campanile ended up in storage. After the war, construction of the Relief Society building took priority, and it wasn't until September 29, 1966, that the campanile was finally completed.

One facet of Relief Society, that of welfare service, continued to expand because of increasing wartime needs. Sisters donated more than three thousand pieces of clothing to the Central Bishops Storehouse in Salt Lake City as the result of a sewing project managed by Donna Sorensen. Women also knitted clothing for the war effort, and ward Relief Societies sewed hospital gowns in their work meetings. Relief Society members taught Red Cross classes and assembled first aid kits. The *Relief Society Magazine* carried frequent announcements and articles about wartime problems of both youth and adults.

The Church Welfare Committee, then in its early stages of development, also included the Relief Society presidency in its meetings. Amy actively supported this program, working closely with Elders Harold B. Lee and Marion G. Romney.

During Amy's term as president, she received numerous honors, including election to the Social Science Honor Society of America, the Distinguished Alumnus Award from Brigham Young University, honorary membership in the American Association of Mental Deficiency, and the Honorary Life Membership Award from the Utah State Conference of Social Work (which she helped organize in 1925).

Changing Seasons

In November 1943, Amy suffered a terrible personal tragedy when her husband, Richard, was released from the Quorum of the Twelve Apostles and excommunicated from the Church. Although Amy was devastated by these events, she kept her personal feelings to herself. Following the counsel of her father to master unpleasant situations, she continued her daily activities and reminded her family not to look back but to go forward as much as possible. She continued to serve as general president of the Relief Society and performed her duties as the stress mounted within her. In September 1944 she asked to be released, and President Grant complied the following spring.

Richard and Amy worked through their private problems, made more difficult by their service in such public positions, and their marriage survived. Five years before Amy's death, Richard was rebaptized. His full priesthood blessings were restored posthumously in 1970.

Amy's strong testimony of the gospel of Jesus Christ guided her life and helped her surmount the family tragedies she faced:

> My testimony has been my anchor and my stay, my satisfaction in times of joy and gladness, my comfort in times of sorrow and discouragement. I am grateful for the opportunity of serving, . . . particularly in Relief Society where during most of my mature life I have worked so happily and contentedly with its thousands of members. I have visited in their homes, slept in their beds, and eaten at their tables and have thus learned of their beauty of character, their unselfishness, their understanding hearts, their faithfulness, and their sacrifices. I honor beyond my power of expression this great sisterhood of service.[18]

Familiar activities filled the last fifteen years of Amy's life. Originally a founder of the University Women's Club, she joined with the group again and continued her activity in the Friendship Circle and the Authors' Club. The Alice Louise Reynolds Club asked Amy to write a biography of Dr. Karl G. Maeser, her BYU professor, mentor, and life-long friend. The book, entitled *A Lighter of Lamps*, was published in 1947. In 1958 she had the honor of unveiling a memorial statue of Dr. Karl G. Maeser on the Brigham Young University campus. Amy also continued to serve in numerous social-services organizations, taught the literature lessons in her ward Relief Society, sewed, bottled fruit, and cared for friends and family members.

On December 5, 1959, while convalescing from a fall, Amy died at age eighty-seven at the home of her daughter, Margaret. Soon after-ward, Richard commissioned Vera W. Pohlman, Amy's longtime secretary and friend, to write a biography of his "marvelous and matchless companion for sixty-two years."[19] The book, *In Memoriam*, was published in 1960.

Amy Brown Lyman served as an officer of the Relief Society for a total of thirty-two years, including two years as a member of the general board, two years as assistant secretary, fifteen years as general secretary-treasurer, eight years as first counselor to Louise Y. Robison, and five years as eighth general president. The healing efforts of this dedicated humanitarian brought peace to many who suffered, hope to the despondent, and the charity that "never faileth" to the sisters of the Relief Society.

Notes

1. Amy Brown Lyman, *In Retrospect: Autobiography of Amy Brown Lyman* (Salt Lake City: General Board of Relief Society, 1945), p. 9.

2. Ibid. p. 166.

3. Ibid., p. 167.

4. Ibid., p. 4.

5. Ibid., p. 7.

6. Ibid., p. 38.

7. Ibid., p. 18.

8. Ibid.

9. Ibid., p. 21.

10. John Zimmerman Brown, *Autobiography of John Brown* (Salt Lake City, 1941), p. 429.

11. *Autobiography of Amy Brown Lyman,* p. 30.

12. Ibid., p. 36.

13. Ibid., p. 42.

14. Ibid., p. 43.

15. Ibid., p. 48.

16. Ibid., p. 61.

17. Ibid., p. 83.

18. Interview with Amy Lyman Engar, April 20, 1988.

19. Richard R. Lyman to Vera W. Pohlman, December 26, 1962, in possession of Vera W. Pohlman.

9

BELLE SMITH SPAFFORD
1945–1974

Even after Belle Smith Spafford was released as Relief Society general president, the president of the National Council of Women, seeing her familiar face in the crowd of women awaiting the start of a council meeting in New York City's Waldorf-Astoria Hotel, hurried over and asked Belle to sit at the head table. But Belle declined, saying that she had been released as Relief Society general president and from the executive board of the National Council of Women. The president insisted, however, and Belle was seated at the long table of illustrious women from around the world, including a princess and the presidents of several prominent women's organizations.

As the meeting began, the president introduced each of the women by name, country, and organization; but when she came to Belle, she simply said, "You all know our dear Belle." The women at the table rose to give Belle a standing ovation.[1]

They knew her indeed—as a woman, a sister, and a friend who truly belonged to the world.

The three decades that Belle Spafford served as Relief Society general president, from 1945 to 1974, saw sweeping changes in the world and in the status of women. She was a constant and steady guide through this turbulent era, both in the Church and in the national and international world of women. During her administration, the Relief Society grew from a largely English-speaking organization of one hundred thousand members to a worldwide organization of nearly a million sisters in sixty-five countries. As a young woman, however, she had to be converted to Relief Society herself.

Childhood and Youth

Belle was born on October 8, 1895, the seventh and last child of Hester Sims and John Gibson Smith. Hester named her Marion Isabelle Sims Smith, but she was always known simply as Belle. Seven months earlier, Hester was enjoying a happy marriage, security in John's business, and six children with another on the way. She felt that her "cup of joy was full." Then suddenly John had died, and Hester went through her pregnancy without his love and support. Though she had many struggles, she managed to raise her family with faith and courage. A friend of hers said, "I don't think I've ever encountered a woman who knew better where she was going or who had greater strength in controlling her sense of direction. She always appeared to me as a woman who was at peace with herself."[2]

"Mother never allowed us to feel that we were without a father," Belle said. "She would often say to us (and all of us remember this), 'Why, you're not without a father. You have a father. He's not with us, but he is taking care of us, I'm sure. And you have a Heavenly Father, and you have the father of the ward who is the bishop."[3] The oldest son was sixteen and held the Aaronic Priesthood when John died. Hester asked him to sit at the head of the table in "Pa's chair." Then she told her children, "We do have the priesthood in our home. And he sits at the head of the table."[4]

Although Hester received a monthly income from John's business and did not have to work outside her home, money was generally in short supply. She taught Belle and her other children to work and to be careful with money, but she also told them, "I don't want you to be stingy. I want you to be thrifty, and there's a difference between thrift and stinginess."[5]

Belle learned that Hester's philosophy toward money did not necessarily mean spending it on the most practical thing, but on the most significant. When Belle was in high school, the student body president invited her to the junior prom. Excited about the date, Belle talked to her mother about a new dress. Hester replied that she did have four dollars, enough to buy satin for a party dress, but she reminded Belle that a textbook she needed at school also cost four dollars. When she asked her daughter to choose between the dress and the book, teenaged Belle chose the dress. Hester enthusiastically made a pink satin dress and bought pink slippers to match.

"That was a very wise decision," Belle later said, "because for a girl in high school it was important. And then I recall mother very quietly said to me, 'You know that textbook is in the school library.' So she was a wise mother."[6]

Belle recalled another important lesson her mother taught her. One of Belle's childhood friends was the daughter of the president of a neighboring stake. One night when Belle joined the family for dinner, the conversation focused on some of the General Authorities. Family members told amusing—but uncomplimentary—stories. When Belle repeated the stories to her mother, Hester exclaimed, "Oh, don't we feel sorry for those children, that their parents would allow them to tell stories like that about the General Authorities? Tonight in our family prayer we must remember to pray for those children."[7]

Hester shared with her children her love of music, art, and good books and firmly implanted in their minds the importance of education. Belle and her brothers and sisters took music lessons, served missions, and earned college degrees. They also learned practical lessons from the sayings their mother often quoted:

> Never speak or act out of the wealth of your ambition and ego and the poverty of your knowledge and experience.

> An eighth of an inch makes a difference, especially if it's at the end of your nose.

> Never point out your own faults. Others recognize them soon enough.

> Take what God gives and build a house of happiness.

> No investment pays dividends as high as kindness.

> Many a man who is too weak to climb to the mountaintop can point the way for another man to reach it.

Never fight a mad dog. You will lose.

Accept people as you find them, not as others represent them to be.[8]

Hester's Scottish mother, Isabella McMurrin Sims, for whom Belle
was named, significantly influenced Belle's life. She lived with the
Smiths after Belle's father died. A very strong personality, Grandmother
Sims was the final word in advice or counsel. She often told her grandchildren that whenever they received praise or a compliment, they were
to "see that ye're desairvin'."

Belle could not remember a time when her grandmother did not
wear a black silk dress to church meetings, and as a young girl she used
to sit and look at her in Sunday School and think she was the most
elegant woman in the Church.[9] Isabella often pinned to her dress a
gold watch, which Belle always admired. One day she approached her
and said, "Grandmother, when you die will you will me your beautiful
watch?" Isabella replied, "By the time I'm gone the watch will be gone
also. I want to leave you something far more precious that I brought
from Scotland. I want to leave you my testimony of the truthfulness of
the gospel."[10]

Although Isabella had a firm testimony of the gospel, her testimony of the Word of Wisdom did not develop until she was nearly
eighty, when she finally gave up drinking tea each morning with her
bowl of Scottish oats. Afterward, someone reminded her that she had
heard the Brethren preaching observance of the Word of Wisdom
since the time of Brigham Young. Belle said that her grandmother
had taught her a great lesson when she replied, "I know, but now I'm
converted."[11]

The Smith family lived in the Pioneer Stake on the west side of
Salt Lake City until Belle graduated from the Latter-day Saint High
School and finished a two-year Normal School course at the University
of Utah. During the influenza epidemic of 1918, the wife of Belle's
brother John died while pregnant with her third child. Hester moved
to Provo to care for the children and John, and Belle moved with her,
continuing her studies at the Brigham Young University Training
School.

Courtship and Marriage

The Smiths' move to Provo profoundly affected Belle's life, for there she met Willis Earl Spafford, who had just returned from service in World War I and enrolled at Brigham Young University. Handsome and athletic, Earl played basketball at the university and enjoyed tennis and ice skating. He and Belle met at a school social function and soon found that they had much in common. They were married on March 23, 1921, in the Salt Lake Temple.

Early in her marriage, Belle taught courses at Brigham Young University in remedial work for handicapped children—what would later be known as special education. This experience laid the foundation for her deep interest in social work and her ongoing concern for human needs.

Belle and Earl had two children: a daughter, Mary, born in 1923; and a son, Earl Smith, born in 1926. The year that young Earl was born, the family moved to Salt Lake City, where they bought a home on Fifth East and Garfield Avenue. Earl was employed by New York Life Insurance Company and later became a deputy collector for the Internal Revenue Service.

Mary and Earl grew up in a home where their mother believed that "the most valuable contribution that a woman can make to society is to rear children who have internalized a sense of worthwhile values through the family teaching that would enable them to function as responsible citizens."[12] Mary became a teacher and social worker. She and her husband, Clarence W. Kemp, resided in Chicago and were the parents of five sons. Earl graduated from the University of Utah College of Law and practiced law in Salt Lake City. He and his wife, Iris Montague, had three sons and two daughters.

When their children were small, Earl suggested that Belle take classes at the University of Utah. He hired help for her at home, which gave her time to pursue her studies in social work. Whether formally or informally, she continued to learn throughout her life. Whenever she received a new call or assignment that she felt unprepared for, she took classes to learn what she needed to know. For example, when she became editor of the *Relief Society Magazine,* she enrolled in English composition; and while serving as chairman of a Church history curriculum committee, she took a class at the University of Utah on the westward movement. Her friends and family members knew they should not telephone after nine o'clock in the evening, for that was her study time. She read the scriptures and books on whatever subject she was currently interested in. When asked why she formed this nightly study habit, she replied: "One, because it is a commandment, and two, because when I get to the other side I want to have something to talk about with some of the prominent men and women in history."[13]

When her grandchildren came along, Belle established "scholar night," a one-on-one night with each of them. She would invite a grandchild to dinner, and then they would study or play together, depending on her perception of the child's needs. Each of the grandchildren felt that he or she was the favorite grandchild. They all knew they could call their grandmother at any time, even during important meetings, and she would take time for them.

Her son Earl recalled Belle's devotion to her family as her most important assignment:

> Throughout my life mother has enjoyed a position of prominence and respect in both the church and world community, but those of us who are close to her, her children, her grandchildren, and her husband, when living, have always viewed her not in the light of prominence, but as a warm and affectionate woman who always seemed to have time for the little things. She has cooked with her daughters and granddaughters, she has taught us social graces, she has been our tutor, our comforter, our counselor and our confidante.[14]

Belle's warmth and affection were also apparent in her keen sense of humor. She enjoyed telling humorous stories, and she and her son particularly liked exchanging jokes. One of her grandsons commented, "Grandma is the only person I know that could tell the same old joke over and over again and get a laugh every time." She even got the last laugh by attaching a humorous poem to her will.

Belle's sense of humor not only brightened her family life but also helped her to cope with the many demands placed upon her and to put others at ease. Often when she received a compliment for something she accomplished, she jokingly replied, "I've done pretty well for a little girl who lived on the wrong side of the railroad tracks." Once at a women's club luncheon as she began to speak, loud music issued from the intercom. When the music stopped, she started her speech again; but almost on cue, the music sounded out again, and no one knew how to turn it off. When her talk was interrupted for the third time, she said, "Don't let this trouble you. I'm used to giving musical readings; many people prefer them, so I will just go on."[15]

A Relief Society Convert

Belle's conversion to Relief Society began when the Spaffords moved to Salt Lake City in 1926. As a young woman she taught Sunday School and a religion class, a forerunner of seminary, and at age seventeen, she was president of a ward YWMIA. She was thirty when she settled into the Belvedere Ward in Salt Lake City, and participating in an "old women's organization" like Relief Society was the furthest thing from her mind. She was more interested in accepting an invitation she had received to join a literary club. When her visiting teachers invited her to Relief Society, however, she remembered her own mother's devotion to the organization and agreed to go to the Tuesday morning meetings.[16]

Though Belle attended the meetings regularly, she was shocked when Bishop George Bowles called her to be a counselor in the Relief Society presidency. She responded by saying, "That organization is for my mother, not for me." She told him that she had no experience for the calling and said, furthermore, that she had "no desire to learn."

Although she accepted the call, her experiences did not soften her feelings toward Relief Society. Because the chapel was being remodeled, weekday Relief Society was held in the furnace room in the basement. After three weeks of taking her children to Relief Society in the cold, drafty, cement-floored room, she decided to quit, saying, "Never, never will I come another day." She asked the bishop to release her. He listened patiently to her complaints and then said, "Sister Spafford, you know I somehow don't feel impressed to release you. I wish you would try a little longer, and eventually we'll have our meetinghouse finished and the furnace fixed. And I just don't feel to respond to your request." Belle agreed to stay on.

She agreed, that is, until her accident. When the Spaffords' car hit a telephone pole, Belle's face was severely cut by shattered glass. The pain from the resulting infection was so intense one Sunday evening that Earl called a doctor to come to the house, but because the abscess was too close to her facial nerves, the doctor could not lance it. Bishop Bowles stopped to see Belle that evening and gave her a blessing. Belle asked, "Bishop, now will you release me from Relief Society?" He told her he would pray about it. A few days later he returned and said, "I'm not impressed to release you from Relief Society. You stay." Belle conceded, saying, "Well, if that's your feeling under these circumstances, I'll stay and I'll quit complaining and I'll do my best."[17]

Belle continued to serve in her ward Relief Society presidency. Then the stake president indicated that he wanted to issue a call for her to serve on the stake Relief Society board, but her ward Relief Society president wouldn't agree to Belle's release. Sometime later, however, the ward president suddenly changed her mind, telling Belle that one day she would explain why. Just before her death, the ward president asked Belle to visit her and related a dream that had prompted her change of mind. "In it," Belle recalled, "she said she saw me try to climb the stairs. She had been holding me back. And she saw I couldn't climb till she let go. At length she let go and I climbed the stairs and then she saw me one step from the top. And she said, 'I knew as well as I knew anything that that's where you would be, at the top in the Relief Society work.'"[18]

After Belle received a call to the Relief Society general board in 1935, her former bishop, George Bowles, who was serving as a stake patriarch in California, telephoned her when he came to Salt Lake City for general conference and said he wanted to give her a blessing. In the blessing she was told, "I would use the night for the purposes for which the Lord designed it—for sleep, for rest, for restoration of my body—so that I would waken in the morning refreshed and ready to undertake the labors of the day."[19] She enjoyed that blessing all her life.

Called to the general board during Louise Y. Robison's presidency, Belle was much surprised with her specific assignment. Later, she recalled:

> Sister Robison immediately assigned me to the one division of work for which I was not qualified—home-making. I used to go to the quiltings in my own ward

and the sisters wouldn't let me quilt. So when Sister Robison asked me which committee I would prefer to be on I said, "Any but the homemaking. They won't let me quilt and I'm not a good seamstress, and I'd rather be on one of the educational committees." So I was assigned to serve on the homemaking committee. What a wise president to give me that opportunity to catch the vision and the importance of the homemaking program. I worked very hard to make a contribution on this committee. I think the Lord prepares us every step of the way for our callings. He puts the opportunity before us, and if we take it and make the most of it we see the time when it was important for us to have it.[20]

Two years later Belle became editor of the *Relief Society Magazine*, a position she held for eight years. She went to her mother for advice and reassurance, and Hester said: "Well, I'll tell you what your experience will be. The big problems and the big obstacles in the way won't bother you. The big trees on the path will not deter you. You will go around them, you will climb over them, or you will hack them down. But the vines will trip you. Watch for the vines."[21]

Belle wanted to improve the quality of the magazine and make it more readable. Hester, who had worked for a book publisher before marriage, advised her to select good paper and an appropriate typeface for the magazine. Belle chose a type large enough for the older sisters to read easily. With regard to content, Belle believed that the magazine should be an outlet for the literary efforts of the sisters and should contain the history of the Relief Society. Often through her editorials she taught lessons on such topics as graciousness and composure. Under her editorship, the magazine doubled its circulation.

Amy Brown Lyman became general president in January 1940, and two and a half years later, in October 1942, Belle became a counselor in the presidency. She also continued to serve as editor of the magazine.

Ninth Relief Society President

When Belle was asked to come to the office of President J. Reuben Clark, Jr., in April 1945, she expected to be released as a counselor. To her surprise, however, she was called to be the ninth general president of the Relief Society. Prior to her call, she had heard a rumor that the auxiliaries would be reorganized and that presidencies would serve for a term of five years. When she asked President Clark about the rumor, he peered at her over the rim of his eyeglasses and said, "You may not last that long, Sister." Then he added, "We hope that as you administer the affairs of the Relief Society, you will do so with the concept that the Relief Society is a companion organization to the Priesthood."[22]

Belle chose as first counselor Marianne C. Sharp, a daughter of President Clark and her closest friend. She remained as first counselor for Belle's entire term of office. As second counselor Belle selected Gertrude R. Garff. Velma Simonsen succeeded Sister Garff in September 1947, followed by Helen W. Anderson in January 1957 and Louise W. Madsen in August 1958.

At the Relief Society conference in October 1945, the first conference over which Belle presided and the first to be held in three years due to World War II, President George Albert Smith spoke on the purpose and blessing of Relief Society. Belle was emotionally stirred by his prophecy that in a few years women from Europe, South Africa, China, and the South Seas would attend Relief Society conference in the Tabernacle and that they would come by airplane in just a few hours. Belle asked President Smith after the meeting if he thought this could happen during her administration. When President Smith replied, "It very well could happen during your administration," Belle asked how women could possibly come to Salt Lake City from various parts of the world in just a few hours. President Smith responded, "I don't know that you need to worry about that. The Lord will take care of that."[23]

Three years later, the Relief Society presidency hosted a special session for international sisters during general conference. Belle noted that every part of the world President Smith had mentioned in his prophecy was represented.

One of Belle's significant and most tangible accomplishments as president was the construction of the Relief Society Building. Nineteenth-century Relief Society sisters had dreamed of having their own building in the shadow of the temple. In 1901, the First Presidency donated a building site, but that land was used instead for the Presiding Bishop's Office. At the 1945 Relief Society conference, the First Presidency approved a home for the Relief Society across the street from the Salt Lake Temple, literally in its shadow. Belle, with her board, suggested that every member of the Relief Society in the Church, which then numbered one hundred thousand, donate five dollars to the building fund. She also encouraged men to make gifts to honor their wives, mothers, or sisters. With sacrifice and effort, the Relief Society reached its half-million-dollar goal, and construction began in 1953. At the dedication on October 3, 1956, Belle spoke of "the beauty of its artistic decor, the simple elegance of classic design, the beauty of the bronze, marbles, and woods, and its spirit of love and peace. . . . The building is a magnificent symbol of faith, diligence, and devotion of all women."[24]

Along with her work in Relief Society, Belle became an influential leader in women's organizations throughout the world—most notably the National Council of Women and the International Council of Women, organizations established in 1888 to promote women's suffrage, to examine current women's issues and problems, and to protect the interests of women and children.

Belle's first experience with the National Council of Women was not a pleasant one, however. As a general board member, she represented the Relief Society at meetings of the council at its headquarters in New York City. At a luncheon in the mid-1970s, Belle attempted to find a seat at several tables where there were empty chairs, but at each table, the women, knowing she was a Mormon from Utah, told her the seats were taken. After being refused a seat at every available table, Belle approached the council president and said, "Where would you like me to sit? It seems that all the chairs are taken." The president, assessing the situation, graciously asked Belle to sit next to her at the head table.[25]

Belle had been skeptical of the value to the Relief Society of membership in the council, so when she became the Relief Society president, she recommended to President George Albert Smith that the Relief Society withdraw. "President Smith thoughtfully read through our statements," she recalled. She further defended their position, saying:

> "President Smith, it's costly for us to go to New York
> to attend their annual meetings and we really get

nothing from the councils, either the National or International Council.". . .

He said "You surprise me. Do you always think in terms of what you get? Don't you think it's well at times to think in terms of what you have to give? Now I feel that Mormon women have something to give to women of the world and I believe also that you may learn from them. Rather than to terminate your membership, I suggest you take two or three of your ablest board members and attend the meetings and continue your membership in these organizations." . . . As I arose to leave, he extended his hand across the desk and grasping my hand firmly he said in a positive voice, "Attend the forthcoming meetings and make your influence felt in those organizations."[26]

Belle followed his counsel and made her influence felt. She was a member of the National Council of Women for forty-two years, serving on the executive committee and as vice president from 1948 to 1956. She was also a delegate to the International Council of Women triennial meetings at Philadelphia in 1947, Montreal in 1957, and Washington, D.C., in 1963, and chairman of the U.S. delegation to the ICW triennial meetings at Helsinki, 1954; Tehran, 1966; and Bangkok, 1969.

In 1968, Belle was nominated to be president of the National Council of Women. She turned the nomination down, believing that she could not serve effectively as president of both the council and the Relief Society. The council refused to accept her answer and asked Belle to talk with the president of her church about the matter. When she discussed the matter with President David O. McKay, he counseled her to accept the nomination and promised her more help with her Relief Society work, adding that his door would always be open to her. Belle was unanimously elected and served as president from 1968 to 1970, the first Latter-day Saint to hold that position.

In all her spheres of influence, Belle was skillful in handling differences of opinion without compromising her standards and beliefs.

Elder Marvin J. Ashton of the Council of the Twelve said of her, "She knew how to disagree without being disagreeable. She wore a velvet glove yet her grip was of steel."[27]

Mayola R. Miltenberger, who served as Relief Society general secretary for many years, noted how Belle's influence was felt in the National Council of Women:

> I recall being with Sister Spafford in a large Eastern city at a meeting [when] she was a member of the executive committee. The room was filled with distinguished women, each of whom was a strong, articulate leader in her own right. A particularly thorny and difficult issue was being debated heatedly. Finally, the presiding officer turned to President Spafford and asked her to voice an opinion on the problem. In her thoughtful, measured way, Sister Spafford analyzed the matter, stating the issue fairly, without rancor or confrontation, and offering, at the same time, reasonable options that could be accepted by all present. After a few moments' silence, one of those present rose and in a subdued voice said, "What Mrs. Spafford has just proposed calls to my mind our insignia [a lighted candle with the words 'Lead Kindly Light' written in the smoke trail]. We have today been led by the 'kindly light' of Belle S. Spafford."[28]

A special interest of Belle's during these years was social service. As Relief Society president, she directed social-service agencies in Utah, Arizona, Nevada, and Idaho, and supervised programs for abused children and unwed mothers, adoptive services, youth guidance services, and Indian foster-care services. She was instrumental in getting legislation passed in the state of Utah to establish university programs to educate social workers, legislation that became a model for other western states. For her pioneering efforts in social services, the Utah State Conference of Social Work awarded her an honorary life membership and the University of Utah established the Belle S. Spafford Endowed Chair in Social Work.

Her community service included a wide range of organizations. She was a member of the National Advisory Committee to the White House Conference on Aging and served as vice president of the American Mothers Committee and Advisory Board. She was the first female member of the Board of Governors of LDS Hospital and of the Board of Trustees of Brigham Young University, a member and then an officer of the board of directors of the National Association for Practical Nurses, and a special lecturer at the School of Social Work at the University of Utah. Her numerous honors included honorary degrees and service citations from Brigham Young University, Ricks College, and the University of Utah; the Distinguished Service Award for the Crusade for Freedom; and the Pursuit of Excellence Award from the LDS Student Association. She was one of ten outstanding women from Utah cited in *Famous Mothers in American History, 1776–1976*, and one of seven named to the Salt Lake Council Women's Hall of Fame. While she was grateful for such honors, she was quick to attribute them to those who gave her so much behind-the-scenes support, especially her coworkers in the Relief Society and her family.

When Belle assumed her responsibilities as general president of the Relief Society, she determined that she would maintain a close and happy relationship with her family (Mary was twenty-two and Earl nineteen at the time). Her husband, Earl, suggested that she meet him every day for lunch, and over the years the Spaffords claimed they "found every eating place in town, both good and bad."[29] Earl was completely supportive of his wife's Church and community work and freed her from worrying about many home details. Marianne C. Sharp said: "Without the tender care with which he has guarded her, without his unselfish acceptance of the calls which have been made upon her time, increasing with the passing of the years, without his full support and wholehearted cooperation, it would not have been possible for President Spafford to have continued her Church duties and at the same time to have cared for her family."[30]

In 1963, Belle's beloved husband, Earl, died of a heart attack, and within a year her daughter, Mary, also died. Belle was deeply grieved by these deaths, yet she adapted courageously to her change in lifestyle. Earl had taken care of so many details for her that as a widow she found it hard to remember to do such things as filling her car with gas. But she knew that adjusting to loss was part of living. She took an active part in raising Mary's five boys and became even more immersed in Relief Society.

In 1970, the *Relief Society Magazine* was discontinued as part of the revision of the Church magazine system. In the future, all adult members of the Church would be encouraged to read the *Ensign,* which would incorporate features for women as well as the kinds of articles and features found in the *Improvement Era.* The *Children's Friend* was renamed the *Friend,* and a new magazine for youth, the *New Era,* was established. When Belle reported the discontinuance of the *Relief Society Magazine* to her general board, she said, "I've always been sure of two things: death and taxes. Now I'm sure of three things: death, taxes, and change."[31] Though she regretted that the women had lost their magazine, she supported the decision to consolidate the Church's periodicals, commenting, "Adjustment is painful in changing an old pattern into a new one, but we must make the new pattern fit."[32]

In addition to writing articles and editorials for the *Relief Society Magazine,* Belle coauthored with Marianne C. Sharp *A Centenary of Relief Society,* a history of the first hundred years of Relief Society. She also wrote numerous articles for other Church publications and national women's magazines and in the 1970s published two books: *Woman in Today's World* (1971) and *A Woman's Reach* (1974).

Another change the Relief Society adjusted to was the loss of its financial independence when the priesthood correlation program was established in the 1970s. Belle agreed with the General Authorities that Relief Society members would be able to devote more time to compassionate service and teaching the gospel if they were no longer concerned about generating and managing their own funds. She said: "This life is a life of choices. We sometimes don't like to get out of the groove that's been pleasant for us and step into a new groove that might present a few adjustments for us. We have to consider which in the ultimate is going to be the greatest benefit for the greatest number. Always I find that the decisions of the Brethren are right."[33]

Unprecedented Changes

The three decades of Belle Spafford's administration were years of unprecedented change in the world and in the lives of women. A few months before her release, she said in an interview in the *Ensign:*

Tremendous changes . . . have taken place in the social, economic, industrial, and educational life of most countries in the world since Relief Society was founded. And I don't think any change in the world has been more significant than the change in the status of women. At the time the Relief Society was founded, a woman's world was her home, her family, and perhaps a little community service. Today a woman's world is as broad as the universe. There's scarcely an area of human endeavor that a woman cannot enter if she has the will and preparation to do so.

Yet in the midst of all this change, the organizational structure of the Relief Society, the basic purposes for which it was established have remained constant, and the Church programs that have implemented these purposes have been adaptable to the needs of women in each succeeding era. Through the years, Relief Society has been just as constant in its purpose as truth is constant. The purposes that were important for a handful of women in Nauvoo are still important to women worldwide. That is the miracle of Relief Society. I've worked in Relief Society many years, and I'm just beginning to get an insight into its greatness.[34]

President Spencer W. Kimball, the sixth prophet under whom Belle served, announced her release at the Relief Society conference on October 3, 1974. He said of her presidency, "It is most difficult to find words to express to these sisters our admiration for them and our gratitude to them." Of Belle Spafford, he noted that she was "a beautiful Latter-day Saint wife and mother. Her voice has been heard in places where it has taken insight, courage, and forthrightness at times when she has stood almost alone."[35]

The evening she was released, Belle wrote in her midnight letter to herself:

Twenty-nine and a half years have passed since that day, during which I have served under six of the Prophet-

Presidents of the Church: Presidents Heber J. Grant, George Albert Smith, David O. McKay, Joseph Fielding Smith, Harold B. Lee, and Spencer W. Kimball and their great and inspired counselors. What a rare and marvelous blessing!

These have been busy, demanding, challenging years, yet rewarding beyond my powers to measure. The members of each of the First Presidencies, the Twelve and other General Authorities have been good to me. The Lord has been good to me! Many, many times he has put ideas into my mind and even words into my mouth that have enabled me to meet difficult situations or remove resistant obstacles that otherwise might have impaired the work of the Society for which I had been given responsibility.

Today this office and calling was terminated by a Prophet-President of the church. A deep-seated feeling of gratitude engulfs me that I have been blessed and honored to have had such a glorious calling; that now my great mission is honorably completed, as attested by the Lord's prophet. A sweet feeling of relief and joy pervades my being that the responsibilities of this exacting calling have been placed on younger shoulders but whose calling is from the same divine source. There is within my soul a feeling of peace and good promise for the future—my personal future and that of my beloved Relief Society.[36]

After her release, Belle continued to serve as an advisor for several major enterprises of the Church. She also remained active in the National Council of Women and the American Regional Council of the International Council of Women until 1979. When she retired from her positions with the NCW, the council designated October 23, 1979, as "Belle S. Spafford Day" in honor of "her capable, influential, and gracious leadership." The council also endowed a fellowship at

New York University that was later called the Belle S. Spafford Archival Research Program Fund at the New York Public Library. In 1988, the National Council of Women also presented a posthumous award for her work in establishing the American Regional Council of the International Council of Women.

On her eighty-first birthday, October 8, 1976, Belle wrote the following in response to her son Earl's question, "Mother, what have you learned during these eighty-one years?"

> During the four score and one years of my life I have learned . . .
> That life is very short.
> That time is extremely valuable and should not be dissipated.
> That the teachings of the Church are sound and reasonable. Obedience to them brings sure rewards. Disobedience brings naught but sorrow.
> That the body is a fine precision instrument designed for accomplishment. It is folly, indeed, to neglect or abuse it.
> That adversity is the common lot of everyone. Life's testing lies in whether or not one is able to overcome and rise above it.
> That family ties are sacred. No effort is too great to safeguard them.
> That friends are the savor that brings flavor and sweet refreshment to life.
> That liberty is a priceless heritage. It should not be allowed to perish from this earth.
> These things I know of a certainty.[37]

As she approached her eighty-second birthday, Belle became fearful about her health. Elder Boyd K. Packer of the Quorum of the Twelve Apostles related the following experience:

> On Sunday morning, September 19, 1977, I awakened in the early hours of the morning greatly troubled over a

dream that concerned Sister Spafford. My wife also awakened and asked why I was so restless. "Sister Spafford is in trouble," I told her. "She needs a blessing." When morning came, I called her. She was deeply troubled indeed. I told her I had a blessing for her. She wept and said it came as an answer to her fervent prayer the night long. She had not been well. There had been tests. The day before, the doctor told her the results. They were frightening—ominous indeed. There was a tumor and other complications. Steven Johnson, an attentive young neighbor, assisted me in the blessing. It was most unusual. Her life was not over. Her days were to be prolonged for a most important purpose. Promises, special promises were given; among them that her mind would be sharp and alert as long as she lived. There would be no diminution of her mental capacities. . . . When further tests were made that next week, the tumor was not there.[38]

Belle lived another four and a half years and was not only alert until the day she died, but also maintained her warm humor. The last two months of her life she lived with her granddaughter's family, Mel and Janet Spafford Nimer and their three children. Mel redecorated a bedroom in their home to match Belle's own bedroom, so that she was never really moved out of her home—her home was simply moved to another location. Two-year-old Janelle Nimer often climbed up the rails of Belle's hospital bed so she and her grandmother could nap together or share stories. When she couldn't go to church, church was brought to her. Aaronic Priesthood members would come to the home to serve her the sacrament, after which she would say, "Now, you young men, will you preach to me?"

Belle gradually became weaker and finally asked to be taken to a hospital. She died on February 2, 1982, within hours of her admittance.

Belle had often said of people, "There are no strangers, only friends we have yet to meet." After her death, many women came to visit her family, each saying that Belle was her best friend. They echoed the sentiments of a nonmember friend, who once wrote to her: "Many claim you in your church and in your family, but my dear Belle, you belong to the world."[39]

At her funeral Elder Packer said, "When all of the tomorrows have passed, Belle S. Spafford will stand as one of the greatest women of this dispensation."[40]

Belle Smith Spafford, once converted to Relief Society, immeasurably influenced its course for more than half a century. She led women, in both the Church and national and international society, through an era of tremendous change. A dynamic leader, she was understanding and tactful, but forthright on principles and issues. A woman, a sister, a friend, and a church leader, she truly belonged to the world.

Notes

1. Telephone interview with Edythe K. Watson, March 30, 1989.

2. Belle Spafford Oral History, LDS Church Archives, p. 1. Hereafter cited as Oral History.

3. Oral History, p. 2.

4. Ibid.

5. Ibid., p. 3.

6. Ibid., p. 4.

7. Ibid., p. 5.

8. Ibid., p. 3.

9. Ibid., p. 23.

10. Ibid.

11. Ibid., p. 22.

12. *Church News,* February 24, 1973, p. 5.

13. Janet S. Nimer [Wilson], Relief Society Legacy Lecture, March 1982, p. 3.

14. "Tribute to Belle S. Spafford by Her Family," family scrapbook, in possession of Janet S. Nimer Wilson.

15. Joann Woodruff Bair, "Belle Spafford: A Sketch," *Dialogue,* Summer 1971, p. 72.

16. Ibid., p. 73.

17. Oral History, pp. 11–13.

18. Ibid., p. 24.

19. Ibid., p. 15.

20. Ibid., pp. 25–26.

21. Ibid., p. 30.

22. Ibid., p. 80.

23. Ibid., p. 86.

24. Gayle M. Chandler, "Belle S. Spafford: Leader of Women," master's thesis, Brigham Young University, 1983, pp. 18–19.

25. Telephone interview with Florence S. Jacobsen, April 28, 1989.

26. "Belle S. Spafford: Leader of Women," p. 23.

27. Ibid., p. 24.

28. Foreword in Belle S. Spafford, *A Woman's Reach* (Salt Lake City: Deseret Book, 1974), p. ii.

29. Relief Society Legacy Lecture, p. 3.

30. "Belle Smith Spafford Called to Be Ninth General President of Relief Society, April 1945," *Relief Society Magazine* 32 (May 1945): 259.

31. "Belle S. Spafford: Leader of Women," p. 20.

32. Ibid.

33. Oral History, p. 206.

34. "Relief Society: A Conversation with Belle S. Spafford," *Ensign,* June 1974, p. 15.

35. "Report of Relief Society Conference," *Ensign,* November 1974, p. 120.

36. Relief Society Legacy Lecture, p. 4.

37. "Belle S. Spafford: Leader of Women," p. 142.

38. Boyd K. Packer, funeral address, February 5, 1982, in family scrapbook, p. 17.

39. Relief Society Legacy Lecture, pp. 3–4.

40. Ibid., p. 5.

10

BARBARA BRADSHAW SMITH
1974–1984

"I have come to call you, Sister Smith, to be the new general president of the Relief Society of the Church worldwide," said President Spencer W. Kimball as he sat in Barbara Smith's living room. Barbara felt overwhelmed, in spite of the feeling she had had for three weeks prior to this visit that she would be called to serve as general Relief Society president and that President Kimball would come to her home.

"I couldn't believe that such a thing would happen," Barbara later said, "because I thought even if there were a remote chance that President Kimball would call me, the prophet of the Lord wouldn't come to my home; he would ask me to come to his office. But here he was at my home. I think the Lord must have done that for me so that I would know that he wanted me to serve, because I certainly didn't feel capable. I was grateful for that affirmation."[1]

Even with this personal confirmation, Barbara felt nervous as she sat in the Salt Lake Tabernacle on an autumn day in October 1974 and tried to prepare for the reaction of the congregation to the announcement that Belle S. Spafford, who had served as president for almost thirty years, was to be released. Barbara later recalled:

> When President Kimball said that he had come to make a change in the general presidency of the Relief Society, the whole audience said, "Oh, no." When they said that, my heart sank, because I knew they would feel that way. I felt that way myself. I started to cry. Then the words to "How Firm a Foundation" came to

mind, especially the verse that says, "Fear not, I am with thee; oh, be not dismayed, for I am thy God and will still give thee aid. I'll strengthen thee, help thee, and cause thee to stand, upheld by my righteous, omnipotent hand." Those words gave me courage and I was able to stand and speak.[2]

Barbara Smith did stand and speak at that conference, the first of innumerable times she would stand and speak to and for the women of the Church. With Barbara, the first president born in the twentieth century, a new era of Relief Society had begun. Sustained with Barbara were her counselors, Janath R. Cannon and Marian R. Boyer and as secretary-treasurer, Mayola R. Miltenberger. Marian became first counselor in the presidency in 1978 when Janath was released to serve a mission to Nigeria with her husband. Shirley W. Thomas served as second counselor until 1983 when she was released to accompany her husband as a mission president in Australia, and was succeeded by Ann S. Reese.

Members of the Relief Society would find in Barbara Bradshaw Smith an extraordinary advocate during the crucial years of unrest as the United States debated, and eventually defeated, the proposed Equal Rights Amendment to the Constitution. Her success in this role can be attributed to the forceful combination of her integrity, courage, faith, energy, and optimism—traits she would hasten to attribute to the influence of her family, especially her mother and grandmother.

Heritage

Barbara's grandmother, Caroline Daniels Mills, possessed similar traits. When she decided to return to school and become a doctor, Caroline took her three children with her to Iowa City, Iowa, where she attended medical school. She tried to care for the children and carry on her work as a student, but after the first year she realized it was too difficult. With the support of her mother, who came and cared for the children, and her husband, who remained home and earned enough money to keep her in school, Caroline received a degree in medicine, specializing in surgery. Her life served as an example of independence and interdependence to Barbara.

A Happy Childhood

Dr. Caroline Mills was the attending physician at Barbara's birth on January 26, 1922, in Salt Lake City, Utah. Though it was midwinter, the weather was as mild and sunny as in springtime. Barbara has enjoyed retelling the events of that day, which have been the source of good-natured laughter over the years: "My father came home from work and asked my mother, 'What's the matter? Don't you feel good?' My mother said, 'No, I haven't been feeling too well today.' He then leaned over to kiss her and there I was. I began to cry. That was the first time he realized that I had been born."[3]

Barbara was the third of six children born to Dorothy Mills and Dan Delos Bradshaw: Carolyn, Robert, Barbara, George, Frank, and Thomas. Her mother was a woman of rare optimism. If she saw any of her children climbing a ladder, instead of shouting at them to come down, Dorothy encouraged them to climb carefully and see how high they could reach. Her optimism transferred into the practical areas of the Bradshaw family. "I knew we didn't have a lot, but my mother just seemed to make the money stretch," said Barbara.

> I remember going to the pantry and saying, "What are we going to have for dinner? There's nothing here." Mother would say, "Don't worry about that, dear. Anyone can fix a wonderful meal if they have everything to begin with, but it's the sign of a good cook if you can start with nothing and then prepare a delicious meal." So it was fun to watch her as she made biscuits, hot bread, scones or other good food for us for dinner.[4]

Dee Bradshaw, Barbara's father, was a barber. "Those were days of the Depression," said Barbara. "He would cut the hair of whole families for a dollar, so he would often work all day long cutting hair and much of his night, too."[5]

While Barbara learned optimism and independence from her mother and grandmother, she gained an important perspective on life from an experience with her father. Once, as she ran into his barber shop and started looking for him, she became confused by the large mirrors. No matter which way she moved, he seemed to get farther away from her instead of closer. Fear and frustration grew in her until her father called out to her. Immediately she knew which way to turn—just as one learns how to turn to the Father by listening to the voice of the Spirit. "I have often thought of that frightening experience I had as a child and recalled the significant lesson I learned from it concerning the eternal processes of life," said Barbara.[6]

As a young girl, Barbara was selected as one of the models for a small bronze statue of a boy and girl, a statue that now stands in front of the Salt Lake City and County Building; and during her teens, her silhouette appeared on the cover of one of the Mutual Improvement Association manuals. These events appropriately coincided with Barbara's life as she set an example for others during her school years and foreshadowed the day when she would become an example for millions of women.

Barbara's sister Carolyn recollected that "Barbara was always an obedient girl. I remember she loved to achieve and excel in things. Because of this, she had many friends. I think Barbara takes after Mother, who was very talented and often busy with roadshows and one-act plays. Barbara has always loved to plan things and then carry out the plans."[7]

Popular and confident at both Lincoln Junior High School and South High School in Salt Lake City, Barbara served as a student body officer in both schools. She credited a health teacher in junior high school with helping her realize the importance of a smile, later one of Barbara's trademarks. This teacher pointed out to her that she should smile more. "I remember putting forth additional effort," said Barbara. "Because of her I became more outgoing."[8]

Marriage and Family Life

Barbara met Douglas Hill Smith while she was on the debate team at South High School. He was attending the University of Utah and had been asked to judge a debate meet in which she participated. He was impressed not only with her beauty but also with her maturity and a special spiritual quality about her.

"When I first met Barbara," said Douglas, "her mother told me she was someone very special. Throughout our life together I have come to know that Mother Bradshaw's statement to me was far more than parental pride."[9]

After a two-year courtship, Douglas and Barbara were married on June 16, 1941, in the Salt Lake Temple. They spent the energy of their early years of marriage establishing a home and rearing a family. They were the parents of seven children: Sandra, Lillian, Barton, Lowell, Blaine, Catherine, and Sherilynn. Once Barbara overheard a friend of their young son Blaine ask, "Is your mother and dad rich?" Blaine answered, "Yeah, we're rich in kids."[10]

When the children were small, Barbara and Douglas divided the night into two four-hour segments to guarantee each of them at least four hours of sleep without interruption while the other took care of any child who might wake up crying.

Creative in her discipline, Barbara described her years of rearing her children as "a constant path of being on an even keel. There were sicknesses and problems that came from time to time but I wasn't up in the clouds nor down in the dumps."[11] She remembered once overhearing a Primary teacher say that her son was the worst child in her class. For a short time Barbara was hurt and decided not to send her son to Primary anymore, but that didn't last.

> I realized that unless I did something to help him be better, he would continue to be difficult to manage. I determined that I would send a report card with him to Primary and I called and told the teacher I wanted her to mark it honestly and then give it back to him to bring home. Then, I thought as long as I was giving one to him I would send report cards with his two brothers too. The next thing I heard was that he was good in class and that the other members of the group were better too. . . . I had been hurt and offended but I knew it was my responsibility to do something constructive to take care of the problem.[12]

Whenever Barbara was away from home, she tried to leave things in order. She wanted her children to learn that although she sacrificed for the Church, she was also willing to sacrifice for them. She wanted them to realize that she trusted them, and she typically left them with chores and assignments to be completed. Her daughter Lillian remembers that both her mother and her father were busy with church, business, and community responsibilities.

> However, my memories of my mother are of her being home, not of her going. She often had friends and people who wanted to talk to her. It was very common to have someone out on the porch at night visiting with her. Listening to others and giving them the desire to go on and be better than they have been is probably mother's greatest talent. Somehow she has the gift to be able to see the good in others and to help them to see the best in themselves. Mother taught us to always do our best and that we were not competing with other people, only ourselves. I think her attitude was why should you be less than you are? Why not develop your talents and yourself to the very fullest? We learned to work hard and not waste our time.[13]

As a young mother, Barbara gained a strong testimony of Relief Society. After she received a call as social relations teacher, she determined to do her best in spite of her feelings of inadequacy. Many years later, she wrote about the experience in her book *A Fruitful Season:*

> I knelt down in my kitchen, and as the sun streamed through the window I prayed for a strong testimony of the lesson I was to teach and for directions as I prepared and presented the material. I will never forget the powerful feeling of warmth and light that came to me. The sun's rays were as naught compared to that warm sensation that filled my whole being. There I was, on my knees, . . . and finding myself in tears, knowing that the lesson I was to teach really had the ratification of my Heavenly Father.
>
> My commitment was sure. I wanted to seek for me and mine that godly seed; Relief Society was for me. I knew it—deep inside me. I wanted to be an active, involved

Relief Society sister and have my service ascend to the Lord and be a cause for eternal glory. I wanted with all my heart to have the graces of rare womanhood and glorious motherhood radiate from me.[14]

"It didn't surprise me when my mother was called to be the president of the Relief Society," said Lillian, "because all my life I have felt her spirit lifting others. Her only desire her whole life has been to do good."[15] Reflecting later on her service as president, Barbara said, "The very first thing that the Lord made known to me after I became the general president of the Relief Society was that the Lord loves every son and every daughter and that he has given them each talents and abilities."[16]

Soon after her call as president, Barbara received a blessing from President Kimball in which she was promised that she would be able to lead the women of the Church and have an influence upon the women of the world. The fulfillment of this blessing would unfold as Barbara became a strong advocate for women both in the Church and in the world.

Advocate for Women

The first seven years of her presidency, 1974 to 1981, were filled with media attention, due to interest in the Equal Rights Amendment. Few women in the United States were left untouched by the ERA controversy. Many struggled to define their roles as women and to decide whether they were treated with equality in their varied responsibilities. Inner turmoil often resulted from this introspection—sometimes temporary, sometimes permanent. The result was growing diversity and disparity among women, including many Latter-day Saints.

In November 1975, Barbara met with Phyllis Schlafly, then the most prominent and articulate voice in the battle against the ERA nationwide. "We talked about the ERA," Barbara recalled, "and I told her that I didn't think the Church would make a public statement against the ERA because it only took a position on moral issues. She said to me she felt that the ERA was one of the greatest moral issues of our day and that it would be very destructive to the family. If I would just study it, I would understand how destructive it could be."[17]

As Barbara studied the Equal Rights Amendment, she gained a clearer understanding of its pros and cons. The time had come for her, as leader of the women of the Church, to announce her position. Her first opportunity, which received full media coverage, was a fireside talk at the Institute of Religion adjacent to the University of Utah in December 1974. With that fireside address, Barbara B. Smith assumed her role as an advocate for women as she spoke against the ERA.

Barbara stated on several occasions:

> I stand as a representative of an organization that is in favor of women's rights. I may differ with some people, however, on the best way or ways to achieve these rights. The Equal Rights Amendment is not the way. The national ERA is so broad that I am convinced it would bring us much more trouble than has been envisioned by even the most pessimistic of its opponents. In many instances women would be hurt, not helped. A very substantial concern for those of us who care about helping women is that the ERA would, in fact, cause women to lose previously hard-won rights.*

She believed, moreover, that the ERA would "lock us into a system that did not provide for the emotional, physical, or biological differences between the sexes."[18]

Barbara acknowledged that many forms of discrimination against women did exist, such as unequal opportunity for promotion in paid employment, unequal pay for equal work, unequal job benefits, restrictions in the use of credit, inequalities in property rights, inheritance, and the administration of a child's estate. For all the inequities, though, she believed that drafting specific legislation to correct specific problems offered a better solution than the one broad and vague statement of the proposed amendment.

---

* So that this statement would accurately reflect the sentiments Barbara repeatedly expressed, Barbara edited it herself in October 1988, when this chapter was originally being drafted.

An October 22, 1976, a statement from the First Presidency opposing the ERA gave direction and peace to many sisters, but others felt anger and a sense of displacement. Women's issues and the ERA thus became Barbara's greatest challenge as president of the Relief Society, as she walked a fine line between supporting women's rights while at the same time speaking against the Equal Rights Amendment.

The Church's anti-ERA viewpoint was a point of controversy for several years. When Sonja Johnson, formerly an active Latter-day Saint, was excommunicated, the media focused particular attention on the Church. This led to an appearance on ABC television's *Donahue* show for Barbara. Beverly Campbell, also a Latter-day Saint and a leader of the anti-ERA effort in Virginia, appeared with her.

Barbara considered the television appearance one of the most unforgettable experiences in her term as general president of the Relief Society. Just prior to leaving for Chicago, where the show was to originate, she learned that her pregnant daughter, Catherine, had been taken to the hospital with toxemia. In Barbara's hurry to get to the hospital, she slipped on icy steps at her home and fell down the entire flight of stairs. Miraculously, she was uninjured and able to make it to the airport on time after visiting her daughter. Later that evening, she received word that her daughter and new grandchild were fine.

Barbara's anxiety was further relieved the next morning when Phil Donahue explained that the show was to be taped instead of broadcast live. She was pleased because "we didn't have calls from people we couldn't see. We could look at and respond directly to every person that questioned us from the audience. I was grateful for that."[19] She was disappointed, however, that in the course of the interview she had little opportunity to say anything specific about the role of women in the Church. At the conclusion of the program she started to name five points of emphasis that make Mormon women different from other women, but time ran out and she was unable to give them all.

Reaction to the show was immediate. Back home in Salt Lake City, Barbara received thousands of letters from people requesting those five points, wanting to know more about the Church, and feeling grateful that questions had been met honestly.[20] The five points she intended to give were: first, the importance of Relief

Society visiting teaching; second, no tobacco, tea, coffee, or alcohol; third, a year's supply of food; fourth, family home evening; and fifth, the Book of Mormon.

In connection with her willingness to speak out against the Equal Rights Amendment, Barbara also spoke out against young women joining the military. Recruitment tactics at the time were urging more and more women to enlist. Using "equal pay for equal work" as one incentive, the military tied itself to the women's movement and benefited from its momentum.

Barbara was asked to speak on the hazards of women joining the military at Brigham Young University on February 17, 1976. Military personnel associated with BYU would be in the audience, so BYU President Dallin H. Oaks asked for a copy of the talk in order to prepare them for her message. However, when she arrived, she learned that President Oaks had not been able to get advance copies to them. She felt heartsick as she thought of the shock awaiting them.[21]

Although she was directly facing high-level military officers, Barbara spoke forthrightly. "I would not encourage any young Latter-day Saint woman, especially one just out of high school, to become a military enlistee," she counseled. "I feel that the regimentation of military life places a great strain upon most women who enlist in the military services. It is difficult for them to live under the pressures of putting their lives so completely into another's charge, resigning their actions to another's discipline." She then acknowledged the great good of the military and the fact that, in times of war, women have always been able to rise to the need. "I hope women will do in the future as they have done over and over again in the past: save families!"[22]

The speech invoked controversy, and Barbara Smith received numerous letters and telephone calls. Nevertheless, she continued to speak out on that subject as well as the ERA and other women's issues. About these challenges, she said:

> It is very hard to have so many people against you. Once I had a whole group raise signs and parade against me personally when I gave a talk against abortion. I gained much of my strength to face these challenges from my mother who helped me feel that I

could do whatever I had to do. Also, the example of my great-great-grandfather gave me courage. After the Saints had been driven from Missouri, he was asked by the leaders of the Church to go back and sell the land still owned by the Saints. After he'd sold the first piece of property, a mob gathered around him and said, "Give us the money, give us the deeds to the property, and leave or you're going to be a dead man before night." My great-great-grandfather said, "This land has been acquired according to the laws of the state and the country and we have every legal right to sell it. Some who own this land are widows, the handicapped, and the elderly. I am going to do all that I can to sell every piece of property before I leave. If you feel anything different about it, you might just as well shoot me." Slowly, the mob left and he was free to sell the property. These examples built in my family and they worked together to help me become strong enough to do what needed to be done.[23]

Eventually, the national tide turned against the Equal Rights Amendment, and several states started proceedings to rescind their passage of the ERA. The emotional controversy began to die down, but in its wake was a general and individual unrest among women. The ERA had divided women into two groups, both committed more firmly than ever to their own points of view.

One of the highlights of Barbara Smith's presidency and, she felt, one of the most effective means of uniting Latter-day Saint sisters, was the Relief Society's Nauvoo Monument to Women. From conception to dedication, it closely paralleled the stormiest years of the ERA movement.

In 1975 the Relief Society general board decided that the bronze plaque in Nauvoo commemorating the organization of the Relief Society in 1842 should be replaced and invited sculptors to present ideas for a new monument. Dennis Smith was one of the sculptors who accepted that invitation. The Relief Society chose his proposal of eleven figures in a garden setting, and in addition they selected two statues to be done by Florence Hansen. Latter-day Saint women throughout the world donated money for this monument to honor the many facets of a woman's life, and in the process, they became united in a common cause.

The Nauvoo Monument to Women was dedicated in the early summer of 1978. Marian R. Boyer, one of Barbara's counselors, remembered the occasion:

> After Barbara and I arrived in Nauvoo for the dedication, we walked down to the garden, just the two of us. We had worked so hard to accomplish this huge undertaking. . . . We walked down over the hill just as the sun was going down behind the Mississippi River. We sat on a bench, and neither of us could speak. We just looked at each other and started to cry with joy. After seeing that beautiful garden, we realized what it represented and what it could mean to the women of the Church if they would only catch its message.[24]

While the ERA and work on the Nauvoo Monument to Women took much of her time during Barbara Smith's ten years as Relief Society president, other facets of the work blossomed during her administration as well.

A Worldwide View

In 1975, members of the Relief Society presidency were invited to participate in Church area conferences held in various parts of the world. They traveled with the First Presidency and their wives to Asia, Canada, Europe, and areas in the United States. With this beginning, Barbara became the most widely traveled of all the general Relief Society presidents. Over the years of her administration, she visited many countries on nearly every continent, from Australia to South America, Europe, Asia, and North America. According to her husband, "Her travels were filled with special feelings of divine guidance and understanding. She was constantly in the arms of the sisters, loving them and crying with them as they were overcome by the Holy Spirit."[25]

As a result of what Barbara saw and learned in her travels, the Relief Society began providing training for health and welfare missionaries and for the wives of mission presidents. In that way, many others could learn from these faithful women how to bestow the tender ministrations of the Relief Society.

In 1976, the Relief Society participated in the celebration of the bicentennial of the United States. The Relief Society Building was filled with displays and was referred to as "The Spirit of '76 North Main" (a play on words referring to its street address), and a reader's theater presentation, *Melt Down My Pewter,* was performed in many wards and stakes.

Involvement in the International Women's Year (1977), the White House Conference on Families (1978), the International Year of the Child (1979), the National and International Councils of Women, and the American Mothers Committee immersed Barbara Smith in meaningful projects for children, in helping the aged to productively meet their challenges, and in teaching women how to be more influential as citizens. Barbara felt proud to sit on these committees and observe how other committee members reacted when they recognized that Latter-day Saint women really did care about what they were doing.[26]

The Relief Society wheat storage program ended in 1978, concluding a "sacred trust" that had been given the sisters more than a century before. It was a tender moment for Relief Society women when, on September 30, 1978, President Barbara B. Smith called for and received a sustaining vote of the sisters in a welfare session of general conference to give the Relief Society wheat and the wheat trust funds to the Church.

In 1983, Barbara was invited to Cape Canaveral, Florida, to witness the space shuttle launch, which included Sally Ride, the first woman astronaut. "It was a thrilling experience and probably the most perfect launching up to that time," Barbara remembered. She was among the guests invited to the buildings where the space shuttle was prepared for launch; there they listened to the directors of the space program and mingled with the astronauts.[27] Later Barbara had an opportunity to explain her views on women's rights and the ERA to Sally Ride.

On several occasions Barbara was invited to the White House in Washington, D.C. The first visit was in 1978. "I felt the hospitality of the old south as I met with First Lady Rosalynn Carter in her office at the White House," she said. "During our half hour visit, she had an opportunity to explain her views on women's issues and I invited her to the dedication of the Nauvoo Monument to Women."[28] Mrs. Carter was unable to attend the dedication, but she sent a representative, Bethine Church, the wife of Senator Frank Church of Idaho.

As a result of her meeting with Mrs. Carter, Barbara was invited to join distinguished women from various religious and ethnic groups in a seminar to discuss employment for women. "We were all supposed to come with ideas," she recalled. "I, of course, took our welfare program, and information about our employment specialists who could help individuals seek jobs and help them with their self-esteem."[29] Her ideas were well received, but the group could not see any way to implement them.

The establishment of a consolidated meeting schedule for the Church in 1980 had a far-reaching effect for the Relief Society. Auxiliary meetings that had been held on weekdays were moved to Sundays to share a single block of time with priesthood, Sunday School, and sacrament meetings. Consequently, the Relief Society curriculum and the visiting teaching plan were simplified so that more women could participate.

The Relief Society observed the Church's sesquicentennial in 1980 by presenting to the Church life-size replicas of four of the bronze statues from the Nauvoo Monument to Women. These statues were subsequently placed on the plaza of the Church Office Building in Salt Lake City. In addition, the general board planted thirty-five redbud trees on the plaza grounds. A jubilee box, patterned after the one made by Sarah M. Kimball in 1881, was also assembled, to be opened in the year 2030.

In conjunction with the 1980 World Conference on Records in Salt Lake City, the Relief Society created a display entitled "Histories Made Fresh Daily." Family memorabilia as a means of enhancing family history was stressed, and fresh-baked homemade cookies were passed out to the thousands who visited the display.

In 1982, a "learn, then teach" program was introduced, emphasizing the need for women to share with others the education and learning experiences provided in Relief Society. As part of this program, women throughout the Church celebrated 140 years of Relief Society with concerts, lectures, and other special observances.

The theme for the celebration was "Legacy—Remembered and Renewed," and concerts spotlighting outstanding LDS female musicians were presented in Dallas, Texas; Oakland and Los Angeles, California; Salt Lake City, Utah, and Washington, D.C. Outstanding art was displayed at the Salt Lake Art Center, and a series of lectures by women was given in Salt Lake City, with many of these talks later published in a book, *A Woman's Choices*. Also published in connection with the celebration was a book entitled *A Legacy Remembered: The Relief Society Magazine, 1914–1970*.

An emphasis on correlating the past and present in Relief Society continued with the dedication of the fully restored Sarah M. Kimball home in Nauvoo in 1982; and in 1984, work was begun on an official, updated history of the Relief Society. With the growth of the Relief Society into a worldwide organization, Barbara Smith wanted the Relief Society Building in Salt Lake City to become a resource center for sisters from around the world. Under her direction, displays were set up in empty rooms and even offices so that women could visit the Relief Society Building and learn not only about their ecclesiastical callings but also about how to develop their talents.

Her policy of openness and sharing reflected the relationship Barbara wanted with the sisters of the Relief Society. "I always left my door open," she said. "Many, many women came because they were troubled. I suppose the discussions on the ERA triggered some of those feelings and so they would phone me or come in."[30] "Barbara's spirit of hospitality was reflected by her open office," remembered Mayola Miltenberger, general secretary. "She belonged to the women of the world."[31]

Indeed, many of the women who worked with Barbara over the years have recognized her strengths. "Barbara Smith is a visionary woman," said Carol L. Clark, a member of the general board for ten years. "She has a vision of womanhood and of Relief Society and has brought a depth to LDS womanhood. We may not yet understand the significance of some of the things she set in place. I believe in years to come her administration will be marked by and remembered for her vision."[32]

Phyllis Marriott was president of the American Mothers Committee when Barbara served as an AMC board member. "Barbara was extremely knowledgeable," she said. "I've never known a woman who gained such universal respect. She was a perfectionist, and people came to admire her for the way in which she carried out assignments."[33] "I used to think I could beat Sister Smith to the office, but I never did," said Mayola Miltenberger. "She has incredible vigor."[34] Carol Clark agreed. "Barbara is tireless, and practically wore us [the general board members] out," she said. "She has remarkable energy."[35]

"Barbara expected the best of her board members and got it," said Ann S. Reese, Barbara's counselor from November 1983 to April 1984. "We felt good after a project because we knew we had given it our all."[36]

Ann recalled a committee meeting where the members discussed a proposed mother-education course of study.

> I drove Barbara home from the Relief Society Building. It had been a busy, mentally tiring day and I was emotionally and physically exhausted. As Barbara got out of the car, she turned to me and said, "Isn't this the most exciting calling? I feel so blessed to be a part of the Relief Society curriculum planning. I can hardly wait for each day to begin—it is so thrilling to be a part of this work." I found this a typical reaction of a woman whom friends and family describe as having remarkable energy and desire to serve her Heavenly Father.[37]

Even with her remarkable energy, Barbara would not have been able to serve as she did without her family's support. "When President Kimball came to our home and asked Barbara to serve as president of the Relief Society," recalled Douglas Smith, "he turned to me and asked if I would sustain and support her. I've been in church positions for thirty years of our marriage and she has fully sustained me. I just determined this would be the time when I would fully sustain her."[38]

From shopping and ironing to housecleaning, Douglas did support his wife. He joked that he could make chicken soup as "well as any man in the Church."[39] He also enjoyed driving Barbara to many of her meetings. "I have never felt I was playing second fiddle," he said. "I've always felt this was my opportunity to return to Barbara that which she has given to me, and I've had great spiritual blessings from it."[40]

All but two of Barbara's seven children were married when she was called as Relief Society president. "We didn't go without her mothering, love, and support," said daughter Sherilyn, the youngest child. "We knew she would be always be there for us. And she included us as much as possible in the things she did."[41]

An Honorable Release

After ten years of service, Barbara B. Smith was released as general president of the Relief Society on April 7, 1984. Membership in the organization had increased from 837,253 sisters speaking seventeen different languages in 1974 to 1,600,000 speaking eighty different languages in 1984.

As she prepared to turn her office over to her successor, Barbara W. Winder, Barbara Smith found herself reminiscing: "Emptying out my desk, taking that last look around my office, I thought of all the events that had taken place in the beautiful Relief Society Building, events again so fresh in my mind as part of a soul-searing, soul-soaring experience. I wanted with all my heart to make the last ten years mine forever, with their innumerable, priceless moments I had shared with my counselors, the board, our staff, and women from near and far."[42]

"So many people feel hurt when they are released from a position," she explained. "I came to the conclusion when I was released that I could either be hurt or I could feel the blessings of those years. I chose to feel the blessings."[43]

Douglas Smith wrote:

> I saw the hand of the Lord in Barbara's hand leading and guiding her and on many occasions giving her great inspiration and direction. The period of her service as the general president of the Relief Society was filled with challenges beyond any mortal expectation. We frequently prayed together supplicating the Lord to inspire her with His Spirit that she might know the will of the Master and go forth to it with all her vigor. Often we would feel and see his Holy Spirit fall upon her in ways of magnificence. She knew the Lord wanted her to love his children and help the sisters of the Church

understand their importance in the sight of the Lord
and their duty to serve him in the offices to which they
had been appointed with all diligence.[44]

After Barbara's release, she relaxed and spent more time with her
family. Drawing upon the knowledge and spirit of her own growth and
experiences as president, she also found time to write several books: *The
Love That Never Faileth* (1984), *The Light of Christmas* (1985), *Growth
in Grandmothering* (1986), and *A Fruitful Season* (1988).

In April 1987, Douglas H. Smith was called to serve as a member
of the First Quorum of the Seventy, and the following year he was
named area president in Asia. Barbara accompanied him to the Far
East on this new assignment, and, under a new program established
shortly after her release from Relief Society, one of her responsibilities
was to represent the general boards of Relief Society, Young Women,
and Primary and to help train leaders in her area. About this she said:

> This new calling was one of the most challenging experi-
> ences of my life, especially because I do not speak any of
> their languages. Even though my husband's assignment
> included almost half of the population of the earth, I
> know the work will go forward in a very significant way.
> I traveled in the Orient during my years as Relief Society
> president, but I came back on a different basis. I tried to
> remember what I had learned through my Relief Society
> service so that I would be able to use it in a way that
> would be a blessing to these wonderful people whom I
> have come to love so much.[45]

After five years of service, Douglas was released from the Quorum
of the Seventy at general conference in April 1992. Barbara was called
to serve as Relief Society president in their home ward, the Ensign
Second Ward, a joyful experience for her to be involved "at the grass
roots." She has been delighted in that her daughters have all served as
Relief Society presidents as well.

With more time to devote to family affairs, Barbara and Douglas
published a history of their posterity. They have been working on a

second volume to include the ever-growing number of great-grand-children. Barbara planned this book with the purpose of helping these children understand who they are and to help bring them closer to the Lord by citing a scripture and a characteristic of God for each child. They visit frequently with each of their seven children and their families. When a wedding or baby shower is held, it is often a learning experience for the family rather than just a get-together.

The Smiths have served one day a week in the Salt Lake Temple, a short distance from their condominium in downtown Salt Lake City. Barbara has continued her involvement with several study groups, including one of her high school friends, who meet quarterly and "study things that will help us keep growing," she said. She has enjoyed meeting with all of the former general presidency and board members each March to celebrate the organization of Relief Society, a tradition started during her administration. As Barbara looked back on the extensive service she and Douglas have given over many years, she called it "a grand experience—not a sacrifice."[46]

Since that morning when Barbara B. Smith knelt in her sunlit kitchen to seek help with her Relief Society lesson, she has endeavored to remember what she has learned through her Relief Society service and to share it with others.

> I really believe that those years of my administration, when women's issues were so prominent, were very critical in the history of the world. The women who lived through those years of turmoil need to know that how they lived their lives was important and to recognize their place in history. Women today also need to feel the importance of Relief Society in their lives and to recognize that they are creating their own place in history so that they will be able to pass this great heritage on to their daughters.[47]

Notes

1. Barbara B. Smith Oral History, interviews by Jessie L. Embry, Salt

Lake City, Utah 1977, The James Moyle Oral History Program, LDS Church Archives, p. 59. Hereafter cited as Oral History.

2. Oral History, p. 63.

3. Ibid., p. 6.

4. Interview with Barbara B. Smith by Sheri L. Dew, January 24, 1984. Hereafter cited as Interview with Dew; also Oral History, p. 1.

5. Ibid., p. 6.

6. Ibid., p. 7.

7. Interview with Carolyn Strong by Sheri L. Dew, May 9, 1984.

8. Oral History, p. 9.

9. Statement from Douglas Hill Smith, October 10, 1988, in possession of LaRene Gaunt.

10. Carolyn Strong interview.

11. Barbara B. Smith to LaRene Gaunt, April 27, 1988.

12. Ibid.

13. Interview with Lillian S. Alldredge by Sheri L. Dew, May 11, 1984.

14. Barbara B. Smith, *A Fruitful Season* (Salt Lake City: Bookcraft, 1988), pp. 19–20.

15. Lillian S. Alldredge interview.

16. Oral History, p. 84.

17. Oral History, p. 65.

18. Editing by Barbara B. Smith on first draft of this chapter, October 1988, in possession of LaRene Gaunt.

19. Interview with Barbara B. Smith by LaRene Gaunt and Janet Peterson, October 5, 1988. Hereafter cited as Barbara Smith interview.

20. Janet Thomas, "Barbara B. Smith: Woman for the World," *This People*, Summer 1980, pp. 13–14.

21. Oral History, p. 85.

22. "Women Should Be Cautious about Military," *Church News,* February 21, 1976, p. 13.

23. Barbara Smith interview.

24. Sheri L. Dew, "A Woman for Her Time," *This People,* June/July 1984, p. 22.

25. Douglas H. Smith to LaRene Gaunt, October 10, 1988.

26. Barbara Smith interview.

27. Barbara Smith notes in possession of Sheri L. Dew.

28. Ibid.; also Mayola Miltenberger, *A Decade of Relief Society, 1974–1984* (Salt Lake City: Relief Society General Board, 1984), p. 22.

29. Interview with Dew.

30. Barbara Smith interview.

31. Interview with Mayola Miltenberger by LaRene Gaunt, September 20, 1988.

32. "A Woman for Her Time," p. 21.

33. Interview with Phyllis Marriott by Sheri L. Dew, May 11, 1988.

34. "A Woman for Her Time," p. 23.

35. Interview with Carol L. Clark by Sheri L. Dew, May 14, 1984.

36. Telephone interview with Ann Reese by LaRene Gaunt, September 5, 1988.

37. Ibid.

38. Interview with Douglas H. Smith by Sheri L. Dew, February 3, 1984.

39. "A Woman for Her Time," p. 26.

40. Interview with Douglas H. Smith by Sheri L. Dew, February 3, 1984.

41. Interview with Sherilyn S. Alba by LaRene Gaunt, April 5, 1989.

42. *A Fruitful Season,* p. 213.

43. Barbara Smith interview.

44. Douglas H. Smith to LaRene Gaunt, October 10, 1988.

45. Barbara Smith interview.

46. Interview with Barbara B. Smith by Janet Peterson, November 20, 2006.

47. Barbara Smith interview.

11

BARBARA WOODHEAD WINDER
1984–1990

When Barbara Woodhead Winder was in the second grade, a boy—the class bully—came to school one morning in a torn pair of pants held together with a safety pin. The teacher, Louella Dover, took him home, then returned to class and explained that the boy did not have a mother and had only one pair of pants. "I remember feeling empathy for him," Barbara recalled, "How hard to have no mother!"[1] It was experiences such as this, combined with the influence of teachers, parents, and grandparents who spent their lives in the service of others, that helped Barbara develop the compassion that was so characteristic of her leadership of Relief Society members worldwide.

Heritage

Barbara's great-grandfather, George E. Hand, began the family tradition of service and sacrifice as a seventeen-year-old convert to The Church of Jesus Christ of Latter-day Saints. The only member of his family to leave England in 1865, George was sent by his parents to Utah to earn money for the rest of the family to emigrate. Although his parents and several of his nine brothers and sisters died before he could send for them, George worked for thirty-nine years to fulfill his parents' mandate to help his family gather to Zion.

Barbara's maternal grandmother, Susie Stewart Hand, served as a counselor and then for nine years as president of the Third Ward Relief Society in Sandy, Utah. Sandy was a mining town in the southeast part of the Salt Lake Valley, and because of the high death toll among miners, many widows had no pensions or insurance benefits. As Relief Society president, Susie took care of their needs, with her own children helping to distribute food and clothing. She would often set extra places at the dinner table for visitors. Since the railroad ran through the center of town, tramps would frequently come to her door for a meal. Susie's daughters said that for many years after her death they heard people tell of their mother's unselfish service to others. Dave Hand, a barber by profession and a gardener by avocation, gave free haircuts and shaves, as well as dahlias and cannas from his prize-winning garden, to the sick and needy.

Although Susie Hand died when Barbara was a little girl, Barbara remembered "the warm feeling of love at her home and the wonderful food she prepared. She had eight children and baked everything—pies, for example, and loaves of bread—by the dozen. Her home was always open to everyone."[2] Barbara also had the opportunity to learn from her Grandfather and Grandmother Woodhead. Her father's mother, Ruby May Stubbs Woodhead, who had also served as a Relief Society president, came to live with Barbara's family near the end of her life. Through many stories about her early life and her experiences with her husband and children, Ruby passed on her values to her grandchildren. For example, she often told of answering the door one evening and finding a stranger standing there. He said, "I don't know if you know what kind of a man your husband is, Mrs. Woodhead, but my family would not have had food or heat this winter if it hadn't been for him."[3]

Because of her age and ill health, Ruby needed to have someone sleep in the same room with her at night, so fifteen-year-old Barbara decided that she would be that person. Because Ruby's need for constant care tended to keep Barbara's parents homebound, Barbara often said to them on a Friday night when she was planning to get together with friends or a date, "Mother, we'll stay here and play games. You and Dad go somewhere and enjoy yourselves."[4]

Barbara's parents, Marguerite Hand and Willard Verl Woodhead, were also fine examples of service to others. "My mother and father are some of the most compassionate people I know," she said. "We often had someone living with us."[5] These included Barbara's aunts on occasion, as well as her Grandmother Woodhead. The Woodheads were also willing to make sacrifices to help others. When Susie Hand died of a heart attack in her early fifties, three of her eight children were still at home, so the

Woodheads left their home and moved in with Marguerite's father in Sandy to take care of him and the children.

Lessons of Childhood

Barbara, the eldest child in the Woodhead family, was born on May 9, 1931, in Midvale, Utah. She was eighteen months old when her brother Willard was born, six and a half years old when Nancy was born, and sixteen when David was born. Because Marguerite needed to work outside the home, Barbara often had to care for the younger children. As she grew up, therefore, she learned many lessons—of work, of family relationships, and of pain and patience.

When Barbara was in the fourth grade, her family moved to East Millcreek, then a rural area of Salt Lake County. Barbara worked every summer in the nearby strawberry and raspberry patches and orchards until she was old enough to get a job in the ice cream parlor around the corner from her home. The Woodheads had a large garden, and Barbara had opportunities to help with that also. She wrote:

> I am grateful now for our family garden—though I wasn't always grateful for it while I was growing up. Mother taught me how to pull the weeds with the root included so the weed would not grow back again—at least not that particular one. And as if the continuous weeding process were not enough work, early each spring we had to "de-rock" our garden, which was developed on top of an old creekbed. "De-rocking" took the combined effort of the entire family and consisted of gathering and collecting the baseball-size or larger rocks that seemed to proliferate during the winter while the rest of nature slept. Then, having cleared the land enough to prepare the soil for planting, I helped Dad load the rocks into our little trailer to take them to the dump.
>
> I didn't know then, as we shelled the peas and snapped the beans preparatory for canning, that more than a winter's storehouse of food was being preserved. We were laying foundations for family relationships that

would be much greater than our year's supply. In fact, we are still being richly fed from those seeds planted many years ago.[6]

Although the Woodheads had a loving relationship, Barbara wanted her family to be strong in the Church and to be sealed in the temple. Marguerite and Verl were not married in the temple and did not participate often in Church activities during Barbara's childhood. "However, I was encouraged to go to church, and always did," Barbara said. She continued:

> I chose friends who were active in the Church. We had neighbors who were close to the Church, and I can remember one Sunday evening going next door. Mother said, "Why do you always go over there?" I enjoyed the spirit there and the gospel discussions. I was learning; I was seeking to be edified. I remember clearly the Sunday evening the father in that home taught about the three degrees of glory in a family discussion. I had never heard of this before. It was wonderful how the Spirit bore witness to me of its truthfulness.[7]

A Primary teacher reached out to Barbara and took her to Primary each week, and when she was eight years old, the same teacher took her to be baptized. Later, Barbara admitted:

> About the time of my baptism, I must have been quite unbearable to live with because I was constantly admonishing my parents about what they should be doing. But as I matured, I came to recognize that perhaps my approach to my parents' problem of being less active was not the right one. Through those teen years, I started learning acceptance of other people, and I began to understand why people behave as they do. I came to recognize that Mother and Dad had real financial struggles during the Depression years, and as I was growing up they really had a hard time. Mother worked a good

part of the time, and Dad worked shift work and on weekends, and as a result they were often very tired. Because of their work schedules, they weren't able to participate with me, but rather encouraged me and cheered me on from the sidelines.[8]

Barbara learned another important lesson in maturity and spirituality as a student at Granite High School. When she was elected president of the girls' association, the group's adviser, Ann Pehrson, asked her "to fast and pray with her for girls who were having problems." According to Barbara, "She really taught me the meaning of fasting and prayer."[9]

Miss Pehrson also suggested to Barbara that she attend the University of Utah. Because of the expense involved, Barbara and most of her friends had not planned on college after they graduated from high school. But Miss Pehrson persisted, so Barbara took the entrance examination for the university and was admitted. The shorthand and typing skills she had gained in high school helped her secure a part-time job as a secretary during her freshman year. She often met her father, who was teaching on campus, for lunch.

Marriage and a Family

Barbara decided to major in home economics, and she found that she enjoyed her classes and the other activities in which she was involved. She once commented to her mother that if she were to continue her schooling, she had better not date any returned missionaries because "all they wanted to do was get married." But several weeks before Barbara was to begin her sophomore year, a friend, Ned Winder, persuaded her to go out with just one more returned missionary—his brother Richard, who had recently returned from a mission in Czechoslovakia. Rich took Barbara to a family party and afterward told his mother, "I've met the girl I'm going to marry." Two and a half weeks later, he proposed. Nineteen-year-old Barbara and twenty-six-year-old Richard William Winder were married January 10, 1951, in the Salt Lake Temple.

Barbara's parents were not able to go the temple with her on her wedding day—a difficult day for her mother especially. Five years later, however, Barbara's lifelong desire was fulfilled. Her parents renewed their interest in the Church and started attending a temple preparation class arranged by friends and taught by their son-in-law, Rich Winder. During the next two years, they became involved in their ward: Verl, a machinist, was excellent with outdoor projects, and Marguerite, an expert cook, helped in the Relief Society with food assignments. Just before Barbara's fourth child was born, Verl and Marguerite and their children were sealed in the temple. Barbara believes that the experience of her parents' inactivity and subsequent return to the Church gave her "empathy and a broader understanding of a wide range of challenges."[10]

The newlyweds' first home was in a new subdivision in Granger, a suburb southwest of Salt Lake City. With no telephone and Rich needing their car to get to work, Barbara felt quite isolated. That isolation took a serious turn when their first child, Richard W. Winder, Jr., was five days old. Barbara developed a high fever and was even too ill to seek help from her neighbors. However, in one of the small miracles she believes are so typical of Relief Society work, her visiting teachers happened to come to her home and were able to get Barbara and her new baby the help they needed.

A year and a half after their marriage, Barbara and Rich moved to Winder Lane, a tree-lined, rural road on the Winder family dairy farm. All up and down Winder Lane were members of the Winder family: Rich's parents, Edwin Kent and Alma Cannon Winder, who had a home next door, and his brother and sisters, who lived on both sides of the lane. Barbara, who said she "never felt like an in-law," was grateful to become part of the Winder family. She found security in her husband's "rich heritage of strong, stalwart Church members."[11]

Rich and Barbara's four children arrived within five years: Richard in December 1951, Susan in January 1953, George in July 1954, and Robert in April 1956. The children had nineteen cousins who also lived on the lane. Barbara said of their familial arrangement, "We raised our children together. Cousins were more like brothers and sisters to our children than cousins. They were free to go into anyone's home and were always welcomed. It was a real source of strength to have each other."[12]

Rich and Barbara both love the out-of-doors and found hiking to be a good way to enjoy nature and spend time with their children.

Family vacations were planned to such places as Glacier National Park and the Grand Tetons. The children began hiking when they were little and as they grew older, they climbed several of Utah's major peaks, including Mount Olympus, Lone Peak, Twin Peaks, Mount Timpanogos, and Mount Nebo. Barbara was part of many of those adventures, although Rich and the boys enrolled in a climbing school and ascended the Grand Teton in Wyoming without her.

The Winders continued the hiking tradition with their married children and grandchildren. Their son Rick said that at least once a year the entire family hiked together and viewed those occasions as "a time to grow together, to learn more about each other, to laugh together, and to share feelings."[13]

"Ice Cream Sunday" became another Winder tradition, especially when the children were teenagers. With the abundant supply of cream available from the dairy, Rich and Barbara churned homemade ice cream every Sunday and invited all the Winder relatives and the children's friends to their home each week.

A Compassionate Woman

Barbara's children experienced her sensitivity for the needs and feelings of others as they grew up. Her daughter, Susan W. Tanner, recalled her first day of kindergarten. She was frightened and clung to her mother, but Barbara noticed another little girl who was just as frightened and suggested to Susan, "Oh, look at that little girl. Go make her happy." Susan said, "After that, I didn't worry about being nervous myself. I've often thought how right that was and how typical of Mother."[14] Barbara became aware of some children in the neighborhood whose parents were divorced and who, with their mother working, needed extra attention. Even though her own children were teenagers or had left home and gone out on their own, she organized a weekly summer-school class in her home for those children and taught them grooming, cleanliness, and basic cooking and sewing skills.

Susan says that she and her brothers learned from their mother's example of generosity and good humor. The kitchen was always available to bring friends in for a snack or to make cookies or a meal to take to someone. One evening just before Halloween, girls from the Granger High School Pep Club strewed toilet paper around the Winders' house and yard, a local custom that was usually done surreptitiously. Much to the girls' surprise, Barbara brought out candied apples to treat them.[15] Her children also remember her as being the first one to help out when there was a birth of a new baby or a death in the neighborhood. As Relief Society general president, Barbara lamented to her family, "I wish I could have a day off every now and then so that I could give service."

Rich's work at the Winder family dairy and bakery required long, hard hours. Through the years, the dairy, established by his great-grand-father John R. Winder, had developed into a successful business. When the suburbs started encroaching on property around the farm, Rich developed part of the dairy property into a cemetery, so that the farm would remain somewhat isolated. For Rich and Barbara, the farm was a wonderful place to raise their children.

Throughout their marriage, Rich and Barbara have worked together and helped one another. While Rich has served in his Church callings, Barbara has wholeheartedly supported and assisted him. For eighteen years he served either as bishop, counselor in the stake presidency, or stake president of the Jordan North Stake. Rich, in turn, supported Barbara when she became involved in PTA, Cub Scouting, and a dairy council. She also served as international president of Lambda Delta Sigma, the LDS sorority for college girls, along with her various other Church callings, such as president of the Primary and of the Young Women and chorister for several organizations. In 1973, she was called to the Melchizedek Priesthood MIA general board, where she served for three and a half years. She then served on the Relief Society general board under Barbara B. Smith for five years.

While Barbara was a member of the Relief Society general board, she sat at a board meeting one afternoon and looked at the portraits of the previous presidents hanging on the wall. In her mind she heard the words, "You need to know about those sisters," but she did not understand the significance of this thought until several years later.

In 1982, Rich was called to preside over the California San Diego Mission, and Barbara became the "mission mother." Serving a mission together was "our sweetest experience," said Barbara, "because we worked so closely together."[16]

In January 1984, while in the mission field, Barbara had what she described as "some funny feelings." She could not determine what they signified but wondered if perhaps they meant that she should be doing genealogy work, even though her schedule was so busy that she scarcely had time to prepare the numerous talks she had to give. She called her daughter, Susan, who was living in the Winder home, and asked her to locate the genealogy materials. Susan did, but then called her mother back and suggested that the genealogy wait until after the mission; she didn't feel that Barbara should add more to her already full schedule.

About the same time, Rich experienced more than "funny feelings," and not about genealogy. He received a strong impression that his wife would be the next general president of the Relief Society. When he described this impression to Barbara, she responded, "Don't even talk to me about it. We have work to do." Still, the telephone call in April from President Gordon B. Hinckley, then a counselor in the First Presidency, came as a surprise. President Hinckley didn't ask if Barbara would accept the call. He only asked, "Are you worthy?"

The Winders spent a restless, sleepless night. Barbara said, "If you ever wonder what it's going to be like at Judgment Day, that must be it. I lay there and my whole life passed before me. It was not funny—it was scary."[17] The next day they flew to Salt Lake City. When she met with President Hinckley, he told her that her administration was to be for "a different time." He requested that her counselors be sisters who would be able to create a new pattern and tradition in Relief Society. He also indicated that he would like all of the women's organizations to be housed together.

Following her meeting with President Hinckley, Barbara, feeling the weight of the responsibilities of the call, found sanctuary in the quiet of the empty boardroom in the Relief Society Building. Again she looked at the portraits of the ten Relief Society presidents. She realized that they had each walked the path she would walk. Although she had not yet selected her counselors and felt very much alone at the moment, she knew she would not be alone in her calling as Relief Society president, for she felt support from the women who preceded her.

"A New Time"

On April 7, 1984, Barbara B. Smith was released, and Barbara W. Winder was sustained as the eleventh general president of the Relief

Society. She selected Joy F. Evans and Joanne B. Doxey as her counselors and Joan B. Spencer as secretary.

Between April and August, when the first meeting of the newly organized presidency and general board would be held, Barbara felt overwhelmed at the thought of her new responsibilities, which were not yet clearly defined. At that first board meeting in August, Elder Dean L. Larsen of the First Quorum of the Seventy echoed President Hinckley's admonition: "This Relief Society presidency and board are coming into service at a landmark time, a time when their role will be to be a resource to and to advise priesthood leadership so that they will be more able to effectively touch the lives of sisters throughout the world."[18] Elder Larsen defined the role of the Relief Society as "to counsel and to sit in council," suggesting that the new leaders should become skilled in counseling with the priesthood councils and in teaching Relief Society stake and ward officers.

That August, President Hinckley announced the formation of thirteen geographic areas of the Church, with an area president and two counselors, all members of the First Quorum of the Seventy, presiding over each. He emphasized that the Church's rapid growth required flexibility to meet the challenges of such growth.

Barbara recalled, "The day we went to the meeting when the area presidencies were announced, it was like a light coming on."[19] She then understood that her role as Relief Society president was to administer the Relief Society program not as an end itself but as a means of accomplishing the mission of the Church—to invite all to come unto Christ by preaching the gospel, perfecting the Saints, and redeeming the dead. The goals of Relief Society in support of this mission were therefore refined, with emphasis on helping women to build faith, to live and share the gospel, to give service with concern for each individual's spiritual and temporal welfare, to strengthen families, and to sustain the priesthood in helping all to receive sacred ordinances and covenants. The Relief Society would have to reduce and simplify wherever possible to more fully accommodate the widely varying needs of Relief Society sisters throughout the Church, particularly in the developing areas. As Joseph Smith shared a vision of the purpose of Relief Society, he said, "The Society is not only to relieve the poor, but to save souls."[20] Barbara was determined to make these words a reality by focusing on basic needs and basic resources to assist women worldwide.

In 1978, at a Regional Representatives' meeting, President Spencer W. Kimball had defined the priesthood line, explaining, "The Church does not have several organizational lines running from headquarters leaders to their local counterparts. There is only one fundamental organizational channel, and that is the priesthood channel."[21] Now Barbara received further insight into what President Hinckley meant by a "different time." In order for the auxiliaries to function under President Kimball's guidelines, she said, "There had to be a willingness to let go." The auxiliaries were to be gathered under the umbrella of the priesthood and no longer viewed as independent entities. "Now we see ourselves not as a separate organization telling the sisters what to do, but we see ourselves as Primary, Young Women, and Relief Society organizations counseling with the priesthood line and keeping the Brethren aware of the needs of the children, young women, and women of the Church. The Church is governed and directed by priesthood power. We are there to be a resource, to counsel and to sit in council."[22]

Closer cooperation of the Relief Society, Young Women, and Primary organizations was facilitated as their offices were moved into the same building and the presidencies held joint weekly meetings. While the Relief Society Building was being remodeled, they worked and met in the Church Office Building. Then, during the first quarter of 1987, the auxiliaries moved into their new offices to be ready for general conference in April. All three organizations were placed under the same General Authority as managing director instead of having three separate managing directors, and a new General Women's Executive Committee began meeting weekly to discuss the needs of children, young women, women, and families. Further, the presidencies and general board members of the auxiliaries drew closer as they began to travel together to visit stakes.

Joanne B. Doxey, second counselor in the Relief Society presidency, said of the new coordination of the auxiliaries: "We are all women working for the same purpose of saving souls, sharing the same concerns for families. We want to become principle-oriented instead of program-oriented. It is our fondest hope that there will be no transitional gap for young women from Primary to Young Women and from Young Women to Relief Society. We all must have the vision, but it takes time for changes to be made. We have felt guided that this is the time."[23]

Barbara Winder added, "If there is anything for me to teach at this time, it is working in harmony and in unity. I know that we are to work together and that we are to be supportive of one another and we must learn to work together in councils."[24]

Shortly after Barbara became Relief Society president, she traveled to Argentina, Brazil, and Peru and visited sisters in their homes as well as in ward and stake meetings. As she attended Relief Society and saw the sisters struggling with English poetry in cultural refinement lessons, the Spirit told her, "This is not what they need."

The Relief Society presidency announced a new format for Relief Society for the 1987 lesson year. The manual was smaller in size and had a new name—Personal Study Guide. A second spiritual living lesson each month took the place of the cultural refinement lesson; mother education lessons were replaced by home and family education lessons; and the social relations and compassionate service lessons were combined. One of Barbara's concerns was her desire for the sisters of the Church to become more familiar with the scriptures and to see that answers to everyday problems and challenges can be found in them. Beginning with the 1988 Personal Study Guide, which began production in 1985, all of the Sunday lessons for Relief Society became scripturally based and correlated with the gospel doctrine course of study.

Beginning January 1, 1987, a major organizational change took place on the stake and ward levels of Relief Society, with the elimination of stake boards and greater flexibility in ward boards. Barbara explained:

> We're simplifying staffing and making the programs more adaptable to various countries. In most areas of the world, it is difficult to staff the stake board. With the added flexibility of the organization, the women of various cultures and age groups can adapt the program to their circumstances. The ward board is structured so

it may expand or contract as needed. In large wards, the standard Relief Society organization could be augmented by many positions, such as homemaking specialists, nursery assistants, special events chairmen, and enrichment specialists for optional midweek activities. This would give as many sisters as possible a chance to serve. In very small wards or branches, the organization is designed to function with only a president—adding counselors, secretary-treasurer, and teachers and board members as needed and available.[25]

With the elimination of the stake board, only the Relief Society presidencies and secretary-treasurers attended stake leadership meetings, thus reducing time, expense, and travel for ward board members. Information from quarterly stake meetings was conveyed to ward boards at their monthly board meeting. Another reason for eliminating the attendance of Relief Society teachers at quarterly stake meetings was to motivate teachers to become more self-reliant and more dependent on the Spirit and to adapt the lessons to the particular needs of their classes.

Another need Barbara observed as she traveled throughout the Church was flexibility in the visiting teaching program. For many women in developing areas of the Church, monthly personal visits required tremendous sacrifice. In Kenya, for example, doing visiting teaching cost some sisters a day's pay and a day's time to reach women many miles away. In Europe, too, with the cost of gasoline at several dollars a liter, driving great distances to meet with the assigned sisters imposed a financial burden. Further, Barbara believed that visiting teaching efforts should be concentrated on women who need it most. In September 1988, the Relief Society announced new flexibility in the traditional visiting teaching policy, which had required a monthly personal visit to each sister. The new policy suggested that a personal visit should take place a minimum of once a quarter, and other contacts could be made by telephone call or letter. Barbara said: "We desire to meet the needs of the worldwide Church. We want to help show love and compassion to every sister, particularly where there are special needs, and to make it more possible for visits and contacts that will bless lives." The ultimate goal, she explained, is to "place more emphasis on ministering."[26]

Barbara's compassionate nature was an integral part of her administrative style. Joan B. Spencer, general secretary of the Relief Society, observed:

> She comes across quietly, but she has great depth of character. She understands people and is caring, compassionate, and concerned about everyone. Barbara doesn't hesitate in making decisions but in the process weighs the matter carefully in a gentle, tender way and makes the people involved feel good about the decision. She sets aside her own desires and has the interests of others at heart. She would rather be the scapegoat than hurt someone's feelings.[27]

Joan noted, too, that Barbara made every effort to be sure that her family did not suffer because of her heavy responsibilities. Her children felt free to call or drop in to the office. Monday night was open for the family to gather at the Winder home, often for a barbecue or a swim. "Barbara is a wonderful influence on her grandchildren," said Joan. "They just love her—she is so dear."[28]

Her family responded with total support for her, especially her husband, Rich. Barbara's daughter, Susan, observed that her father is "not a person who needs to be in the limelight." He did the grocery shopping, often having dinner ready for Barbara after one of her twelve-hour days. Even more significant to Barbara, he provided emotional support. "When I came home and told him I'm tired, he would say, 'I'd be surprised if you weren't.' I think he was my greatest asset in handling the pressure."[29]

Joanne B. Doxey, second counselor in the Relief Society presidency, said at the time they served together:

> Barbara is a happy person who laughs, lifts, and loves. I see her absolute care for other people on a daily basis. She has such compassion for everyone and does not move the work forward by stepping on someone's toes. When she receives letters from sisters in the Church relating their problems, Barbara's eyes fill with tears

because she puts herself in their shoes and really feels empathy for them. She wants to know what we can do to help people feel comfortable about themselves, their situations, and their lives. Although she is very busy, Barbara takes the time to make phone calls or talk with women in person. Quality visiting teaching is one of her great concerns. She wants every sister in the Church to know that someone loves and cares about her. Through working many years in Lambda Delta Sigma, Barbara has a particular love for the Young Adults and relates well to those young women. She is not a competitive leader; rather she is a compassionate leader. In working with the other auxiliaries, she is not protective of her own program nor of any programs, but of people.[30]

Joanne also observed that Barbara is an effective leader because she is a detail person. "Nothing slips between the cracks; she remembers what needs to be done."[31]

Barbara's first counselor, Joy F. Evans, stated:

She has an infectious laugh, a merry smile, a happy disposition; more than that, her personal values are sound and her faith strong. She loves the Lord and seeks in every way to truly follow Him—and while doing so, helps all of us to try a little harder. She wants so much for the sisters of the Church to recognize their divine worth and their great potential, and wants to see Relief Society as a sweet, strengthening, helpful organization that assists them to do so. She is and will be a great blessing to the women of the Church and through them to the families of the Church, and the communities in which they live. Service and love, caring and concern, faith and courage—these are her bywords.[32]

Beyond the organizational administering of the worldwide Relief Society, Barbara viewed her responsibility as ministering, "to help with the healing that needs to go on." She stated:

It is a new time, it is a change of direction, it is a time to heal, a time to bond women to women and women to men. We can have unity in diversity and diversity in unity. We don't have to be like one another to enjoy sisterhood.

One of the important things we must do is to help the daughters of God know who they are and that they have had an important part in building His kingdom throughout all generations of time. Another of the most important things we can do is to learn to be accepting of one another and overcome judging one another, to learn to love each other and build each other more. That's what women are traditionally so good at doing. I recognize that we are all imperfect, but we can be there to help each other and to have understanding. If we don't do that, we're not going to be ready for His coming. We won't be able to tolerate His coming until we can learn some of those kinds of things. We have a lot of work to do.[33]

Continuing Church Service

Richard Winder received a call in February 1990 to return to the area where he had served a mission as a young man—Czechoslovakia—this time to serve as president of the new Czechoslovakia Prague Mission. Thus, Barbara was released as general president of the Relief Society at general conference on March 31, 1990. Elaine L. Jack succeeded her as president.

The Winders arrived in Prague in July 1990, where they found living conditions to be very difficult due to the many harsh years of the former Communist regime. Housing was hard to obtain, and Barbara spent much of her time standing in line for such basic commodities as bread and meat. When she contracted pneumonia that winter, needed medicine was not available.

Initially, eight missionaries were assigned to serve in Czechoslovakia; that number grew to twenty by mid-1991. Rich and Barbara contacted the small group of Saints who had remained faithful during the forty years that the mission had been closed. Barbara found that the Czech people "were hungering for the gospel. Love is what we had to try to bring to them. The gospel is a happy thing."[34] By the end of 1991, Church membership there grew to 600 people.[35]

Following the Winders' return home in July 1993, they were called to be first counselor and assistant matron of the Jordan River Temple. Having had pneumonia and foot surgery during their mission, Barbara had thought she was "heading home to heal." She found that "the temple proved to be a very healing time."[36]

After their temple service ended in 1996, Barbara was called to be the Laurel adviser and Rich, the priests quorum adviser in their ward. Barbara also delved into family history, learning how to work with computer programs. From 1999 to 2002, the Winders presided over the 350 family history missionaries working at the Family History Library in Salt Lake City. They moved downtown from their home in West Valley, which, according to Barbara, was "especially fun" during the 2002 Winter Olympics.

In April 2002, Barbara and Rich were still unpacking boxes in their new home near the Jordan River Temple when President Hinckley telephoned saying, "Richard, I understand you're unemployed." He then extended a call to both of them which he said would be "the jewel in your crown of service"[37]—to be president and matron of the Nauvoo Temple. They left immediately to help prepare for the temple's dedication on June 27, 2002, the anniversary of the Prophet Joseph Smith's martyrdom.

The Winders' daughter, Susan Tanner, was called to be the Young Women general president at the October 2002 general conference. Barbara and Susan are the only mother and daughter who have both served as general auxiliary presidents.

Their Nauvoo Temple service was completed in October 2004 and, at last settled into their home, Barbara and Rich have taught temple preparation and missionary preparation classes in their ward and serve at the Jordan River Temple.

The examples and experiences Barbara W. Winder had as a young girl have helped her become a compassionate, loving person committed to the gospel of Jesus Christ. As a young woman and mother, she had opportunities, both within the Church and community, to develop leadership skills. As a mature woman and grandmother, she was called at a "new time" to preside over the largest Relief Society in the history of the Church—two and a half million sisters. Her life and her spirit indeed made her a compassionate leader who cared deeply about the one and who had vision for the many.

Notes

1. Jan U. Pinborough, "Barbara Woodhead Winder: A Gift of Loving," *Ensign,* October 1985, p. 29.

2. Janet Peterson, "Friend to Friend," *Friend,* May 1985, p. 7.

3. Interview with Barbara W. Winder by LaRene Gaunt and Janet Peterson, June 3, 1988. Hereafter cited as Barbara W. Winder interview.

4. Telephone interview with Marguerite H. Woodhead, June 8, 1988.

5. Interview with Barbara W. Winder, May 31, 1989.

6. Barbara W. Winder, *A Joyful Mother* (Salt Lake City: Deseret Book, 1988), p. 5.

7. Barbara W. Winder interview.

8. Ibid.

9. "Barbara Woodhead Winder: A Gift of Loving," p. 29.

10. Barbara W. Winder interview.

11. Ibid.

12. Gerry Avant, "A Woman with Purpose," *Church News,* May 6, 1984, p. 14.

13. Telephone interview with Richard W. Winder, Jr., July 1988.

14. "Barbara Woodhead Winder: A Gift of Loving," p. 29.

15. "A Woman with Purpose."

16. "Barbara W. Winder: Relief Society General President," *Ensign,* May 1984, p. 97.

17. Barbara W. Winder interview.

18. Minutes of Relief Society General Board Retreat, August 1984, in possession of Barbara W. Winder.

19. Barbara W. Winder interview.

20. Minutes, June 9, 1842.

21. Spencer W. Kimball, "Living the Gospel in the Home," *Ensign,* May 1978, p. 101.

22. Barbara W. Winder interview.

23. Telephone interview with Joanne B. Doxey, August 22, 1988.

24. Barbara W. Winder interview.

25. "Relief Society Organization Simplified," *Ensign,* November 1986, p. 100.

26. "Visiting Teaching Policy Clarified," *Church News*, November 26, 1988, p. 6.

27. Telephone interview with Joan B. Spencer, August 1988.

28. Ibid.

29. "Barbara Woodhead Winder: A Gift of Loving," p. 31.

30. Telephone interview with Joanne B. Doxey, August 22, 1988.

31. Ibid.

32. Statement of Joy F. Evans, August 27, 1988.

33. Barbara W. Winder interview.

34. Interview with Barbara W. Winder by Janet Peterson, October 11, 2006.

35. Kahlile B. Mehr, *Mormon Missionaries Enter Eastern Europe* (Provo: Brigham Young University Press, 2002), p. 189.

36. Interview with Barbara W. Winder, October 11, 2006.

37. Ibid.

12

ELAINE LOW JACK
1990–1997

In 1975 Elaine Low Jack faced one of the most exhilarating but frightening experiences of her life when she rappelled down the face of a cliff in the mountains near Provo, Utah. "I just jumped off the cliff," she recalled. "I tried not to anticipate falling, but to have confidence in my niece, who had tied the rope at the top. I knew I could hang onto the rope. But I liked that feeling. Once I felt I could do it, I wasn't frightened anymore."[1]

When Elaine was called as the twelfth general president of the Relief Society, she exhibited many of those same traits of optimism, confidence, courage, and love of adventure as she had during that first rappel. "This calling is a challenge to be met joyfully," she said. "I have confidence in the one who is holding the rope, that is, our Heavenly Father. I will just do what I need to do and 'hang on.'"[2]

"I believe Elaine Jack was raised up for this particular time," commented Ardeth Greene Kapp in 1990, then Young Women general president and a longtime friend of Elaine's. "She has a work to do to lead the women of the Church at a time when there are many challenges and many opportunities. I have confidence that during her tenure as general president, all that can be done will be done. This period will be marked by one of significant growth among the women of the Church."[3]

Growing Up in Canada

Elaine was born in the small Latter-day Saint community of Cardston, Alberta, Canada, one of four children of Sterling O. and Lovina Anderson Low. She enjoyed a happy childhood with her two brothers, David and Bruce, and her sister, Jean. The family lived a quarter of a block from the Cardston Alberta Temple. Like most families in the community, they had a big garden and a cow. Lovina Low often told her children, "You can be anything you want to be when you grow up, if you are willing to work."[4] The effect of this philosophy became evident in the lives of the children as they learned to work hard, set high goals, and help one another.

Lovina suffered from a heart condition most of her life, but she was a good manager, and the children did much of the work around the home. By the time Elaine was twelve, she was washing clothes and doing much of the cooking, including baking bread. "I knew what needed to be done," she recalled. "We canned fruits and vegetables in the summer and put carrots and potatoes in the storage pit in the fall. At the time I didn't always enjoy the work, but later I recognized that those extra responsibilities were an advantage."[5]

Church and school activities helped to give Elaine confidence. She played the organ in Sunday School and learned to lead music. She also served as a student aide in the principal's office in high school. "When someone has confidence in you," she said, "you rise to the level of their expectation. Because many people had a good influence on me in Cardston, I accomplished more than I might have otherwise. I am thankful for teachers and Church leaders who gave me opportunities for growth."[6]

Heritage

Elaine was greatly influenced by her maternal grandparents, John and Mary Ann Ross Anderson, who lived two doors away from the Lows. As young adults, they had emigrated through the Perpetual Emigration Fund from Scotland to America in 1882. John and Mary Ann waited to get married, however, until they arrived in Salt Lake City so their marriage could be performed in the Endowment House. John, a stonemason from Aberdeen, helped build both the Salt Lake and Cardston Alberta temples. Elaine remembers Mary Ann Anderson as "genteel" and John Anderson as faithful and "solid as the granite of Aberdeen."[7]

John Anderson always tried to follow the promptings of the Spirit in decisions affecting his life. He recorded in his journal concerning his decision to move from Utah to Canada in 1902, "I prayed for guidance concerning my future. Then one spring morning in March . . . from a pamphlet which came in my mail, I read of a settlement in Raymond, Canada, and turning to my wife said, 'Mary Ann, I feel impressed to move to Raymond, Canada.' My wife felt as I did that the impression was from the right spirit."[8] They later moved to Cardston.

John and Mary Ann served in the Cardston Alberta Temple. John also served as a stake patriarch. When Elaine was in high school, she recorded the patriarchal blessings he gave in a small room near the lobby of the temple. "Grandma and Grandpa would stop in almost every day on their way home from the temple," she remembered, "and there was always a warm reception for me at their house. I have fond memories of the aroma of finnan haddie, which they cooked on Fridays, and of their garden, where they grew vegetables and gooseberries and rhubarb. If I wanted a little extra money, I could offer to do some extra work for Grandma."[9]

Elaine's paternal grandfather, Sylvester Low, was born in Scotland, where he joined the Church. He then emigrated to Utah and married Mary Smith, who was of English descent. Settling on a farm in the Cardston area, the Lows demonstrated a combination of the tenacity, strength, and commitment needed to survive on the virgin Canadian prairies. Sylvester died before Elaine was born, and Mary died when Elaine was a young girl.

College, Employment, and Romance

Elaine graduated from Cardston High School as valedictorian of her graduating class of thirty-five. That fall she left for Salt Lake City to attend the University of Utah, where she majored in English. Homesick at first, she found comfort in the company of her sister, Jean, who was employed in Salt Lake City.

It wasn't long until Elaine adjusted to school and took a part-time job at a retail credit firm. "I didn't realize how unskilled I was," she recalled, "but I had an understanding boss who trained me. And it paid off for him. By the end of three months I had become proficient. I was a hard worker, too, because of the work ethic my parents, especially my father, instilled in me."[10]

During that first year of college, Elaine also met her future husband, a senior medical student named Joseph E. Jack. Joe had taken a trip with some friends the previous summer to attend sessions at the Logan, Idaho Falls, and Alberta temples. In Cardston he met a friend of Elaine's who suggested that he give Elaine a call when she went to the University of Utah. In February he did just that and asked her to the Founder's Day dance. They had a good time, but Elaine didn't see him again until she went to pick up her grades at the end of the winter quarter, and there was Joe, handing out the report cards. As he handed over her card, he asked her out again. They dated steadily until the end of the school year, when Elaine went home to Cardston for the summer.

After Joe's graduation from medical school in August 1947, he visited Elaine in Canada, and they became engaged. Though her parents had known him only a short time, they sensed his good character and trusted Elaine's judgment. "They let me know they had confidence in my choice," she said, "and that trust became part of the strength they gave me as well."[11]

Joe had to leave for New York in September to begin his internship at Staten Island Hospital, so Elaine returned to the University of Utah. Over the next year, they wrote to each other every day.

Life in the Mission Field

Joe and Elaine were married in the Cardston Alberta Temple on September 16, 1948. They then moved to New York so he could resume his internship at Staten Island Hospital. He decided to go into surgery after his internship and was one of four selected out of sixty-four applicants to do his residency at Bellevue Hospital in Manhattan. The Jacks attended the Manhattan Ward, where Elaine served as Junior Sunday School coordinator. It was there that she first realized that she had a testimony. Joe worked every other night and every other weekend so Elaine often had to travel alone from Staten Island to Manhattan, a trip that took an hour and a half by bus, ferry, subway, and on foot. She remembers sitting in church and thinking, "I wouldn't be doing this if I didn't believe it."[12]

Two years after her marriage, Elaine was eligible to become an American citizen. She remembers well going to the county courthouse on Staten Island to take the citizenship test and oath of allegiance. "It was a big step to take," she said, "but I think it was essential since I was going to live in the United States."[13]

After completing the first year of his residency at Bellevue, Joe joined the Public Health Service to fulfill his military obligation during the Korean War. The Jacks were sent to Boston, where Joe served in a medical corps for the Coast Guard. There they became members of the Cambridge Branch of the New England Mission, and their first baby, David, was born on February 7, 1952. That spring, when Joe was assigned to temporary service on the icebreaker *East Wind,* Elaine took David to Canada so she could care for her mother, who had suffered a heart attack. While in Canada, she received a letter from the president of the Cambridge Branch asking her to serve as a counselor in the branch Relief Society presidency. With a new baby, Elaine didn't think she would have the time, but when she returned to Boston she accepted the call, and her Relief Society service began.

The boundaries of the branch extended into Maine, and only six to eight sisters regularly attended Relief Society meetings. "The distances were long," remembered Elaine, "but we wanted to visit the sisters, so I just put the baby in the car and drove wherever I needed to. I had a wonderful time. I loved witnessing the growth of our Relief Society and the sisters in it."[14] By the time Elaine was released, sixty-three sisters were attending Relief Society regularly. Joe served for a time in the Cambridge Branch presidency, and the couple was an integral part of the branch. When he completed his military service in Boston and they returned to New York, Joe and Elaine took many happy memories with them.

Back in New York, Joe continued his residency in surgery, and the Jacks became parents of two more sons: William (Bill), who was born December 1, 1954, and Eric, born June 20, 1955. Elaine was called to serve in the Young Women's Mutual Improvement Association (forerunner of Young Women) in the Short Hills (New Jersey) Ward. A year later she was called to serve in the New York Stake Relief Society presidency, and for a time she served in both callings. Her Relief Society calling involved considerable travel since the stake encompassed all five boroughs of New York City and extended east to Long Island, north into Westchester County, and west into several counties of New Jersey. Again her attitude was "this is what we have to do, so let's do it." Fortunately, Joe's work schedule allowed him to watch the boys more often while Elaine carried on her Relief Society assignments.

The Jacks continued their commitment with the Public Health Service in Mount Edgecombe, Alaska, moving there in 1956. At that time Alaska was still a U.S. territory, and Mount Edgecombe had only a handful of Latter-day Saints. However, the first person to visit the Jacks after they arrived was one of the few other Latter-day Saints in town, who brought them a hot huckleberry pie. For the next two years, the Saints met in the Jacks' home. Elaine and Joe remember this as "a time of testimony strengthening." "Those years of relative isolation were a time of family unity for us," said Joe. "With no television, we made our own entertainment by picking berries, biking, picnicking, hiking, and participating in neighborhood activities. At Christmas time, we even took our family out to cut down our own Christmas tree."[15]

Settling in Salt Lake City

In 1958 the Jacks moved back to Salt Lake City, where Joe established his surgical practice. A fourth and final son was also born to them: Gordon, on March 30, 1962.

The Utah mountains provided opportunities for activities the family could enjoy together. Although Elaine had never skied before, she learned after her fourth son was born and then she skied for many years. In the summers, the family often went backpacking. There were trips to the Wind River Mountains in Wyoming, the Sawtooths in Idaho, and Glacier National Park in Montana. One day in the Uintah Mountains in Utah their hiking trail took them over three 12,000-foot-high mountain passes. As they hiked, Elaine often pointed out the wildflowers by name, a hobby inspired by a Relief Society home-making lesson.

"My mother was always a good sport," said Elaine's eldest son, David. "Sometimes, when we were hiking, we would hide rocks in her backpack. She would discover them after we got to the bottom and laugh right along with us."[16] Even today her sons like to joke about having a mother who wore army boots when they went hiking.

When Joe bought golf clubs for himself, he bought some for Elaine, too. As each of the boys got old enough to play golf, they joined Joe and Elaine. Joe even pulled their youngest son, Gordon, around the course on his golf cart before Gordon was old enough to play so he could join the fun too. Golfing is still the family's favorite activity.

Elaine enjoys organizing family get-togethers. One summer she and Joe planned a family reunion in Sun Valley, Idaho, for their sons, daughters-in-law, and grandchildren. Days were carefully planned so everyone was involved with such activities as hikes on guided nature trails, heritage nights, slide shows, costumed performances, naps, and ethnic-food assignments. Of course, family golf tournaments were also held.

Music plays a significant role in Elaine's life. One of her prized possessions is a Steinway piano that a cherished friend willed to her. When the family gets together, Elaine sits down at the piano and the children and grandchildren gather around her and sing. She especially enjoys these times since she remembers well the years she didn't have a piano. Playing the piano is a talent she enjoys developing, and piano lessons have been a part of her life off and on since she was a little girl. She has studied popular music as well as the classics.

Elaine likes people—she is gracious, laughs easily, and puts others at ease. She enjoys entertaining friends in her home and cooking for them. Carol L. Clark, who later served as Elaine's administrative assistant, said:

> I started working with Elaine Jack when I was called to serve on Belle S. Spafford's general board in 1973. Elaine chaired the Curriculum Committee at a season when the Relief Society chose authors and evaluated every lesson. We met at 6 a.m. Sunday mornings for many months of each year around her kitchen table to discuss those lessons.
>
> I learned early some wonderful qualities Elaine possesses. She has always been "class" embodied. From the cut of her clothes to the set of her table to her hand-written notes, Elaine is blessed with a natural graciousness and charm. Ever the loving wife and mother, Elaine shares her home and family and fun

and food (always fabulous—she's a gifted cook) with so many others—both extended family and those she adopts in.[17]

Elaine also has worked quietly in private relationships to provide support and help to those in need. Her sons remember the support and encouragement she gave them as they were growing up. She thanked them when they helped around the house and praised them for their accomplishments at church and at school. When David was in college and working two jobs, he would sometimes come home late at night to find his mother still up and working. "I was impressed that she was willing to help me by typing my thesis and other papers even late at night and when she had other projects she needed to finish," he said.[18]

"Elaine's service comes from a lifelong attitude of sacrificing for others," according to Joe, who is proud of her for her willingness to serve and for many other personal qualities. "She genuinely loves and cares about people. Her poise and confidence make her a real lady, and her sense of humor in raising four boys has been a tremendous asset. She has been a wonderful wife whom I love."[19]

"Elaine is spirited and cheerful," said her sister Jean L. Collett. "Her positive attitude and gratitude for her blessings have helped her meet the personal challenges in her life. She is energetic, works fast, and stays ahead of her obligations. In fact, I think work is fun for her. We've had an especially close relationship—she's my best friend."[20]

Church and Community Service

Elaine has enjoyed her involvement in church and community service. As an American citizen, she feels strongly about her need to be involved in endeavors that improve the community. She was a lay speaker for the American Cancer Society, showing educational films to many groups; served in both county and state medical auxiliaries; was a member of the Utah State Board for Unproven Health Practices; and served as a delegate to a state political convention. She was also a member of the board of directors of Deseret Book Company.

In the Church, Elaine's service in Utah has alternated between Young Women and Relief Society, just as it did in New York. (And with four sons, she also served often as a den mother in Cub Scouts.) On a ward level she taught Relief Society and was counselor to three ward Relief Society presidents, and on a stake level she was a board member and president of the Holladay South Stake Relief Society. During the years she taught cultural refinement lessons, she really went the extra mile. Two mornings a month she invited women in her neighborhood, including nonmembers, to her home for "mingles"—talks by friends who were experts in such topics as art appreciation, children's literature, and publishing a newspaper.

In September 1972, Elaine was called to the Relief Society general board of Belle S. Spafford. When Sister Spafford was released in 1974, the new general president, Barbara B. Smith, called Elaine back to the board, and she served in this calling until April 1984, when Sister Smith was released.

Elaine's service shifted again to Young Women in April 1987 when she was called to serve as second counselor to Ardeth G. Kapp in the Young Women general presidency. Feeling overwhelmed, Elaine called Sister Kapp the next morning and asked, "How could you choose me?" Sister Kapp simply said, "I didn't choose you; the Lord did."[21]

Speaking of their service together, Sister Kapp said, "It was a great joy for me to have the privilege of working with Elaine. While she can dream of the ideal and set her sights on the stars, she has the ability to be realistic and practical as she keeps her feet on the ground. As a counselor, Elaine was faithful, loyal, dedicated, and wonderfully optimistic."[22]

Leading the Worldwide Sisterhood

On March 31, 1990, Elaine Low Jack was sustained as the twelfth general Relief Society president, succeeding Barbara W. Winder. Chieko N. Okazaki was sustained as first counselor and Aileen Hales Clyde as second counselor. Commenting on Elaine's call, Ardeth Kapp stated, "We anticipate an even closer relationship between the Young Women and Relief Society, and trust that the bridge needed for young women to move from one organization to the next will be strengthened through a carefully planned transition."[23]

"I'd like the 1990s to be a decade when women extend themselves, exemplify righteousness, and teach in compassion and love," the new president said of her hopes for Relief Society. "I want each woman to find her own individual happiness as a result of her belief in the gospel. If women are solid and secure in their personal testimonies and live according to what they know is right, they will be blessed individually and will make a difference in the world." Then she added, "My testimony is my whole life. It is the foundation for my decisions and my judgment. It is simply the standard I live by."[24]

Elaine viewed her call as

> an exciting time to be representing Relief Society women worldwide. There are great blessings and opportunities available—personal blessings that come through unshakable faith and opportunities that come through giving Christian service. I have confidence that our Latter-day Saint sisters will continue in their enthusiasm to promote righteousness, both in themselves and in others.
>
> Women internationally can share faith, values, experiences, and ideas. I have respect for the diversity among women and acknowledge the strengths, abilities, and talents they possess. We can relate to all women through the Spirit.[25]

A group of Spanish sisters attended general conference and were in the Tabernacle when Elaine was sustained as general Relief Society president. Afterwards, Renee Canals, a member of the Young Women general board who speaks Spanish, invited Elaine to meet with these sisters. "We found that we didn't need to rely on language to understand one another," Elaine noted. "The Spirit helped us to communicate."[26]

President Thomas S. Monson, then Second Counselor in the First Presidency, gave Elaine as the newly called president this counsel: "This is a time of great change in the world and in the Church as we observe modifications in family style and family characteristics. We recognize that there are many single-parent families; there are other families where difficulties exist between husbands and wives, and furthermore, we find the encroachment of the drug culture and other challenges which cause stress in families. You at this hour of need have been called . . . to direct the organization which can provide that ameliorating influence, that balm of Gilead to unite all sisters in the Church."[27]

Relief Society Sesquicentennial

Almost immediately, the new presidency, along with the twelve general board members, began planning the Relief Society Sesquicentennial to be celebrated on March 17, 1992. The major thrust of the Sesquicentennial was celebrating through service. Elaine felt that "service projects beyond our own borders" would be very beneficial to the sisters and to the communities in which they lived. She explained:

> Every local unit determined what service would be best suited to their community. The services varied so much. In Samoa, sisters painted the clock tower and planted flowers. In Africa, they swept a path to the waterhole. In South Africa, they made lap rugs for the elderly. Myriad homeless shelters were painted and fixed up. Books were collected. In one area of California when a Relief Society president asked community leaders what kinds of projects would benefit the community, one leader said, "You mean to tell me that 18,000 units are each going to give service in their local communities?" She said yes. "Then you'll change the world." I think we did.[28]

Other features of the celebration included local units presenting "A Society of Sisters," vignettes about their sisters, and creating histories of their own Relief Societies. The book *Something Extraordinary*, a collage of photos submitted by sisters around the world, was published.

On March 17, 1992—one hundred and fifty years after the Relief Society was organized by the Prophet Joseph Smith in the upper room of the Red Brick Store—sisters worldwide joined by satellite uplinks to five continents celebrated together. In her address that day Elaine said, "With this broadcast, we join as we never have before. Never in the history of the Church have the women of Zion been linked so closely together. This is symbolic, reminding us that we come together in the greatest of all causes, the gospel of Jesus Christ."[29]

During the broadcast, sisters from Zimbabwe, Mexico, Korea, Australia, and Germany—representing the five continents—each spoke in their own languages about what Relief Society meant to them. Elaine's counselors, Chieko N. Okazaki and Aileen H. Clyde, and President Thomas S. Monson also addressed the worldwide gathering.

Part of the broadcast included a film of Elaine speaking to Relief Society sisters from Nauvoo in which she said:

> The experiences of women in Nauvoo and in every Relief Society throughout the Church prove that women individually can be a great force. Alma described the value of our contribution, stating, "By small and simple things are great things brought to pass." (Alma 37:6.) Women's lives are full of small and simple things . . . Small and simple things that define relationships and build testimonies. Small and simple things that grow strong men and women. . . .
>
> We are part of a grand whole. We need each other to make our sisterhood complete. When we reach out to clasp the hands of our sisters, we reach to every continent, for we are of every nation. We are bonded as we try to understand what the Lord has to say to us, what He will make of us. We speak in different tongues, yet we are a family who can still be of one heart. We work, play, give birth, nurture, dream dreams; we cry, pray, laugh, sometimes clap for joy, and find that mortality teaches us our need for our Savior, Jesus Christ.[30]

Looking back on the Sesquicentennial commemoration, Elaine remarked, "I think that was the happiest time of our whole administration."[31] Aileen H. Clyde, second counselor, felt that "the focus of the Sesquicentennial helped unify us as a presidency and gave us a real goal. In doing that we grew very quickly and strongly together."[32]

Gospel Literacy Effort

As the culmination of the Sesquicentennial, the Relief Society launched the Gospel Literacy Effort at the end of 1992. "It has two purposes," Elaine explained. "First, to provide basic gospel literacy skills for those who cannot read or write; and second, to encourage lifelong personal spiritual study and self-improvement."[33] She further stated, "The ability to read is more than just an earthly skill. It's important to our eternal progression as well. If we're going to bring souls to Christ, they must be able to understand the basic commandments and gospel principles that are in God's word—the scriptures."[34]

Literacy is not learned just in school settings; the home is vital in teaching reading skills. Since the ability of a mother to read has such a great influence on her children, the Relief Society wanted to help women especially to become more literate. Elaine added, "If the education of a woman makes such a difference, that's enough reason to encourage literacy."[35] Particularly in developing areas of the world, economic concerns often prevent girls from receiving adequate educations.

Relief Society leaders, working under the direction of the priesthood, implemented the ongoing Gospel Literacy Effort in their units not only to help ward or branch members but also to reach out to the community. Some sisters tutored prison inmates to help them earn high school diplomas. Others donated books to libraries or tutored at an after-school program for low-income youth.

Elaine had the opportunity to visit literacy classes when she traveled to Guatemala. "These sisters washed their clothes on stones in a town square yet attended literacy classes to help their children," she recalled.[36] Following that trip, she was particularly gratified to learn that in the Mexico South Area, 183 literacy classes were held with 870 members attending.[37]

The Family

President Gordon B. Hinckley, speaking at the conclusion of the general Relief Society meeting on September 23, 1995, praised the organization of Relief Society and the three-and-a-half million women who comprised it worldwide, thanking Latter-day Saint women for their faithfulness and goodness. He stated that with so many opportunities for education, this is "the best season for women in all the history of the world." He also said that there has never been a time of more "challenging problems,"[38] particularly for the increasing assaults on the family and the campaign of many to redefine the institution of the family. President Hinckley, the prophet, chose to introduce and read "The Family: A Proclamation to the World" at that 1995 Relief Society general meeting, where sisters would hear it first.

Along with several members of the Quorum of the Seventy, Elaine attended and spoke at the World Congress on Families held in Prague, Czech Republic, in March 1997. These leaders emphasized Church doctrine of the family as a divine institution and worked with other international representatives to find ways to combat the growing danger of groups redefining the traditional family.

Throughout her administration, Elaine encouraged women to strengthen one another and themselves that they might better be able to strengthen their families and all "come unto Christ."

"One of our most important roles as Relief Society members is to strengthen each other, so all of us are better able to help our families," she said in an address to the women of the Church. "We come together. We learn from each other. We go home and strengthen our families. It's that simple, yet how profound it is that we have this organization to be our balm of Gilead."[39]

Other Relief Society Matters

Because of her service in the Young Women general presidency prior to her call in Relief Society, Elaine was particularly concerned about the transition of young women into Relief Society. As Ardeth Kapp had anticipated, the Relief Society and Young Women leaders worked together closely in addressing this need. Elaine said, "Our Relief Society should be a place where members are nurtured through the many transitions they face as adult women. Entering Relief Society is only the first of many changes that will come to each woman. . . . Relief Society leaders can do much to help young adults feel important and needed."[40]

Elaine desired that leadership training for local leaders be more equitable. Intermountain West Relief Societies often had visits by general auxiliary leaders but those in outlying areas of the Church did not have as many. Furthermore, when the presidency and board members were asked to give training sessions, they queried local leaders as to what their needs were, such as help with visiting teaching or teacher training, and then presented workshops to meet those specific needs. Many times the day after leadership training sessions, a member of the presidency and a general board member held focus groups, whose purpose was to learn of sisters' experiences in Relief Society— what has helped them and what they might change. Aileen H. Clyde, second counselor in the general presidency, observed that all over the world, women's first concern was the well-being of their families. The second main concern was economic pressure, whether it was having enough food for supper or stability of income to provide for education and missions for children.[41] The general leaders learned from sisters that Relief Society was a spiritual strength and support to them.

As Relief Society general president, Elaine traveled to many areas of the world, to every continent except South America, visiting sisters in their homes whenever possible. "You learn more about women in their homes than in any other place," she noted.[42] "I learned firsthand the circumstances of the sisters and their children and how they minister to each other. I learned they are capable, sensitive and, more important, they are realistic about what can be done."[43] She also felt sisters in these various areas developed a personal connection with Relief Society leaders. "I think one of the best compliments I received was, 'Sister Jack, you're real.'" She laughed, but she wanted very much for the sisters to realize that "we are all here for the same purpose," to strengthen families, to serve one another, to "come unto Christ."[44]

At President Hinckley's invitation, Elaine had the wonderful opportunity of speaking at two temple dedications in Canada. The Toronto Ontario Temple was dedicated in 1990, and the following year the temple which influenced her so much as a young girl—the Cardston Alberta Temple—was rededicated after being remodeled.

"Collegial" describes Elaine's leadership style, according to Carol L. Clark. "Ebullient by nature, she enthusiastically sought ideas from her counselors and board members," said Carol.[45] Aileen H. Clyde noted that when the presidency discussed their concerns, Elaine was "a good listener. There was never a time that she didn't say, 'Thank you for telling me that.' Another strong leadership point was her view of our remarkably fine board members as wonderful resources and utilizing them."[46]

"Elaine is a very gracious person," said Chieko N. Okazaki, having observed her interact with Relief Society sisters in large gatherings and one-on-one. Chieko also felt that Elaine was very effective in working with the other general auxiliary leaders and with the General Authority advisors to the Relief Society in vigorously representing the needs of and concerns for the women of the Church.[47]

Release and Return to Cardston

Elaine's release as Relief Society general president was announced at general conference on April 6, 1997. Mary Ellen W. Smoot was then sustained as the new Relief Society general president. In Elaine's concluding address she referred to her stonemason grandfather, John F. Anderson, laying the very last stone for the Cardston Alberta Temple. He recorded in his journal, "It was not the capstone, but a small stone at the front gate entrance." Elaine said, "My grandfather offered to the Lord the stone he had placed so carefully. Today, I offer my years of service in the general Relief Society."[48] She likened building a temple to fulfilling a calling and that

> each administration builds on the solid bedrock of the past.
>
> For the past seven years this Relief Society presidency has been building. We have added a Churchwide literacy effort to our education focus; we have emphasized the principle of watching over and caring for our sisters through visiting teaching; we have continued to place home and family at the center of our attention and honored the divine nature of women as they nurture, sacrifice, teach, and inspire.[49]

Throughout Elaine's years of service, Joe, as she described, with "his steadiness, his sense of humor and good judgment, and his righteous hands,"[50] wholeheartedly supported her—although he didn't "do dinner."[51] Likewise, her four sons and daughters-in-law and grandchildren helped in a variety of ways. One of the boys in typical Jack good humor said, "We've been training Mom to be a Relief Society president for a long time, and she finally got it right!"[52]

Joe and Elaine received a call in 1997 to serve as president and matron of the Cardston Alberta Temple, a joyful experience for the Jacks, and a return home and fulfillment of her patriarchal blessing, which said that she would receive the blessings of the temple and be a worker in the same temple. "It was a wonderful assignment," said Elaine. "My grandparents were temple workers. I knew so many of the people in Cardston, having grown up there."[53] After many years of Elaine's full-time Church service and Joe's busy surgical practice and leadership callings, being able to serve together was particularly a happy time for the Jacks.

Released from the temple in the fall of 2000, Elaine and Joe returned to their home in Salt Lake City to spend more time with their family, especially with eleven of their sixteen grandchildren living in the area. Visits back and forth with the five Massachusetts grandchildren have been fun and more frequent.

As an advocate for literacy, Elaine not only initiated the Gospel Literacy Effort on the general level, but also seeks to improve literacy in her own neighborhood by volunteering weekly as a reading tutor at a nearby elementary school. She has participated in a book club for many years.

Elaine has served on the board of directors for Hale Center Theater in Salt Lake City and is a member of the National Advisory Council for the University of Utah, which she and Joe and all four sons attended.

A Mia Maid adviser in the Holladay Eighteenth Ward, Elaine enjoys teaching and friendshipping the young women. She participates fully in the Young Women program, including Mutual activities— even attending girls' camp. Eden Jensen, a Mia Maid, commented, "I absolutely adore Sister Jack. One of the things I love about her is that she is such a real person—not a person who was put up on a pedestal. She is a great teacher and shares her testimony all the time. You can tell that she loves to be in Young Women and that she loves each one of us. And she is fun!"[54] The ward Young Women president, Annette Weed, said that having Elaine serve in this capacity has provided the girls with "an incredible opportunity to hear her perspective on the worldwide Church. She has also taught us leaders the importance of planning with a purpose, of asking 'What do we want to have happen?' instead of 'What do we want to do?'"[55]

Shortly after being sustained as Relief Society general president, Elaine commented that she hoped her administration would be "one of substantive matters."[56] Indeed, it was. The Sesquicentennial's focus of celebrating through service, which expanded Relief Society sisters' view and opportunities of giving to others, and the ongoing Gospel Literacy Effort have touched the hearts and lives of countless people, both members and nonmembers, throughout the world. With firm belief in the goodness of women and faith in the Lord, Elaine graciously led the Relief Society to new heights during the last decade of the twentieth century.

Notes

1. Interview with Elaine L. Jack by LaRene Gaunt and Janet Peterson, April 1990. Hereafter cited as Elaine L. Jack interview, 1990.

2. Ibid.

3. Written statement of Ardeth G. Kapp to LaRene Gaunt, May 1990.

4. Elaine L. Jack interview, 1990.

5. Ibid.

6. Ibid.

7. Ibid.

8. Diary of John F. Anderson, 1902, in possession of Elaine L. Jack.

9. Elaine L. Jack interview, 1990.

10. Ibid.

11. Ibid.

12. Ibid.

13. Ibid.

14. Ibid.

15. Telephone interview with Joe E. Jack by LaRene Gaunt, April 1990.

16. Telephone interview with David B. Jack by LaRene Gaunt, April 1990.

17. E-mail from Carol L. Clark to Janet Peterson, December 11, 2006.

18. Telephone interview with David B. Jack by LaRene Gaunt, April 1990.

19. Telephone interview with Joe E. Jack by LaRene Gaunt, April 1990.

20. Telephone interview with Jean L. Collett by LaRene Gaunt, April 1990.

21. Elaine L. Jack interview.

22. Ardeth G. Kapp to LaRene Gaunt, May 1990.

23. Ibid.

24. Elaine L. Jack interview, 1990.

25. Ibid.

26. Ibid.

27. Elaine L. Jack, "Relief Society: A Balm in Gilead," *Ensign,* November 1995, p. 90.

28. Interview with Elaine L. Jack by Janet Peterson, December 14, 2006. Hereafter cited as Elaine L. Jack interview, 2006.

29. Elaine L. Jack, "Look Up and Press On," *Ensign,* May 1992, p. 98.

30. Elaine L. Jack, "Charity Never Faileth," *Ensign,* May 1992, p. 91.

31. Elaine L. Jack interview, 2006.

32. Telephone interview with Aileen H. Clyde, December 28, 2006.

33. LaRene Gaunt, "The Gift of Words," *Ensign,* March 1994, p. 32.

34. Julie A. Dockstader, "Goal of Learning to Read: To Expand the Horizons of Gospel Understanding," *Church News,* October 1, 1994, p. 4.

35. "The Gift of Words," *Ensign,* March 1994, p. 32.

36. Elaine L. Jack interview, 2006.

37. Julie A. Dockstader, "Auxiliary Leaders Take 'Discovery Trip,'" *Church News,* May 27, 1995, p. 3.

38. Gordon B. Hinckley, "Stand Strong against the Wiles of the World," *Ensign,* 1995, p. 98.

39. Jack, "A Balm in Gilead," p. 90.

40. Carol L. Clark, "Knit Together in Love," *Ensign,* October 1993, p. 25.

41. Telephone interview with Aileen H. Clyde, December 28, 2006.

42. Elaine L. Jack interview, 2006.

43. "Auxiliary Leaders Take 'Discovery Trip,'" p. 3.

44. Elaine L. Jack interview, 2006.

45. E-mail from Carol L. Clark to Janet Peterson, December 11, 2006.

46. Telephone interview with Aileen H. Clyde, December 28, 2006.

47. Telephone interview with Chieko N. Okazaki, January 7, 2007.

48. Elaine L. Jack, "A Small Stone," *Ensign,* May 1997, p. 73.

49. Ibid., p. 74.

50. Ibid., p. 74.

51. Elaine L. Jack interview, 2006.

52. "A Small Stone," p. 74.

53. Elaine L. Jack interview, 2006.

54. Telephone interview with Eden Jensen by Janet Peterson, January 3, 2007.

55. Telephone interview with Annette Weed by Janet Peterson, December 21, 2006.

56. Elaine L. Jack interview, 1990.

13

MARY ELLEN W. SMOOT
1997–2002

During her first major address as the new Relief Society general president, Mary Ellen Wood Smoot stated, "I humbly stand before you in my present capacity, having few credentials by the world's standards. But I am not on the world's errand. I am on the Lord's errand."[1] Mary Ellen had completed just one year of college before marrying. She became the mother of seven children, but she did not acquire degrees or "credentials." Midway through her five-year administration when she received the assignment to speak in the first general conference held in the new Conference Center in April 2000, she marveled, "Me, this humble little canning factory girl. I cannot believe it, but I pray the Lord will make me equal to the task."[2]

Mary Ellen, through years of service and devotion to her family, community, and The Church of Jesus Christ of Latter-day Saints, had been well prepared for her call as the thirteenth Relief Society general president. She said, "I bring to this calling a lifetime of experiences as a daughter, wife, mother, and servant within the kingdom."[3] She knew that with His help, she could accomplish the Lord's errand as a leader of Latter-day Saint women as the twentieth century closed and a new millennium dawned.

A Noble Heritage

As Mary Ellen grew up, she often heard the stories of her ancestors joining the Church during its early years, leaving homes behind, enduring persecution, trekking west with the Saints, and settling in Davis County, Utah. Throughout her life, learning more about her family's history has been one of her passionate endeavors.

Paternal Ancestors

In 1833, Daniel Wood, Mary Ellen's paternal great-grandfather, a Methodist minister in Loughboro, Canada, was baptized by Brigham Young. Daniel's sixth wife, Sarah Grace, joined the Church in Liverpool, England, in 1850. While their son, James Grace Wood, served a mission to the Central States from 1916–19, he dreamed of property that was to be his. Upon his return, James took the train from Salt Lake City to Layton and walked around until he recognized a particular piece of land. There he farmed, built homes for his two wives, and served as mayor of the city and as the first bishop of the Clearfield Ward. James and Susan Stoddard Wood's fifth child, Melvin Grace Wood, was Mary Ellen's father.

The lineage of Mary Ellen's grandmother, Susan Stoddard Wood, traces to Israel and Sarah Stoddard, who were baptized in 1842 in New Jersey, then moved to Nauvoo. Shortly after the Stoddard family joined the exodus of Saints from Nauvoo, Sarah, a new baby, and Israel all died from exposure. The three were buried in Montrose, Iowa, on the west bank of the Mississippi River. Susan Stoddard Wood, Mary Ellen's grandmother, wrote: "This left five Stoddard children homeless and almost penniless but not friendless as the Saints were good to them."[4] Charles, one of the surviving children, married Matilda Duncan, whose Scottish parents, James Duncan and Huldah Jones, were converted in St. Clair County, Illinois. While residing in Nauvoo, James gave a prize horse to Joseph Smith, which the Prophet named "Jo Duncan" after himself and James and rode as head of the Nauvoo Legion.

Maternal Ancestors

On Mary Ellen's mother's side, William Blood heard Mormon missionaries preaching on the street in Barton-under-Needwood, Staffordshire, England. When he returned home he said to his wife, Mary Stretton Blood, "Mary, I have heard the truth tonight and I want you to go with me tomorrow night."[5] Baptized on March 1, 1843, they were disowned by William's family, then sold their bakery and store and sailed to America in January 1844. The Prophet Joseph met them on the banks of the Mississippi River when they made their way to Nauvoo. Just three weeks after their arrival, William died of swamp fever. Four days later, Mary gave birth to Emma, who lived only a month. Compounding Mary's sorrow, Joseph and Hyrum were martyred eight days after Emma's death. Speaking of her great-great-grandmother, Mary Ellen said, "With her husband and child gone and the leader of her chosen people murdered, Mary could have turned on her heels and gone back to her family in England, where she would have had security and help. . . . Instead of shrinking, she looked forward to a better day."[6] Mary Blood trekked westward to Utah, remarried, and settled in Kaysville, Utah.

Mary Zillah Crockett, born the same month and year as Joseph Smith, converted in England in 1844, the year the Prophet was martyred, and married William Smith in 1846, when the Saints left Nauvoo. The Smiths' only son, William Edward, fell in love with Jane Blencowe, who was baptized in 1869 in Birmingham. William, promising to send for Jane, sailed for America that year with his widowed mother. Thirteen days after Jane docked in New York City, Jane and William were married in Salt Lake City, and then sealed in the Endowment House in 1873.

Jane and William's son—Mary Ellen's grandfather—Albert Thomas Smith, was born in Kaysville in 1875, and married Ellen Colemere Blood in 1895. Albert worked as a sewing machine salesman, railroad section hand, and store clerk, before obtaining a farm in Clearfield. He helped construct the first chapel in Clearfield. At age thirty-five, Albert received a call to the Birmingham England Mission, where he supervised construction of the first chapel there. Prior to leaving, he added rooms to the home, planted grain, and arranged for Ellen to have help with the orchard and farm. Ellen joined Albert the last few weeks of his mission, leaving their four children with family members.

Albert purchased an eighty-acre farm in Clearfield, which produced so abundantly that he started his own canning company in 1919. This enterprise, along with developing properties, made Albert a successful and influential community leader. He served faithfully in the Church as a bishop's counselor and high priests group leader.

The second of Albert and Ellen's seven children, LaVora Blood Smith, was born in 1898. Somewhat unusual for her era, she served a mission to Sacramento, California, spending most of her mission in

Oakland and Berkeley. When she returned, she dated a number of young men, but it was Melvin G. Wood who won her heart. Melvin had served in the Central States Mission in Texas, when there were only two Latter-day Saint families in Dallas. LaVora and Melvin were married October 24, 1923, in the Salt Lake Temple.

Lessons Learned in Childhood

LaVora and Melvin Wood adored their four little girls, Maurine, Allene, Norma Jean, and Beverly. Still, Melvin hoped that the baby due in the summer of 1933 might be a boy to carry on the Wood name. On August 19, the nurse at the hospital in Ogden, Utah, came from the delivery room and announced, "It's another girl, Melvin." LaVora and Melvin named her Mary Ellen. In 1935, a sixth daughter, Ruth Ann, joined the family. Later, Melvin would say, "I had to wait for my sons until my daughters married, but I love every one of them as if they were my own."[7]

Although Mary Ellen's early childhood years spanned most of the Great Depression, which caused financial hardship for many families throughout the United States and the world, the Wood family survived fairly well due to Melvin and LaVora's abilities and hard work. Melvin loved gardening, planting abundant vegetables and fruit trees as well as beautiful flowers. He also raised a cow, a pig, and chickens, and the Woods usually had plenty of milk and eggs to share with their neighbors. LaVora was very careful to use and store what they produced. Mary Ellen recalled, "Provident living and self-reliance were virtues instilled in us from an early age as we all took part in placing seeds in the ground, watering, weeding, harvesting, and canning or bottling in preparation for the winter months."[8] She remembered, "Our storage room was like a small grocery store. Everything had its own label and we were all a part of the organization of the storage room every fall."[9]

Mary Ellen and her sisters grew up ten miles south of Ogden, in the small town of Clearfield, which she described as "little more than a bend in the road."[10] Next door to the family home was the canning factory that her Smith grandparents owned and her father managed. Her mother served on the board of the Smith Canning Factory, hiring the two hundred women workers. Mary Ellen and her five sisters all worked at the factory starting about age fourteen.

On the other side of Mary Ellen's home was the church, which her father presided over as bishop. The school and a small store were located across the street. Of her youth, Mary Ellen said:

> Our home life was happy. We had a kind loving father and mother with an earnest desire to live the principles of the gospel in their home. Our father would never permit us to talk back to our mother and kindness prevailed other than a few spats of sibling rivalry.
>
> My parents taught us to work hard and prepare for the Sabbath. Mother always baked bread on Saturday, we cleaned through the house Friday and Saturday, did our shopping, and prepared our clothing for Sunday. Then our hair was washed and put up in ringlets. Each was given a dime and we would run out our front door, past the chapel to the recreation hall to watch a weekly movie or stage play.[11]

Ruth Ann W. Christensen, Mary Ellen's younger sister, remembered "the fun things we did were with our family." A yearly tradition involved a one-day excursion to a warm springs near Huntsville, Utah. "Mother would fix fried chicken and potato salad. We played in the water," said Ruth Ann. "Even after our older sisters got married, their husbands went with us. On the way home, Dad bought us a popcorn treat." The extended family gathered at the cemetery each Memorial Day and then enjoyed dinner together at one of their homes. "Christmas at Grandmother's house," according to Ruth Ann, "was magical."[12]

LaVora taught her six daughters how to organize and to accomplish goals. When she needed to shop in Ogden, she would take only one girl with her and say to the rest, "Now you surprise me, you know what needs to be done. See how much you can get accomplished while I'm away and I will check it as soon as I return." The girls delighted in watching her return to see what they had achieved. LaVora often told her daughters, "Whatever you do, do with your might, jobs done by halves are never done right."[13]

When Mary Ellen was six or seven years old, she learned firsthand a lesson on honesty. Seeing a five-dollar bill lying on her sister's dresser, Mary Ellen took the money and walked across the street to the store to buy candy. Thinking the amount of change she received was more than she had taken, she put it back on the dresser. When questioned about the missing money, she confessed she had taken it. Her father took her down to the basement to talk to her, all the while sharpening his razor on a long leather strap. After he simply counseled her about being honest and not taking things that did not belong to her, she cried and made up her mind she would never go through that experience again.[14] As a young teenager she also learned that honesty meant keeping commitments. Mary Ellen gained her first paying job picking peaches but soon found that it was hard, itchy work. With other workers, she decided it would be more fun to cool off in the canal and not pick any more peaches. But the fun was short-lived when her father saw her and reprimanded her for not completing her obligation.

Mary Ellen knew that her parents were united in their desire to teach their children principles of the gospel. However, the most powerful teaching took place as she observed her parents' example in living those principles. Mary Ellen learned at an early age the importance of daily family prayer. Each morning while her mother prepared breakfast, her father gathered the children to the table for prayer. If one of them preferred sleeping a few extra minutes, he would tickle her and say they could not hold family prayer without her. She heard her parents pray for each of their daughters individually, other family members and grandparents, the missionaries, and leaders of the Church. She said, "Prayer changes things, and I am a witness that it changes hearts and convinces you there is a Father listening and caring about you as a child because your parents exemplified this principle in their lives."[15]

She also recognized the value her parents placed on fasting as they observed not only fast day each month but also fasted when someone was ill or needed spiritual blessings. Mary Ellen recalled, "They believed in the spiritual and physical blessings that came from observing the fast and many answers to life's challenges came through fasting and prayer." Often Melvin would give his daughters blessings when they were faced with challenges or were ill.[16]

The Woods taught their children many other gospel principles, including tithing and keeping the Sabbath Day holy. For nine years, Mary Ellen's father served as bishop of their ward. At that time, the bishop handled all matters concerning tithing. The children knew that tithing was sacred and his rolltop desk was off limits, for that was where he kept the receipts and monies until they were sent to Church headquarters. When teenage friends wanted Mary Ellen to go to movies or dances on Sundays, she relied on the earlier teachings of her parents on Sabbath observance and would not go along with them.

Though Mary Ellen didn't realize it at the time, she was taught that service was "a way of life." She said, "We delighted 'in service and good works.' We never gathered our own eggs but that we gave some of them away. We didn't plant our own garden but that some of the harvest was given to others. And neighbors did the same for us." She came to understand firsthand "how service is a fundamental principle of gospel living."[17]

Throughout her growing up years, Mary Ellen enjoyed a sweet relationship with her grandparents and cherished hearing the stories of her pioneer ancestors. "We were taught love and respect for our grandparents and all of our relatives. They loved one another and shared the positive things about one another," said Mary Ellen.[18] Grandma Wood, a widow, came to dinner every Sunday. Grandma Smith talked daily with LaVora, her only living daughter. Mary Ellen admired the courtesy and respect that Grandpa Smith showed as he opened the car door or carried things for her grandmother. Their devotion to each other left a lasting impression on young Mary Ellen. The Wood sisters were often called upon to help their grandmothers. Mary Ellen remarked, "If Grandma needed her raspberries picked, Mother would awaken her daughters at 5:00 A.M. in the morning to start in Grandma's raspberry patch before it was light. There was no such thing as requesting to remain in bed because you were tired. Work needed to be done and we all were a part of the team."[19]

Through her experiences at home and in the "quaint little chapel," Mary Ellen's testimony developed. She doesn't remember "ever doubting if the Church was true" because her parents had such strong testimonies. Nevertheless, it was at a time of great need in the Wood family that Mary Ellen's faith was tested and grew. When she was twelve years old, she had to forgo attending a Valentine's party to travel to the Northwest. Melvin and LaVora were helping their oldest daughter, Maurine, and her baby girl move to Washington state to join her husband. Mary Ellen and Ruth Ann were needed to help unpack boxes. On the way, LaVora, driving on rainy roads in Oregon, lost control of the car, which rolled two and a half times. Melvin and Mary Ellen, with minor injuries, crawled out the driver's side of the car. They found that Maurine and her baby were all right, but LaVora and Ruth Ann were pinned under the hood of the car. The road was deserted and the nearest town twelve miles away.

"Then something happened that I will never forget," recalled Mary Ellen. "I watched my father, who always had a great deal of faith, bow his head in prayer and ask for the Lord's help."[20] He said, "Mary Ellen, as I lift the car, you pull your mother out." She watched her father lift the heavy Buick enough for her to pull her mother out. Ten-year-old Ruth Ann was able scramble out herself, having only sustained bruises. LaVora, however, was seriously injured with a broken pelvis, ribs, and collar bone. Mary Ellen, with cut and bleeding knees, knelt beside her mother, who, in terrible pain and near death, said, "Mary Ellen, always remember who you are and be a good girl."[21]

Mary Ellen witnessed miracles in her mother's medical care and recovery. Through several blessings given to her and through the faith and prayers of many, LaVora eventually did heal from her injuries and walk again, despite doctors' predictions that she would not. She told her family she had pleaded with the Lord that if she could just live long enough to see all six of her daughters married in the temple, she would dedicate her life to Him and then be willing to go.

Mary Ellen later stated, "I am convinced that our Father in Heaven heard her promise because that is exactly what happened. After six months recuperating she resumed her busy active life [including many years of service as stake Relief Society president]. . . . I knew we were following the promptings of the Holy Ghost through important decisions that were made at that time. In my heart I knew that the Lord knows us, loves us and is there for us in times of great need."[22]

During LaVora's six-month recovery, the Wood daughters still at home learned to manage the household entirely. Mary Ellen remembers that her father never complained about "the food they served or burned."[23]

A Leader and a New Friend

All through Mary Ellen's adolescence, she was a natural leader, both in school and church settings. A cheerleader, she also held positions in student government throughout junior high, high school, and her freshman year at Utah State University. When her class of young women in Mutual was not particularly attentive or respectful to their teacher, the wise teacher took Mary Ellen aside. She told her she noticed what a strong leader Mary Ellen was and realized that her actions would influence the rest of the class, so she needed Mary Ellen's help. Musically talented, Mary Ellen was called during her high school years to be the organist and later chorister in Primary, then held on weekdays. The Primary president made her feel confident and needed.

When she was a ninth-grader, Mary Ellen met Stan Smoot, a senior and the Davis High School student body president. Stan was impressed with her "beautiful, bright smile and her personality."[24] Mary Ellen recalled of their dating experiences, "It just seemed right, but we never went steady."[25] Stan attended Utah State University for two years before receiving a mission call to Hawaii. During his absence, they wrote to each other regularly. Near the end of Stan's mission, he invited Mary Ellen and her parents to come to Hawaii, along with his parents, to meet him. After the end of her first year at USU, she returned home to manage her father's ten acres of strawberries, the profits of which provided enough money for Mary Ellen, her parents, and Ruth Ann to travel to Hawaii. The last night of the two-week trip, Stan proposed to Mary Ellen. He had financed the purchase of an engagement ring by selling one of his prize dairy cows.

Marriage

Stanley Millard Smoot and Mary Ellen Wood were married October 8, 1952, in the Salt Lake Temple by Elder Harold B. Lee. Two weeks later, Stan left to serve two years in the Signal Corps. At the end of basic training, Mary Ellen joined him in Morrow Bay, California. Their first child, Stana, was born in July 1953. As Stan had made the camp baseball team, he was not sent overseas, and the Smoots spent the remaining time of his service in Colorado Springs, Colorado. There they made many friends in the Church and in the

Signal Corps. Mary Ellen returned to Utah for the birth of their second child, Steven, in October 1954.

New Home

With two young children in a crowded apartment, Stan and Mary Ellen wanted to move into a home. After the birth of their third child, Sharman, Mary Ellen commented, "I was thrilled at the idea of settling into a home of our own. It was an exciting day when we moved into that little home. I thought I was at the end of my troubles and we would live happily ever after—but I did not realize which end."[26] The "dream home" presented major water problems. The iron-saturated well water tasted and looked terrible; leaks, floods, and repairs were common occurrences. Mary Ellen could not get enough water to complete a whole cycle for her washing machine—and with her growing family, she had lots of laundry. Frustrated, she begged her husband to move but knew they couldn't afford it. She decided to quit whining and make the best of her situation by turning the laundry room into a sitting room and doing their wash at a laundromat. She realized that "the pluses were better than the minuses. We really had a happy life in that small home. Our children could work at their grandfather's dairy, ride horses, build forts, feed baby calves, and pick fruit from the orchard." Mary Ellen felt they all learned patience and long-suffering and that they had "learned to live with some rather unfavorable circumstances that actually helped us to achieve our more important dream of being a happy and united family."[27] (Twenty-five years later, Stan and Mary Ellen moved into another home, which had "a glorious water system.")

The Smoots' home was located in Centerville, Utah, where their lives became "deeply ingrained" in the Church as well as the community. Stan worked full time at the family dairy while he finished his business degree at the University of Utah. Over the years, he received many leadership calls as elders quorum president, bishopric counselor, bishop, stake president's counselor, stake president, regional representative, and Young Men general board member. He also served in the community as county commissioner, national president of the county officials association, and at one time ran for governor of Utah.

Smoot Family Life

Three more children—Shauna, Shane, and Scott—joined the Smoot family within the first four years of life in their Centerville house. Eight years later, Shandell arrived. The Smoots also welcomed five foster children, whom they loved and whose lives they helped to rebuild.

When she had four small children and her mother was suffering from cancer, Mary Ellen wanted to spend more time with her mother and was somewhat frustrated with her family responsibilities. One afternoon as Mary Ellen visited her mother, LaVora said, "Oh, Mary Ellen, you are so blessed. Look at your adorable children. Your husband is working so hard and you are so blessed to have him active in the Church and serving the Lord." Mary Ellen said, "I couldn't remember what I was going to complain about. I started realizing my blessings and how grateful I was for a mother who through her trials could see not only her blessings but mine as well."[28] Mary Ellen was thankful for this time she had with her mother, for LaVora died April 1, 1959, at age 60, having been blessed to live long enough to witness all six daughters married in the temple to worthy men.

One night when Mary Ellen had had a particularly trying day with her five children under the age of six, she began her evening prayer by rehearsing her plight to her Heavenly Father. She received a distinct answer through the Spirit, "Forget yourself and think of others."[29]

The children thought their mother "fun to be around," said Shane, the fifth child. "She enjoyed life and made things fun. She was always doing, always building, and doing something constructive."[30] Mary Ellen often told her children that she wanted her mind to be active "until the day I die." Oldest daughter Stana said, "That's one thing we have learned from our mother, to continually progress. My mother lifted her mind and was never idle. She made sure that her thoughts were on the positive side of life, never tearing apart things or people. That's a conscious choice." Stana remembered that her mother created a thought book filled with scriptures and quotes to share with friends during their morning walks. Discussing uplifting thoughts ensured that their conversations would be positive and stay away from negative things.[31]

Having observed her parents and grandparents, Mary Ellen knew that her support of Stan's business, church, and community involvements was vital to the family's well-being and learned to be independent in caring for the children. She said, "That way when he came home we were happy to have him; however, life continued and we found worthwhile things to do with our time while he was away."[32]

The seven Smoot children enjoyed many worthwhile experiences, with Mary Ellen providing constant encouragement and direction. She also felt that one responsibility of mothers is to help children gain self-confidence through developing their abilities. Thus, the boys participated in Scouts and a variety of sports, raised cattle to show at 4-H fairs, and worked at the dairy. Stana and Shauna, the two girls, enjoyed dance lessons and music; they also helped at the cash-and-carry store next to the dairy. All the children were involved in school activities and student government. Mary Ellen felt keeping her children "busy in the summertime was important at this age."[33] One year Stan and Mary Ellen rehearsed their children to try out for a new Church-sponsored production, *Promised Valley*. For two summers, the Smoot children sang and danced in the nightly musical about the Saints crossing the plains, creating "unforgettable memories for them."[34] Shauna Essig, the second daughter, said, "We gained a lot of confidence from performing on stage in *Promised Valley*."[35]

While Sharman, the Smoot's third child, claimed that "we weren't easy kids to raise," he also noted that living next to the dairy farm provided each of them with ample opportunities to work. He said, "We gained a strong work ethic. We were really needed in hauling hay, feeding calves, and doing all the chores at the dairy. We were truly needed. It was a great blessing in my life."[36]

Just as Mary Ellen's parents had instilled strong values in her, she and Stan made great efforts to teach their children gospel principles and family values. She said, "One of the important things we have done as a family is to set up family values, and one of those is, 'As an eternal family we build, support, and edify one another.' We believe strongly in that."[37] Shane commented, "We always did a lot of things together as a family, which is probably what contributed to us growing together as a family. Mom and Dad were very involved in Church service, and they engaged us a lot in it. We participated in many welfare farm assignments. I remember Mom putting on a cultural fair for which she enlisted our help."[38] Shauna noted that service was taught to the family in many ways, including tying quilts to give away and in participating in welfare projects.[39]

Church and Community Service

Mary Ellen participated in all the auxiliaries of the Church as a teacher, counselor, and president. Following her release as ward Young Women president, she was called to be a Guide Patrol* leader in the Primary, a position she was not overly thrilled in accepting. She changed her attitude when Lucille Reading of the Primary general presidency spoke to ward and stake leaders. Mary Ellen said: "What she said that night hit me with great force. It was just what I needed. Sister Reading said: 'If you are not happy in your calling, don't ask to be released, put more effort into what you are doing and you will learn to love your calling, no matter what it is.' . . . I am so grateful I heard this life-changing challenge."[40]

From 1966 to 1971, Mary Ellen served on the editorial board of the *Children's Friend* magazine. She reviewed all incoming manuscripts and wrote about family home evenings as well as numerous stories. She later was called to a Church writing committee, where she felt her most significant contribution was preparing a priesthood orientation program for 11-year-old boys, known as Priesthood Preview. During this time, while Mary Ellen met every Sunday morning for committee meetings, Stan returned her many years of support to him by caring for the children and taking them to Sunday School.

Blessed with abundant energy and an eagerness to "always stretch herself," as her sister Ruth Ann noted, Mary Ellen worked in community affairs in a number of ways. She served as PTA president in her children's various schools and as district president. She was named president of the Centerville Women's Republican Club, a state committee member, and president-elect of the state Republican Women. A member of the boards of the South Davis Community Hospital and the local

---

* The Guide Patrol was a Primary class for eleven-year-old boys designed to prepare them to become deacons as well as Second Class Scouts.

United Way, she also wrote a teen column for the local newspaper and hosted a teen radio program. One year the Rotarians named her the outstanding citizen of Centerville. Her passion for history led Mary Ellen to organize the Centerville Historical Society and a local chapter of the Daughters of the Utah Pioneers. With her friend Marilyn Sheriff, she co-authored a history of Centerville. The two women interviewed descendants of the original settlers, gathered histories of people and businesses, and published *The City In-Between* in 1975.

Extended Family

As Mary Ellen was only twenty-five years old when her mother died, she realized that only her oldest two children might retain some vague memories of their Grandmother Wood. Thus, she and her five sisters decided to write their mother's life story to share with their posterity. After they finished LaVora's history, they helped their father to write his. The six sisters also organized an annual 24th of July Wood Family reunion with the express purpose "to celebrate their heritage." She observed of this tradition, "A spirit and blessing come through this effort that help family members know who they are and that they belong to and are an important part of the family."[41] Steven, the Smoots' oldest son, said, "Those sisters really did create the tradition of reunions. Those reunions were a big event. It wasn't just a picnic in the park for a couple of hours. We actually met for two to three days. It was more like youth conference. They brought in outside speakers, had dances, competitions, games, activities, and parades. We had great instruction on such topics as how to deal with stress or dress for success."[42] In addition, Stan and Mary Ellen have held reunions for their own family, with a chosen theme, photos, and talent show. But "most important," she said, "bonding has taken place."[43]

Mission to Ohio and Public Affairs

In 1983, Stan was called to preside over the Ohio Columbus Mission. Shandell, thirteen at the time, accompanied them; the other children were married or attending college. Mary Ellen was concerned about transplanting her youngest son and also wanted to help a daughter whose newborn son had severe health problems. Yet she knew this was a call from the Lord, so there was no question in her mind about accepting it. She said that this "single decision to serve the Lord blessed my family in ways that I would not have realized had I remained at home," yet it took "a leap of faith."[44] Shandell made many new friends in Ohio and became a star athlete and national wrestling champion. Other family members and friends assisted Stana and her baby. Mary Ellen and Stan loved serving in the mission field and felt their family grew by 500 missionaries.

"Mom has always been one to set the example in showing everyone how to do things, rather than preaching or lecturing," observed Shandell, who often traveled with his parents to zone conferences, to stake conferences, and to ward and branch sacrament meetings. "She had great relationships with the sister missionaries, in particular, and with all our missionaries. The missionaries loved her."[45]

One year into their mission, the Smoots were asked to open a new mission in Akron, Ohio, which included Church historical sites around Kirtland. Arriving six weeks before the dedication of the restored Newell K. Whitney Store, Stan needed to organize mission affairs and gave Mary Ellen the assignment of public affairs to generate local interest in this event. She also coordinated hospitality for visiting General Authorities, including President Ezra Taft Benson, President of the Quorum of the Twelve Apostles, and President Gordon B. Hinckley, First Counselor in the First Presidency at the time. Mary Ellen prepared press kits for local newspapers to publicize the dedication, invited leaders of other churches to attend, and planned the dinner to follow the dedication. She took to heart the counsel of Karl Anderson, the regional representative, to find descendants of the original settlers of Kirtland. Both she and Stan had ancestors who had lived in Kirtland, and she tracked down Smoot relatives. One woman loaned her a book of Smoot history, which provided her with more than 500 names for which to do temple work.

After being immersed in public affairs in Ohio, in 1986 Mary Ellen was again called to serve in that capacity in Utah. She and Stan served for the next seven years on public affairs committees. Then, in 1993, they were called to be directors of Church Hosting for VIPs. During this four-year assignment, they met with dignitaries and government leaders from all over the world, usually taking these guests to Temple Square, Welfare Square, and the Humanitarian

Service Center. The Smoots accompanied the visitors to meet with Church leaders, often the First Presidency. One particular experience stands out in Mary Ellen's mind. She and Stan escorted Mikhail Gorbachev, former leader of the Soviet Union, and his wife, Raisa, to meet with President Gordon B. Hinckley. She marveled as these two great leaders sat near one another and each expressed the view that they were "just humble men."[46]

Thirteenth Relief Society General President

On March 25, 1997, following a visit with a Russian religious leader and President Hinckley, the Smoots were invited to return to the prophet's office. As they walked back to the Administration Building, Mary Ellen thought that Stan might be given another calling but couldn't dismiss the feeling that she would be called as the new Relief Society general president, though she thought it "ridiculous" as she had not served on a general board. After visiting with the Smoots for a few minutes, President Hinckley extended that very call to Mary Ellen. "I could not breathe and my husband started to cry. The first words out of my mouth: I said to the prophet of the Lord: 'Are you sure?'"[47] Though she felt very humbled and inadequate, Mary Ellen took comfort that this call was from the Lord and that through her faith in Him, He would make her equal to the task. She adopted the motto of President J. Reuben Clark, Jr., for her administration: "The task ahead of us is never as great as the power behind us."[48]

Mary Ellen chose Virginia Urry Jensen as her first counselor and Sheri L. Dew, a single woman, as her second counselor. Knowing that 48 percent of Relief Society sisters were single, Mary Ellen felt they should be represented in the presidency. Following Elaine L. Jack's release at general conference on April 6, 1997, the new presidency was announced and sustained. When President Hinckley set her apart a few days later, he blessed her with this counsel: "This is a tremendous organization, perhaps the largest and oldest of its kind in all the world. Its mission is to do good and to help those in distress and need, to bring about the processes of education, good homemaking and other skills, into the lives of women throughout the world. . . . You have counselors and a board who together will do a great work."[49] Over the next few months, nine general board members were called.

Mary Ellen's tremendous energy set the tone for her administration, observed Virginia Jensen. Mary Ellen's desire "to get out among the women" prompted the presidency and general board members to visit numerous ward Relief Societies, both for Sunday meetings and midweek homemaking meetings. From these visits, they learned much about how the Relief Society programs were meeting the needs of sisters. The local units seemed to appreciate visitors from Church headquarters.[50]

The first training the new administration handled was for a revised curriculum. Previously, the Relief Society had, through writing committees and with priesthood approval, generated its own lessons. Beginning in January 1998, both the Relief Society and Melchizedek priesthood quorums, in their respective meetings, would be taught lessons twice a month from a series of manuals, *Teachings of Presidents of the Church,* of which Brigham Young was the first. The first Sunday of each month a member of the Relief Society presidency (or priesthood leader) would instruct, while the fourth Sunday's lesson would be given from *Teachings for Our Time,* designated by the First Presidency.

Expanding Relief Society Service

"My first glimpse of Mary Ellen's priority of service," said general board member Shauna Frandsen, "was our first Christmas social. The bulk of our responsibility was teaching, whether it was workshops or auxiliary training or traveling to some place in the United States, Mexico, or elsewhere. It was a tradition to have a social with a more relaxed atmosphere where partners could come. At board meeting a week or two before the social, Sister Smoot said she had been made aware of three families who really were not going to have Christmas. She suggested canceling the social and instead meet at Welfare Square and donate whatever we wanted to and then can food for these families. We divided up and delivered the gifts to the families the next night. That was one of the best parts of Christmas."[51]

With the idea of service instilled in her as a child, Mary Ellen wanted her administration to find new ways to expand the reach of Relief Society service. As cosponsors of the BYU Women's Conference, the presidency suggested organizing large-scale service projects during the 1999 two-day event. In between attending sessions, more than

18,000 women assembled thousands of hygiene kits, school supplies, newborn kits, and made quilts and leper bandages. The result was, as BYU President Merrill J. Bateman described, "the largest humanitarian event the Church has ever been involved with in one setting."[52] These service projects have continued with succeeding conferences.

In July 1999, Presiding Bishop H. David Burton asked the Relief Society to provide 30,000 quilts for Kosovo refugees. Sisters around the world responded enthusiastically. Although the Relief Society quit counting after receiving 350,000 quilts, the outpouring has continued, providing quilts as needs arise. When given the assignment, Mary Ellen commented, "We are so happy that the Relief Society has been asked to help with this project. I have found that our sisters have a great desire to serve. . . . This is the mission of Relief Society. That is what we are: a relief society."[53] Mary Ellen had the privilege of personally delivering some of those quilts to needy people in Kosovo. Quilts were also sent to many other disaster areas, including Mexico, Turkey, Venezuela, Mozambique, and Zimbabwe.

Virginia Jensen noted that "service was Mary Ellen's hallmark, particularly in mobilizing people in service. My testimony is that a person is called to a calling for a period of time, and it is their time and the Lord calls them because He knows what is coming up. Those quilts started to come in, and then we had all these natural disasters. They were all used worldwide. The women resonated to that. They loved doing that."[54]

Mary Ellen also strongly believes that service blesses the givers. In her travels to forty countries throughout the world, she often had opportunities to talk to women individually. Her daughter Stana Kjar said, "Everywhere my mother went she would have people talk to her about women and depression. She said, 'I know that service lifts hearts. There's a lot of learning that takes place in that. I know that it lifts the spirit of women when we are serving.'"[55]

Strengthening Families

Strengthening families has been an ongoing effort of Relief Society since its inception in 1842. Particularly in the 1990s, Church leaders felt that the institution of the family was coming under greater attack. The First Presidency, in 1995, issued "The Family: A Proclamation to the World," defining and clarifying the Church's position on the family. In May 1999, Elder Dallin H. Oaks, advisor to the Relief Society, invited Mary Ellen to spend two weeks in Rome, Italy, to help plan the second World Congress on Families. A keynote speaker at the November congress held in Geneva, Switzerland, she received a standing ovation from representatives throughout the world, who also felt keenly the need to strengthen families. Mary Ellen observed that many women admired the way she dressed modestly. Two years later, she participated in planning meetings for the next World Congress.

Throughout her life, Mary Ellen has been passionate about family history and encouraged Relief Society sisters to "find true peace by turning to their own family histories."[56] She often referred to stories from her ancestors' lives in her talks and urged women to find their roots.

Relief Society Declaration and Other Changes

In Mary Ellen's first address to the General Women's Meeting in September 1997, she talked about women of faith and who Latter-day Saint sisters are. She, along with her counselors, felt that a clear and focused declaration would help not only people outside the Church to know what Relief Society represented, but it would also help sisters themselves understand their "meaning, purpose, and direction."[57] Phrased with action verbs such as "increase, dedicate, sustain, and rejoice," the Relief Society Declaration was introduced at the September 1999 General Women's Meeting.

At the same meeting, the name change of homemaking meeting to home, family, and personal enrichment meeting was announced. Effective January 1, 2000, the focus of the midweek meeting for Relief Society was to help strengthen sisters to, in turn, strengthen their families, neighbors, and communities, and to give service. General board member Shauna Frandsen observed, "This presidency felt more emphasis should be put on the home, in gaining skills to strengthen the home and families, which include spiritual as well as homemaking skills. Homemaking, as it was before, did not appeal to all women. The second reason was that often homemaking was synonymous with crafts. The purpose of Relief Society is to bring women and their families to Christ. This midweek meeting needed to be more spiritual, to

build testimonies, and to help women create strong homes."[58] Mary
Ellen stated that "the new home, family, and personal enrichment
meeting provided an ideal setting for sisters to develop the skills
enumerated in the Declaration."[59]

With a worldwide sisterhood of many different backgrounds and
cultures, the Relief Society presidency wanted to implement more
universal visiting teaching messages. Beginning in January 2002, the
new format for visiting teaching messages included selected statements
from Church leaders and verses of scripture focused on a gospel topic
with questions to facilitate discussion. Visiting teachers were invited to
share their experiences and testimonies with the sisters they visit.

When many international travelers came to Salt Lake City in
February 2002 for the Winter Olympics, the Relief Society offered
service by assisting in training volunteers and hosting receptions at
the Joseph Smith Memorial Building. Mary Ellen and her husband
visited the Russian House twice, meeting leaders who they felt might
be instrumental in further opening doors for the Church in that area
of the world.

Stan, who began his lengthy leadership service in the Church as a
twenty-eight-year-old bishop, cheerfully reversed roles to become
Mary Ellen's ardent supporter while she served as Relief Society president. Paying his own way, he occasionally traveled with Mary Ellen to
some of her assignments around the world. Although he had never
been a cook, according to daughter Shauna, "My dad became a great
salad maker."[60] Mary Ellen's children also rallied in support of her
calling, from her daughters putting up her Christmas decorations
every year to adjusting family activities to fit her schedule.

Release and More Family History

At the April 6, 2002, general conference, Mary Ellen, her counselors,
and general board were released. Bonnie D. Parkin was sustained as the
fourteenth general president, with her counselors, Kathleen H. Hughes
and Anne C. Pingree.

Since her release, Mary Ellen has had a little more time to settle
into the new home that Stan built while she served as president. She
and Stan have enjoyed teaching eight-year-olds in their ward Primary.
Her growing number of great-grandchildren and fifty-one grand-

children, whose parents all live within fifteen minutes of the Smoot home in North Salt Lake, appreciate their grandmother's interest in their activities and lives. She creates a bi-monthly newsletter to keep the family, now numbering nearly seventy, informed of family happenings, to impart wisdom, and to bear testimony. The Smoots all meet monthly for family home evenings, often at Stan and Mary Ellen's home. "It's never easy when you put that many kids in one house—it can get pretty chaotic, but it helps the grandkids to be close to their cousins," said Scott, the Smoots' sixth child. "And the grandkids love their grandparents. The door is always open. There's never an inconvenient time to stop at their home. Mom fixes you some food or has a treat for you or gives you something as you go out the door."[61]

Mary Ellen has devoted even more time to family history and shares that love with Shauna. Mother and daughter spend most Thursday mornings together at a family history library and attend the temple often. Mary Ellen traveled to England with a grandson to research her Blencowe line. For the annual 24th of July family reunion in 2006, Mary Ellen presented each family with a professionally published book on this line titled *What Happened to Jane?*, which she worked feverishly to finish in time. Her passion for family history has given her descendants not only an understanding of their heritage but also a deep appreciation of their place in the family and their responsibility to carry on this legacy of faith. Youngest son Shandell remarked, "Mom said our ancestors have paid the price. We are receiving blessings that have been coming from generations of sacrifice, generations of toil, hard work, service, and dedication to the Church. We are definitely receiving blessings from our ancestors."[62]

Mary Ellen Wood Smoot brought to her calling as thirteenth Relief Society general president her remarkable energy, her years of leadership experience in the Church and community, her eagerness to render service, and her devotion to the cause of the family. She sought to help Relief Society sisters worldwide strengthen their testimonies of Jesus Christ and gain a clearer vision of Relief Society, the Lord's organization for women. She said:

> During the five years of our administration we experienced a remarkable time in the history of the Church.

From the groundbreaking of the Conference Center to the Winter Olympics, Relief Society has had the privilege to be involved. We witnessed the beginning of a new millennium, the rapid building of small temples around the world, and the Church growth of over eleven million members with the majority outside the United States.[63]

Notes

1. Mary Ellen Smoot, "The Beacons of His Light," BYU Women's Conference address, May 1997, p. 6.

2. Mary Ellen Smoot, Personal History, p. 34. Hereafter cited as Personal History.

3. "The Beacons of His Light," p. 6.

4. Mary Ellen Smoot, "Come, Let Us Walk in the Light of the Lord," *Ensign,* November 1998, p. 89.

5. Ivy Hooper Blood Hill, *William Blood: Biographies and Posterity,* privately published, 1961, p. 77.

6. "The Beacons of His Light," pp. 4–5.

7. Personal History, p. 1.

8. "The Beacons of His Light," p. 6.

9. Relief Society Scrapbook, p. 3.

10. Mary Ellen Smoot, *Sweet Is the Work: How Relief Society Helps Bring Women to Christ* (Salt Lake City: Bookcraft, 2000), p. 105.

11. Relief Society Scrapbook, p. 3.

12. Telephone interview with Ruth Ann W. Christensen, September 8, 2006.

13. Relief Society Scrapbook, p. 4.

14. Ibid., p. 4.

15. Ibid., p. 5, endnote 7.

16. Personal History, p. 4.

17. *Sweet Is the Work,* pp. 105–6.

18. "The Beacons of His Light," p. 6.

19. Personal History, p. 4.

20. Robyn Lambert, "Friend to Friend," *Friend,* July 1998, p. 6.

21. Relief Society Scrapbook, p. 5.

22. Ibid., p. 6, endnote 8.

23. Ibid., p. 6.

24. Telephone interview with Stanley M. Smoot, September 12, 2006.

25. Interview with Mary Ellen Smoot by Janet Peterson, August 9, 2006. Hereafter cited as Smoot interview.

26. Mary Ellen Smoot, "The Possible Dream," BYU Women's Conference, May 1998, p. 1.

27. Ibid., p. 2.

28. Personal History, p. 23.

29. *Sweet Is the Work,* pp. 108–9.

30. Telephone interview with Shane D. Smoot, September 10, 2006.

31. Telephone interview with Stana S. Kjar, September 11, 2006.

32. Personal History, p. 21.

33. Ibid., p. 28.

34. Ibid.

35. Telephone interview with Shauna S. Essig, September 11, 2006.

36. Telephone interview with Sharman W. Smoot, September 13, 2006.

37. "News of the Church," *Ensign,* May 1997, p. 108.

38. Telephone interview with Shane D. Smoot, September 10, 2006.

39. Telephone interview with Shauna S. Essig, September11, 2006.

40. Relief Society Scrapbook, p. 7.

41. Mary Ellen Smoot, "Family History: A Work of Love," *Ensign,* Mar. 1999, p. 16.

42. Telephone interview with Steven E. Smoot, September 9, 2006.

43. "Family History: A Work of Love," p. 16.

44. "The Possible Dream," p. 8.

45. Telephone interview with Shandell M. Smoot, September 17, 2006.

46. Smoot interview.

47. Personal History, p. 11.

48. *Sweet Is the Work,* p. 18.

49. Personal History, p. 12.

50. Telephone interview with Virginia U. Jensen, September 13, 2006.

51. Interview with Shauna U. Frandsen, August 8, 2006.

52. "For LDS Women, 'Sky's the Limit,'" *Church News,* May 8, 1999, p. 10.

53. Gerry Avant, "Quilts to Ward Off Chill in Kosovo," *Church News,* August 7, 1999, p. 6.

54. Telephone interview with Virginia U. Jensen, September 13, 2006.

55. Telephone interview with Stana S. Kjar, September 11, 2006.

56. Smoot interview.

57. Relief Society Declaration, quoted in "The Visiting Teacher: Welcoming Young Women into Relief Society," *Ensign,* March 2000, p. 71.

58. Interview with Shauna U. Frandsen, August 8, 2006.

59. Relief Society Scrapbook, Preface.

60. Telephone interview with Shauna S. Essig, September11, 2006.

61. Telephone interview with Scott D. Smoot, September 12, 2006.

62. Telephone interview with Shandell M. Smoot, September 17, 2006.

63. Relief Society Scrapbook, Preface, p. ii.

14

BONNIE DANSIE PARKIN
2002–2007

Brigham Young sent Bonnie Parkin's great-grandparents, Jane and Robert Dansie, who had joined the Church in their native England, to settle Fort Herriman, in the southwest corner of the Salt Lake Valley. Robert made a one-room dugout in a hillside for his family of five children. Eventually ten more children were born. Although living conditions were difficult, with the family subsisting for a time on sego lily bulbs, wild rabbits, and occasionally mutton, Jane "was known for making people feel welcome in her home—even if it was in a hole in the hill—and seeing that no one went hungry either for food or a kind word," said Bonnie. "Hers was an example of hard work and service and charity." Jane also handled her situation with humor. Once a cow tromped over the top of the dugout, her legs falling through the mud roof. Her daughter remembered her saying, "Dugouts were very nice, but she did not care to have her ceiling decorated with cow legs."[1]

Jane's traits of friendliness, kindness, hospitality, optimism, and handling life with humor aptly describe her great-granddaughter Bonnie Dansie Parkin, the fourteenth general president of the Relief Society.

Growing Up in Herriman
The middle of five children, Bonnie Rae Dansie was born in Murray, Utah, August 4, 1940, to Jesse Homer and Ruth Martha Butikofer Dansie. She was welcomed by her older sister, Joyce, and brother, Rodney, and followed by two more brothers, Richard and Boyd. "We had a great childhood," Bonnie remarked.[2]

Bonnie grew up on the family homestead in Herriman, where Jesse farmed, raising hay, wheat—and dirt—as family members liked to say. He also worked construction, sold topsoil, and mined by leasing a vein in a nearby mine. Finding good lodes of ore determined success, and some years were lean. The family also operated a little store, Dansie's Place, on their property.

Jesse and Ruth taught their children to honor the good name of their family and to appreciate their gospel heritage. While Bonnie's paternal great-grandparents, Jane and Robert Dansie, were converted in England, the first generation of Church members on her mother's side joined the Church in Switzerland. When her grandfather, Rudolph Butikofer, was eleven years old, missionaries knocked on the door of his family's home in Bern. Rudolph, his mother, and two sisters, Rosina and Anna, were baptized in 1879. The girls, just seventeen and eighteen, emigrated to Utah first. As a young man, Rudolph, with the help of the Church's Perpetual Emigration Fund, left Switzerland to "gather to Zion." When the ship *Nevada* sailed into New York harbor and Rudolph saw the Statue of Liberty, he cried for joy. With other Swiss converts, he traveled to Utah by train, such a slow mode of transportation that at times the young men would jump off and run alongside. Rudolph worked hard at a variety of jobs, including one for the Utah Northern Railroad, to repay his travel loan and to send for his mother and younger sister, Bertha.

Jacob Metzner, Bonnie's maternal great-grandfather, prospered as a stonecutter and contractor in Bern, and built a large home with beautiful grounds for his wife, Marie Burri Metzner, and their five children. After the Metzners heard the elders' message of the restoration of the gospel and joined the Church in 1890, they were outcast, and Jacob could not obtain work. The oldest daughter, Marie, who was Bonnie's grandmother, and her brother Jacob, were sent by the family to Utah. The rest of the family arrived the following year. Rudolph Butikofer met and courted Marie in Salt Lake City, and they were married in the Logan Temple in 1892. The Butikofers later moved to Idaho to farm. Bonnie's mother, Ruth Martha, was one of the youngest of the eleven children. Bonnie said of her grandparents, "They taught their eleven children to work hard, to pay their tithes and offering[s], and to hold fast to the truths of the gospel. The faith of my grandparents in the Lord Jesus Christ is a spiritual legacy that has strengthened and blessed my own testimony and the testimony of my own family."[3]

Bonnie's paternal grandparents, Alma Haleman and Agnes Ruth Kunz Dansie, owned a 500-acre farm in Herriman just a half mile away from Jesse and Ruth's home, so the Dansie children had ample opportunities to develop a close relationship with, work with, and learn from their grandparents.

Bonnie valued the trust her mother placed in her, which she called "one of the greatest gifts that she gave me." Ruth often told her daughter, "It's better to be trusted than loved." Thus, Bonnie tried hard never to disappoint her mother. "I respected her so much that I felt it incredibly important to make sure that I represented my family well," she said. "My mother taught us, 'Do what is right, let the consequences follow.'"[4]

Learning was highly prized in the Dansie home. Although Jesse had attended college prior to his Northwestern States mission, he returned during the Depression years and could not afford to continue school. He especially enjoyed reading biographies, while Ruth often gathered her children around her to read together the scriptures, stories from the *Relief Society Magazine,* and classic litera-ture. Both parents encouraged their five children to set their sights on obtaining a university education, which they all did.

The Dansies also taught their children how to work. Bonnie said, "I am so grateful this day for my mother and father, for the teachings they gave me, for their love, for teaching me how to work."[5] Bonnie and her siblings each worked at the store, tended the garden, harvested corn, hauled hay, and did numerous other chores that rural living required. Nevertheless, Joyce, the oldest in the family, recalled, "We had fun doing it."[6]

While the family knew well that "work on the farm never ended," the Dansies enjoyed good times together. The spring fryers Jesse raised were ready by July. Rodney recalled, "My mom and Grandma would fry chicken for the 24th of July, and we all went to Butterfield Canyon for a picnic to celebrate. My dad would also take us to Yellowstone Park with a trailer and tents. And every year we went to the Butikofer reunion in Idaho. That was a special event, to stay for three to five days."[7]

When Bonnie was fourteen years old, her father was injured in a car accident and spent the Christmas holidays in the hospital. Christmas was an especially tender time that year, for they were recipients of gifts provided by a family in Herriman. Bonnie was delighted to receive a pretty new sweater but appreciated the love extended to them even more. In subsequent years, the Dansies decided to make giving gifts to people in need one of their own Christmas traditions. Although Bonnie said their family "did not have a lot of extra things," one Christmas Eve they became aware of a family who would not have presents at all. Bonnie and her siblings gathered bottled fruit, beef, and oranges for the family, and each contributed one of their own toys or cherished belongings for the children. When Bonnie drove her brothers to deliver the presents, they could see the joy on the children's faces when the door opened.[8] Providing Christmas for others would be a tradition Bonnie carried on with her own children.

Bonnie's friendly, outgoing personality was, as her brother Rodney said, "a magnet for friends."[9] She liked to help her friends, and they, in turn, helped her by working with her to finish chores so that she would be free to go to the movies or on other outings with them. Her leadership abilities were a natural extension of her warmth and caring. Joyce remembered her parents coming home from a meeting with Bonnie's seventh grade teacher, who said, "Make sure Bonnie is on the right track because wherever she goes, she's going to take the whole crowd."[10]

"A Believing Heart"

The small community of Herriman had only one ward and was part of the West Jordan Stake that covered much of the southwest part of the Salt Lake Valley. Large pictures of the latter-day prophets graced the walls of the chapel, which helped Bonnie to memorize their names, just as she did the Articles of Faith. Bonnie felt that "little things like that made a difference in who we became and what we felt as we grew up."[11]

Primary, then held on weekday afternoons, was a testimony-building experience for Bonnie. She said, "I learned the gospel there and felt the Spirit through good music. I remember the leaders who taught us the songs with so much energy. Singing was fun! I don't remember anybody telling me what I was feeling, but it was the Spirit. That's the kind of power that good music has."[12] While Bonnie said she was "born with a believing heart," she felt "many of the things that strengthened my beliefs were things that happened in Primary. It was a joyous time."[13]

Bonnie learned about the blessings of paying tithing. One Sunday when her mother had paid their tithing and fast offerings for the month, which amounted to one dollar, there was no money left over. To raise money for a new building, the ward sponsored a weekly Thursday night movie, which cost one dollar for a family to attend. That week the Dansies simply didn't have another dollar, which was a great disappointment to the children. Bonnie related, "We children said, 'If we hadn't paid our tithing, we would have a dollar for the movie.' Our mother, a woman of faith, said, 'Get ready. Something will happen.' A neighbor knocked on the door, bringing one dollar for some work my dad had done for her. For us kids, that was the message, the lesson, that tithing works."[14]

When she was ten years old, Bonnie learned firsthand that a loving Father in Heaven hears and answers prayers. Her mother, Ruth, became very ill with an infection around the lining of her heart. The five Dansie children went to the hospital but could only stand outside her window, as children were not allowed to visit patients. Bonnie said, "One of my most lasting memories of my father is kneeling with my brothers and sister by my parents' bed in their small room and hearing my father plead with Heavenly Father to bless our mother, who was in the hospital. Hearing my father pour out his heart helped me know that there was a God in heaven who listens."[15]

As a young adult, Bonnie had confirmed to her that there is a living prophet. One winter afternoon, she had just parked her car in front of the Church Administration Building on South Temple and was putting a nickel in the parking meter. A man, dressed in a dark overcoat and wool hat, exited the building. She felt the Spirit stir her soul and realized the man was President David O. McKay. As he passed her, President McKay smiled and tipped his hat. "The Spirit literally filled my being," Bonnie said. "I knew I had seen a prophet of God."[16]

Another soul-stirring experience was the day both Bonnie and her mother received their patriarchal blessings. Bonnie was twenty and

Ruth, forty-nine. Bonnie listened to the patriarch, who was not acquainted with them, describe Ruth's life—how she had been blessed to survive bouts of rheumatic fever, heart disease, and other illnesses, how she had been an instrument in blessing others' lives—and then gave her guidance and promises. "This experience was a witness to me that God lives, that He loves us, and that He knows us individually. I felt the Lord's love for my mother—and for me—on that memorable day."[17]

Bonnie learned to serve by observing her parents and grandparents extending service to others. She also gained a love for Relief Society through her mother and grandmother. She remembers playing under quilting frames as a little girl while her grandmother and other Relief Society sisters quilted. "I knew that this was part of Relief Society— blessing the lives of others," she said. "I was mentored with love for Relief Society by my mother and my grandmother."[18] The way Ruth carried out her service as a visiting teacher for fifty years with "a happy heart" and loved the women in her ward as her sisters taught Bonnie about the important personal connections, the sisterhood, of Relief Society.

Leaving Home

Bonnie was excited to begin college life on a scholarship at Utah State University the fall of 1958, but after two days at school, she recounted, "I became so homesick I was physically ill and feared my heart was going to break. . . . Even though I was attending the same university as my sister and brother, all I wanted to do was go home to the safety of hand-stitched quilts, to the gruff but tender care of my dad, to the gentle arms of my mother in her warm kitchen." When she passed her old two-room school, the chapel, and finally saw the sign for the family store, Dansie's Place, she felt comfort in being home. Bonnie told her father, who was sitting in his usual spot—a brown leather chair—that she couldn't go back to Logan. Instead of reprimanding her, he told her that she could choose whether or not to go back. He also counseled her that she could meet any challenge and that whatever she did, she was still loved.[19] Bonnie renewed her courage and returned to school. She couldn't have imagined that day that years later USU would name her Distinguished Alumna and that a school of education scholarship would be established in her name.

Grandmother Dansie also encouraged Bonnie in her college experience by enclosing a dollar in her letters. Bonnie knew her grandmother was proud of her and that these dollars were a sacrifice because they came from her hard-earned egg money. Though a lifelong learner, Agnes Dansie had not had the opportunity to attend college and vowed her posterity would have that privilege.

Once adjusted to college life, Bonnie enjoyed many great experiences as well as leadership opportunities as president of her sorority, vice president of the senior class, and counselor in her ward Relief Society presidency. Bonnie graduated in 1962 with a B.A. in elementary education and early childhood development. That fall she began teaching third grade in Bountiful.

Marriage and Family Life

A friend lined Bonnie up with James LaMar Parkin, a first-year medical student at the University of Utah. Bonnie recalled that they "shared great conversation," while Jim remembered that Bonnie was a lot of fun and had a tremendous amount of energy. A courtship ensued, and they were married July 1, 1963, in the Salt Lake Temple. The newlyweds moved into a basement apartment in the Avenues in Salt Lake City, and Bonnie continued teaching while Jim completed medical school. Their first son, Jeffrey, was born in 1965.

The Parkin family moved to Seattle in 1966 for Jim to fulfill an internship, residency, and post-doctoral work in otolaryngology. Brett was born the following year, followed by Matthew in 1969, and David in 1972. The six years the Parkins spent in Seattle were busy and rewarding years. They made many new friends among the medical students and ward members. Jim was called to serve in the bishopric and Bonnie as Primary president.

While she had been blessed with a believing heart and had developed a strong testimony, Bonnie realized that she needed to increase her knowledge of the gospel. She and a friend, Louise Nelson, discovered they were on the same level and decided to study the Book of Mormon together, sharing favorite passages and insights with each other. Bonnie recalled that she and Louise "were hungering to know what spiritual women in our ward knew. We wanted righteous children, 'taught by their mothers' to be believing (Alma 56:47)."[20]

Sitting on "an old worn couch," in their Seattle apartment, Bonnie read scripture stories to her little boys. As she did so, she said she found that "a power began to permeate our lives. . . . I learned that God worked miracles in the lives of others, and he could work wonders in mine too."[21]

The Parkins returned to Salt Lake City in 1972 for Jim to begin his practice as an ear, nose, and throat doctor. They purchased a home on the east bench in the Parley's Third Ward, where they have continued to live.

Committed to education and an avid reader herself, Bonnie continued her mother's tradition of reading to her children. "We had tons of children's literature," Jeff remembered. Bonnie and the boys spent summer mornings reading the Book of Mormon together, and in the afternoons when it got hot, the children came inside from playing and heard their mother read a wide variety of books, such as *Where the Red Fern Grows* and *Island of the Blue Dolphins*.[22]

Discipline was kindly taught in the Parkin home. Matt said, "I think a good thing about my mom was that you knew what the rules were, and if you broke a rule, there were consequences. She said, 'If these things don't happen, these things will happen.' That taught us where the boundaries were, and as boys we were always trying to reestablish the boundaries. That consistency was helpful to us and provided security. She was a taskmaster sometimes, too."[23] Jeff recalled that his mother would "not let us get away with stuff"—one morning Bonnie even came to Jeff's schoolroom and took him home to make his bed.[24]

Life in the Parkin home was fun—even when work was involved. Brett said, "There's no harder worker than my mom. She really taught us how to work. We would play games like 'Beat the Clock.' We had a certain amount of time to do a job and we would try to beat the clock." Brett also remembered going out to his grandfather's farm on Friday afternoons to work, commenting, "There's no shortage of work on the farm."[25] Still, there was lots of fun to be had on the farm for the boys in building forts and riding horses. And when the boys walked in the door of their grandparents' home, Grandma Dansie greeted them with a hug, an expression of love, and the question, "What can I feed you?"

Because learning to work was a value Jim and Bonnie wanted to firmly instill in their family, they required that their sons find jobs. Each of the boys had his turn at a paper route. On cold winter mornings, Bonnie often volunteered to drive them to deliver the newspapers. As teenagers, the boys earned spending money with summer and after-school jobs. When one son announced he didn't have time to work as he was going to attend football camps all summer, his parents assured him that he'd be a better football player by hauling hay and secured employment for him at Grandpa Dansie's farm.

Gardening, one of Bonnie's favorite hobbies, also provided meaningful experiences with her sons. "I love to dig in the dirt," remarked Bonnie. "It takes you back to your roots; it settles your head. I gardened with my sons, pulling weeds, one-on-one with them, early in the morning. We talked a lot about life and its challenges. It was a very safe place for my sons."[26]

"Are You Building?" was a phrase the Parkin boys heard often to remind them to have a positive attitude and to be involved in constructive activities. David said, "'AYB?' was definitely a discussion point in our family to make sure that we were positive influences on each other and those around us and in other areas of life. My mom encouraged us to have a positive attitude about life and others rather than a negative one."[27]

According to Matt and Jeff, Bonnie has "a quick wit" and "a wonderful sense of humor, though we tested her limits."[28] David noted, "My mom loves a good laugh. She loves to interact and have a good time."[29] Bonnie even made breakfast fun by cooking green pancakes and green scrambled eggs on occasion. Her quips, called "Bonnie-isms" by her family, included such remarks as, "Fair is where you go to see the pigs," and "The Holy Ghost goes to bed at midnight."

All the Parkins agreed that Bonnie is "a fantastic cook," a skill she learned in her mother's kitchen. Brett has "lots of wonderful memories of hot bread, and good, healthy meals—the meat and potato-type for raising four boys. As much as we had going on, she was always trying to get us to sit down at the dinner table. We learned a lot at the family dinner table."[30] Sunday dinners, particularly, were times for the family to enjoy each other's company, to visit and discuss what was happening in their lives.

Bonnie was "a good sport" who enthusiastically water-skied and snow-skied along with her husband and sons. The Parkins relished a yearly ski trip to Vail, Colorado, where Jim attended medical meetings. The family also enjoyed camping and lots of picnics in the canyons. According to Jim, Bonnie is a natural athlete, who especially loved tennis, playing often with the family or friends. Looking back on their tennis matches, David said, "My mother taught us that you can have a lot of fun competing. She enjoys competition and doesn't like to lose. She felt that tennis was a way to release stress and to have a good time."[31] Bonnie's early morning walks and gardening have been spiritual renewals for her as well as exercise.

The Parkins often shared their home with young men who needed a welcoming place to live—young adults from the singles' ward where Jim served as bishop, a cousin, and visitors from South Africa and New Zealand. Bonnie acquainted them with the way things were run in the Parkin home and helped them move forward in their lives.

"Bonnie has a natural gift for connecting with people and making people feel valued," stated Jim. "She can create a meaningful conversation with anybody. It is amazing how many people think Bonnie is their best friend. Hers is a genuine interest—nothing fake about it. The number of people she maintains connection with is large. She does that better than anyone I've ever seen. Bonnie is also very, very honest and tells what she thinks."[32] "My mom has a great touch with people," noted Brett. "I remember when I was a returned missionary and dating, I liked to take the girls I dated home to talk to my mom. That was a great thing." In speaking of her ability to relate to people she meets through her Church callings, he said, "She has a very tender, empathetic side to her. She is able to relate to other people's pain."[33]

Bonnie has often said, "I got daughters the easy way—my sons married them." Over the next few years following their missions, when Jeff, Brett, Matt, and David married, Bonnie warmly welcomed each new bride into the family. Jana Parkin commented, "I felt so lucky coming into the family, as Bonnie had never had a daughter. She did all those things she wanted to do with a daughter with me— going to the ballet, taking me shopping. My own mother passed away, and Bonnie has been like a second mother to me."[34] Ann Parkin said, "She's a great mother-in-law. She lets us live our own lives, yet she is willing to help whenever any of us need her. She is never critical and loves what we try and our successes. As a mother of four boys, I often think, 'How would Bonnie handle this?' We are so grateful for the way she raised her sons. They are the most amazing men—all of them. And they can cook! Bonnie trained them well, and they're all great cooks."[35]

Bonnie's zest for life makes her a grandmother her eighteen grandchildren adore. She plays tennis with them, hosts tea parties for her granddaughters, cheers at soccer and football games, attends school programs, plans special outings and sleepovers, and reads bedtime stories with great animation. When Bonnie and her grandchildren are separated by distance, she calls, sends packages, and travels to spend time with them. Her grandmothering goes beyond planning good times, for she "has a great desire to nurture."[36] Said Bonnie, "I have . . . grandchildren whose tender little spirits and daily challenges I want to better understand."[37] "A particular joy as grandparents," remarked Bonnie, "is to watch our sons and their remarkable wives parent and teach principles that we tried to teach them and their finding those principles still work."[38]

Extending Service in the Community and the Church

A former school teacher, Bonnie was active in PTA in her sons' schools, serving as a board member and president. She volunteered as a docent for the Utah Symphony for elementary schools and served on the Community Council and the Great Books Foundation. In addition, she was involved with medical auxiliaries.

Bonnie served in their ward and stake in numerous callings. "As I look at my life, every calling has strengthened me," she said.[39] When called as a ward Relief Society president, Bonnie was apprehensive as she was one of the youngest mothers in the ward. But she found "sweet peace," for the sisters in the ward loved and accepted her. She also found this calling helped her to grow. Bonnie later served as a Sunday School teacher, ward Primary president, and stake Young Women president.

Bonnie has carried on her own "personal ministry" as she would describe it, along with her formal Church callings. Daughter-in-law

Jana Parkin noted, "Bonnie is tireless. She has taken in countless meals to families and is constantly doing things for others. When her parents were alive and out on the farm in Herriman, she was out there helping them. Her sister, Joyce, told me that Bonnie is very tuned in to her nieces and nephews. Every once in a while she'll get some insight or inspiration for one of them that she'll pass on to her sister or brothers. She is very generous, too, with financial means."[40]

In September 1990, Bonnie received a call to the Relief Society general board under Elaine L. Jack. Her particular assignment on the board was chairman of the Transition Committee, to help young women as they moved into Relief Society. Aileen H. Clyde, then second counselor in the general presidency, observed that when she and Bonnie went out on assignments together, "Bonnie was thoroughly prepared, both intellectually and spiritually. She is a very spiritual person. I was thrilled every time I listened to her. She is a very gracious person, and her friendliness is genuine."[41]

During the October 1994 general conference, Bonnie was sustained as second counselor to Janette C. Hales, the Young Women general president. Bonnie found that this service was valuable training, especially in learning how a general presidency functions. Sharing insights about the scriptures as they addressed the needs of young women developed a strong bond among the presidency. She served in this capacity until April 1997 when she was released at general conference. Earlier that year, Jim had received a call to preside over the London South Mission, commencing July 1.

"Mission Mother"—The London South Mission

Only ten days after the Parkins' arrival in London, Bonnie became very ill while sitting on the stand for a missionary zone conference. Experiencing nausea and dizziness, she lost her sense of balance and could not hear out of her right ear. After Jim and a missionary administered to her, she was transported to the mission home. Medical tests showed an inner ear blood clot. Bonnie related, "I was scared, worried, and angry. While I believed my husband and I had been called of God, I wondered, 'How can I assist the Lord in this great work if I cannot hear or even walk?' With no other family members or close friends to turn to for help, I felt completely alone. I needed a miracle. . . . I pleaded with Him to make me well. I was sure I had sufficient faith for a miracle."[42]

Bonnie's balance improved over time, but she never regained hearing in that ear. She had difficulty understanding this loss, especially since she was serving a mission for three years. Writing about this experience nine years later, she stated: "I realize that countless blessings have come from those afflictions in England. . . . Like Joseph of old, I was imprisoned—not by bars but by vertigo—in a land far from the help of my extended family. But just as Joseph found support from friends, I found support from my fellow missionaries." Bonnie learned to listen more carefully, to focus on those speaking to her, thus better understanding their words and especially their feelings. She also developed more patience, particularly for those with disabilities. She found faith to accept her affliction.[43]

Bonnie profoundly touched the lives of the London South missionaries through her strong testimony, her compassion, her love, and her gentle humor. When she talked with missionaries, whether individually or in large groups, she made them, according to Noelle Ballard, "feel like you are exactly the person you ought to be. She reached out to the sisters on the mission, built a sweet rapport with them by asking about themselves and their families, by helping them to see their inner and outer beauty. There couldn't be a more appropriate title for her than 'mission mother.' I am sure each one of us left her presence feeling like her favorite."[44] Another sister missionary, Jen Fauset, told of a day when Bonnie tracted with her and her companion. She said, "After my companion and I had each attempted a door approach, Sister Parkin spoke at the third door. She bore her testimony with power and love, and we were let in and allowed to share the first discussion. Sister Parkin revived my spirit that day and gave me a new sense of the great work we were called to do."[45]

Reighlyn Rogers, a senior sister missionary and a widow of only four months when she arrived, related how Bonnie helped her. "Sister Parkin was so loving and sensed my need to talk. She took time to hear my life story and asked me questions to encourage me. It eased my burden and helped me give more to others."[46]

"Sister Parkin has an incredible ability to love," said Will Kruger. "I wanted to do my very best because of her love for me. She had that impact on every missionary! I still remember my monthly visits with Sister Parkin at zone conference. You would walk into the room and were greeted with the warmest smile and the most loving handshake. Those visits would lift me up for the next six weeks until our next zone conference."[47]

Another elder in the mission, Matt Montague, was surprised when Bonnie came to zone conference with cleaning supplies. She instructed the missionaries on how to use the cleaning tools and promised them that by keeping their flats clean and tidy, they would feel the Spirit of the Lord stronger and in greater abundance. Matt also noted that "Sister Parkin's cooking was out of this world"—especially "her famous hot fudge sauce that every missionary loved!"[48] Bonnie's chocolate chip banana bread, which she served after interviews, at zone conferences, and in numerous other settings, was a mission legend.

Bonnie and Jim bade farewell to six grandchildren when they left Salt Lake for London. Two months later the phone rang at 4:00 A.M. It was Brett announcing the safe arrival of his and Angie's twins. Wanting to hold Eliza and Andrew and to help out, Bonnie started to cry and cried after she hung up the phone, but only until 6:00 A.M. She knew the mission motto also included her. At each zone conference all the missionaries stood and personalized the advice President Gordon B. Hinckley's father had given to him as a young missionary in England. She said to herself, "Sister Parkin, forget yourself and go to work."[49]

Brett and Angie flew to London with the twins at nine months to meet their grandparents, a particular joy to Bonnie. Brett observed firsthand how the missionaries loved President and Sister Parkin and watched his mom visit with the sisters and elders after they had finished their interviews with his dad.

During their mission Bonnie gained great insights and experience with the international Church, as not only is London "a melting pot" but also their missionaries came to the London South Mission from all over the world. She especially paid attention to the sister missionaries as they grew in their understanding of Relief Society as a worldwide sisterhood.

For the Parkins, serving a mission was an especially joyful time. "The blessing of missionary service was something Jim and I did together, the highlight of our lives," remarked Bonnie. "We didn't have children with us, so the mission was what we got to do together."[50]

When the Parkins returned home from their mission in July 2000, they were welcomed by twelve grandchildren, "the Lord doubling their grandchildren, doubling their blessings," said Bonnie. She was then called as a ward missionary and Laurel adviser.[51]

Fourteenth General Relief Society President

Jim and Bonnie had stayed up to watch the television broadcast of the closing ceremonies of the 2002 Winter Olympics held in February in Salt Lake City. Early the next morning, a phone call came from President Gordon B. Hinckley's secretary asking them to meet with the prophet that morning. As they got ready, Jim said to Bonnie, "This is about you, not me." They then read their patriarchal blessings and prayed to be able to do whatever was asked of them by President Hinckley.

As the Parkins sat across the desk from President Hinckley, he asked Bonnie about her health. She said that her health was excellent except for losing the hearing in one ear. He then asked how her hearing was in the other ear. When she replied "fine," he said, "Just turn your head."[52] President Hinckley extended the call to Bonnie to serve as the Relief Society general president. When she told him that her family wasn't perfect, he responded, "Whose is?"[53] Bonnie recounted that President Hinckley gave her "an impassioned mandate." He said, "The older sisters in Relief Society must move out of their comfort zones. . . . They must reach out to these younger sisters, making them feel comfortable. They need to help them learn to love Relief Society."[54]

Mary Ellen W. Smoot was released April 6, 2002, during general conference. The new presidency—Bonnie D. Parkin, Kathleen H. Hughes, and Anne C. Pingree—was announced and sustained. Within the next few months, ten sisters, "from all walks of life" according to Bonnie, were called to the general board. Later, Florence Chukwurah, a sister from Nigeria, served on the board for the five months she resided in Salt Lake City.

Following the Saturday announcement at conference, the Parkins' youngest son, David, who was living in Belgium, faxed a note of support and encouragement. "Mother, I know you can do it. You may not remember, but you used to have a scripture on the fridge that said, 'As for me and my house, we will serve the Lord' (Josh. 24:15). I was in and out of the fridge a lot, and I knew that you and Dad meant that."[55]

During the six weeks between being called and sustained, Bonnie had earnestly sought the Lord's direction. She shared the answer she received as she bore her testimony at the Sunday afternoon session of conference: "I know that the Lord loves the women of the Church. If I could have one thing happen for every woman in this Church, it would be that they would feel the love of the Lord in their lives daily."[56] This would become the focus of her administration. Bonnie also desired "with all my heart to have enough charity to genuinely love *every single sister* in the Church . . . 'to be filled with this love, which he hath bestowed upon *all* who are true followers of His Son, Jesus Christ' (Moro. 7:48; emphasis added)."[57]

"Bonnie has great enthusiasm," said Anne Pingree, commenting on their shared experience in the presidency. "She is a capable administrator, is very organized, and is an extremely hard worker. She has a great love for the Lord and for the sisters she represents. To know Bonnie is to love her. To even meet her and to feel her warmth and love and goodness is to love her. She is courageous in taking forward things that she and we as a presidency feel strongly about. She respectfully advocates for the things we believe in and feel represent the needs of women and the family."[58]

Kathleen Hughes remarked: "If you were to characterize Sister Parkin's administration in terms of what she has had on her mind, there are basically two things. Number one would be that the sisters feel like they belong to Relief Society. That has really been a major emphasis of hers. Corollary with that is the idea that women do feel that the Lord loves them because we hear so frequently that women do not feel that the Lord loves them or that they sense they feel His presence very much in their lives."[59]

Bonnie's enthusiasm for Relief Society is heartfelt and contagious. She exclaimed, "I love Relief Society! It has helped define me as a woman. I am who I am because of good women I have associated with in Relief Society—women who have encouraged me, who have loved me, who have believed in me."[60] Another time she promised,

"Come to Relief Society! It will fill your homes with love and charity; it will nurture and strengthen you and your families."[61] She whole-heartedly believes "in the goodness of women to look out for each other in ways that cheer each other on."[62]

While Bonnie described herself as "the farm girl from Herriman" and "the most ordinary person you'll ever meet," those who have inter-acted with her, whether it was a first-time meeting or whether they have known her for years, would disagree. Judy T. Lamphere related her introduction to Bonnie: "I had done the baptism for my mother-in-law at the Salt Lake Temple. I had no makeup on, and my hair was still wet. . . . I was a little embarrassed when I ran into my cousin Kathleen Hughes, who was with Sister Pingree and Sister Parkin. She introduced me and when I explained what I was doing, Sister Parkin said, 'Now here's a woman who has her priorities straight. Ladies, why aren't we out doing work for our ancestors?' And then she asked me all about my life and told me how wonderful it was to meet me. She has a way of fully engaging the person she is talking to and making you feel that you are the most important person."[63] General board member Judy Edwards simply summed up Bonnie's way with people: "She reaches out with love."[64]

Transition of Young Women

With her extensive background of working with young adult sisters, Bonnie focused on helping them feel welcome and an important part of Relief Society. She said while serving as president, "Wherever we have gone as a presidency and board members, we have talked to young single adult sisters—and listened. We have learned that they each need a calling and Relief Society teachers who are sensitive, who value their input. As leaders, we want the single adult sisters to know they have a place in the Church, that what they bring to Relief Society and their testimonies are of value."[65] Bonnie and Young Women general president Susan W. Tanner worked closely together on the transition of young women into Relief Society, a critical time period for girls. They presented workshops to local auxiliary leaders to suggest ways to help make this transition successful. Beginning in February 2007, the First Presidency authorized monthly combined opening exercises for Young Women and Relief Society.

Hearkening to President Hinckley's earlier counsel, Bonnie emphasized how vital it is that sisters of all ages reach out to one another. Developing relationships among different age brackets, however, she noted, often requires careful planning to facilitate. "I have learned that when two hearts connect, age is irrelevant," Bonnie stated. "We desperately need more connections between young and old. And no matter our age, our needs are the same, aren't they? As Relief Society sisters support each other, we share our faith, friendship, and love."[66]

Kathleen Hughes observed, "What Bonnie really tried to do is particularly appeal to the young single adult women in the Church, both the 18-year-olds, who are moving from Young Women into Relief Society, along with those women that are single, particularly those that are in the age bracket of 18 to 30. She really resonates to all ages of these women because not always are the dreams of their lives fulfilled. She feels a very great need to have those women especially feel that they are a part of Relief Society, that there is a place for them, and that the Lord loves them in spite of the fact their hearts' desires are not being realized."[67]

Home, Personal, and Family Enrichment

As the Relief Society presidency traveled throughout the world, they were concerned about the relatively small attendance at home, family, and personal enrichment meetings. With a number of sisters working and long distances to travel for many, they realized it wasn't practical, especially in the developing areas of the Church, to hold monthly meetings. They studied how to "find a way to reconnect women with that meeting," said Kathleen Hughes. The presidency felt inspired to enlarge the activities portion of Relief Society to cut down the number of times enrichment meetings are held. Beginning in January 2006, ward or branch Relief Societies hold quarterly enrichment meetings, and stakes and districts plan two events a year.[68] Such activities, planned and scheduled to meet the needs and interests of the sisters, might include discussions of books, learning sewing and cooking skills, attending the temple together, participating in sporting activities, or working on community service projects.

Bonnie envisioned the flexible home, family, and personal enrichment meetings as a place "where hearts and hands are joined together in a safe, relaxed, and enjoyable environment." She added, "Women of all ages and stages of life can feel a sense of belonging as they participate in activities that build spiritual strength, develop personal skills, strengthen home and family, and exercise charity through service."[69]

Good News Minute

At the April 2005 general conference open house, Bonnie introduced the Good News Minute as a way to build connections among Relief Society sisters and for presidencies to learn what is happening in their sisters' lives. The Good News Minute allows women during the beginning of Sunday Relief Society meetings to briefly share something good that has taken place recently, such as the birth of a grandchild, an engagement, an accomplishment. Many local units reported an increase in the feeling of sisterhood and belonging to Relief Society as they have implemented this.

50th Anniversary of Relief Society Building

The Relief Society Building, located east of the Salt Lake Temple, had been years in planning. Belle S. Spafford, who began serving as Relief Society general president in 1945, suggested that each sister donate $5.00 to the building fund, a considerable sacrifice for many. Church President David O. McKay dedicated the beautifully designed and furnished Relief Society home in October 1956.

Bonnie's grandmother, Agnes Kunz Dansie, was among the 100,000 women who contributed to the building fund. From the money Agnes earned selling eggs and writing a column for the local newspaper, she donated $5.00 for each of her daughters, daughters-in-law, and granddaughters.[70]

As all three auxiliaries have been housed together since 1984, the Relief Society presidency, under the direction of the Presiding Bishopric, worked closely with Young Women general president Susan W. Tanner and Primary general president Cheryl C. Lant and their respective counselors in planning needed remodeling. Renovated and refurbished, the Relief Society Building was reopened March 17, 2006, on the 164th anniversary of the organization of Relief Society. President Hinckley and Bonnie participated in a ribbon-cutting ceremony and each spoke to the group gathered in the Relief Society Building. Quoting Joseph Smith's statement, "If you live up to your privileges, even the angels cannot restrain from being your associates," President Hinckley said, "That is the ideal, I think, that ought to permeate all of the activities of the Relief Society. . . . It is a thing of wonder and a thing to be marveled at, that from the 20 women who met with the Prophet in 1842, there would be an organization today of 5 million of them. It's almost impossible to believe." Bonnie noted, "This building is filled with the spirit of those who have gone before." She also referred to President McKay's dedicatory prayer mentioning the "loyal, faithful, beautiful women" in Relief Society. She said, "Today, our 5.2 million sisters worldwide are equally loyal, faithful and beautiful, and I express my gratitude to those who have gone before, for the legacy they have left, for the tender blessings that are ours as women, as Relief Society sisters."[71]

A Worldwide View

In London Bonnie saw how their missionaries, in particular the sister missionaries, coming from nations around the world, would return to their native lands strengthened and prepared to be leaders. With those successes in mind, the Relief Society presidency suggested that the sister missionaries who serve on Temple Square, most of them converts representing the international Church, receive training on topics such as being covenant women and what their roles are in building the kingdom of God. This assignment was given to the Relief Society general board.[72]

Bonnie's daughter-in-law Jennifer Parkin learned from Bonnie that she "truly wanted to relate to and understand women and their individual needs throughout the world. She felt a great need for women to know that they are daughters of God regardless of their circumstances or where they live."[73]

Bonnie traveled to many areas of the world visiting Relief Society sisters, speaking, training, and sharing her love. She met with women in Europe, Africa, Asia, the Pacific Islands, and South America as well as all across North America, often in their own homes. In November 2004, she, along with the Young Women and Primary presidents, addressed the United Nation's International Year of the Family conference held in

Geneva, Switzerland. The following year she addressed the World Congress of Families III held in Mexico City, Mexico.

In August 2005, Bonnie, as a member of the General Welfare Committee, represented the Church in Mozambique in their partnership with the American Red Cross to vaccinate children against measles and polio, largely eradicated in most areas of the world, but life-threatening in this poverty-stricken African country. While in Mozambique, Bonnie volunteered at clinics and orphanages, hugging and kissing children, and very touched by their plight.[74]

While Bonnie's Relief Society service extended globally, it also took place right in her own neighborhood. Although her husband thought "she was kind of busy downtown," Bonnie still welcomed new neighbors with her banana nut bread or helped out with her ward Relief Society. She felt "she had to do her own part."[75]

Family Support

Each member of her family gave Bonnie complete support and offered help in numerous ways as she served as Relief Society president, a calling which her husband described as "one not designed for rest and recreation."[76] For the many years that Jim served in numerous leadership positions, Bonnie carried much of the load of home and family. Jennifer Parkin noted, "There are times when we sit back and laugh at how the wheels were turned for Bonnie and Jim. He was nothing but supportive and right by her side the whole time."[77] While Jim had manned the barbecue for years, he hadn't spent much time in the kitchen. Matt commented, "He actually figured out how to cook—a surgeon who knows how to cook!"[78] According to her sister, Joyce Taylor, the extended family prayed for her daily and often put her name on temple prayer rolls, that she would be inspired, strengthened, and blessed in her service.[79]

Throughout her years of service as the Relief Society general president, Bonnie D. Parkin sought to help sisters throughout the world to know that the Lord loves each one of them. Her earnest desire was that each sister would "feel the love of the Lord daily" and that she would genuinely love every sister in the Church. Bonnie's administration was an outreach of love, particularly for the single adult members of Relief Society. She also encouraged women of all ages to share with each other their faith, friendship, and love through service, visiting teaching, Sunday lessons, Good News Minutes, and home, family, and personal enrichment activities. Meeting Bonnie, whether on a personal basis or via satellite broadcast, is to feel her love, a genuine and heartfelt expression of the Relief Society motto, "Charity never faileth."

Notes

1. Bonnie D. Parkin, "Choose to Celebrate," BYU commencement address, August 11, 2005, pp. 2–3.

2. Interview with Bonnie D. Parkin by Janet Peterson, February 16, 2007. Hereafter cited as Parkin interview.

3. Bonnie D. Parkin, Idaho Regional Broadcast, November 3, 2006, p. 8.

4. Julie A. Dockstader, "Her Parents' Trust Instilled Desire in Her to 'Do What Is Right,'" *Church News,* November 26, 1994, p. 11.

5. Bonnie D. Parkin, "Feel the Love of the Lord," *Ensign,* May 2002, p. 84.

6. Telephone interview with Joyce D. Taylor, December 28, 2006.

7. Telephone interview with Rodney Dansie, November 14, 2006.

8. "Her Parents' Trust Instilled Desire in Her to 'Do What Is Right,'" p. 11.

9. Telephone interview with Rodney Dansie, November 14, 2006.

10. Telephone interview with Joyce D. Taylor, December 28, 2006.

11. Monica Weeks, "Friend to Friend: Working for Jesus," *Friend,* June 2004, p. 8.

12. Ibid.

13. Ibid., p. 9.

14. Interview with Bonnie D. Parkin, February 16, 2007.

15. Bonnie D. Parkin, "Parents Have A Sacred Duty," *Ensign,* June 2006, p. 96.

16. Bonnie Parkin, "An Anchor for Eternity—and Today," *Ensign,* May 1996, p. 96.

17. Bonnie Parkin, "Eternally Encircled in His Love," *Ensign,* November 2006, p. 109.

18. Bonnie Parkin, "How Has Relief Society Blessed Your Life?" *Ensign,* November 2004, p. 35.

19. Bonnie D. Parkin, "Doing His Will with Faith," BYU—Idaho Commencement address, August 25, 2006, p. 1.

20. Bonnie D. Parkin, "Fat-Free Feasting," *Ensign,* May 1995, p. 90.

21. Ibid.

22. Telephone interview with Jeffrey L. Parkin, September 27, 2006.

23. Telephone interview with Matthew J. Parkin, October 8, 2006.

24. Telephone interview with Jeffrey L. Parkin, September 27, 2006.

25. Parkin interview.

26. Interview with Bonnie D. Parkin, February 16, 2007.

27. Telephone interview with David S. Parkin, November 30, 2006.

28. Telephone interviews with Matthew J. Parkin, October 8, 2006, and Jeffrey L. Parkin, September 27, 2006.

29. Telephone interview with David S. Parkin, November 30, 2006.

30. Telephone interview with Brett D. Parkin, October 3, 2006.

31. Telephone interview with David S. Parkin, November 30, 2006.

32. Telephone interview with James L. Parkin, November 2, 2006.

33. Telephone interview with Brett D. Parkin, October 3, 2006.

34. Telephone interview with Jana Parkin, February 17, 2007.

35. Telephone interview with Ann Parkin, November 1, 2006.

36. Parkin interview.

37. Bonnie D. Parkin, "Choosing Charity: That Good Part," *Ensign,* November 2003, p. 104.

38. Parkin interview.

39. "Bonnie D. Parkin: Relief Society General President," *Ensign,* May 2002, p. 107.

40. Telephone interview with Jana Parkin, February 21, 2007.

41. Telephone interview with Aileen H. Clyde, December 28, 2006.

42. Bonnie D. Parkin, "Lessons from the Old Testament: Blessed in My Afflictions," *Ensign,* March 2006, p. 9.

43. Ibid., p. 10.

44. E-mail from Noelle Ballard, November 8, 2006.

45. E-mail from Jen Fauset, November 9, 2006.

46. E-mail from Reighlynn Rogers, November 9, 2006.

47. E-mail from William Kruger, November 20, 2006.

48. E-mail from Matt Montague, November 9, 2006.

49. Bonnie D. Parkin, "Bearing Record: Nothing Compares to It!" BYU Women's Conference address, May 2001, p. 2.

50. Parkin interview.

51. Parkin interview.

52. "Lessons from the Old Testament: Blessed in My Afflictions," p. 10.

53. Carrie A. Moore, "Service Is Sister Parkin's Priority," *deseretnews.com,* April 2, 2005.

54. Bonnie D. Parkin, "Embracing Sisterhood: Helping Young Women Successfully Transition into Relief Society," Open House, address, Spring 2003, pp. 7–8.

55. Bonnie D. Parkin, "Feel the Love of the Lord," p. 84.

56. Ibid.

57. "Choosing Charity: That Good Part," p. 106.

58. Interview with Anne C. Pingree, October 24, 2006.

59. Interview with Kathleen H. Hughes, October 24, 2006.

60. Bonnie D. Parkin, "Oh, How We Need Each Other!" *Ensign,* March 2004, p. 20.

61. "How Has Relief Society Blessed Your Life?" p. 35.

62. "Bonnie D. Parkin, Relief Society General President," p. 107.

63. E-mail from Judy T. Lamphere, December 18, 2006.

64. Telephone interview with Judy F. Edwards, October 8, 2006.

65. Parkin interview.

66. "Embracing Sisterhood," p. 7.

67. Interview with Kathleen H. Hughes, October 24, 2006.

68. Ibid.

69. Lilian deLong, "A Happy Gathering of Sisters," *Ensign,* January 2006, p. 62.

70. Julie Dockstader Heaps, "50th Anniversary Commemorated," *Church News,* March 25, 2006, p. 3.

71. Ibid.

72. Interview with Anne C. Pingree, October 24, 2006.

73. Telephone interview with Jennifer H. Parkin, November 13, 2006.

74. Carrie A. Moore, "LDS Church Helps Fight Measles in Mozambique," *deseretnews.com,* September 7, 2005.

75. Telephone interview with James L. Parkin, November 2, 2006.

76. Ibid.

77. Telephone interview with Jennifer H. Parkin, November 13, 2006.

78. Telephone interview with Matthew S. Parkin, October 8, 2006.

79. Telephone interview with Joyce D. Taylor, December 28, 2006.

APPENDIX A

RELIEF SOCIETY TIMELINE

1820	First Vision
1829	Aaronic and Melchizedek priesthoods are restored
1830	Book of Mormon is published; the Church is organized on April 6 in Fayette, New York; D&C 25 is revealed; Emma Smith is identified as "an elect lady" (v. 3)
1830–1844	Joseph Smith, first prophet and president of Church
1831–1838	Kirtland period
1831–1839	Missouri period
1834	Zion's Camp
1835	Doctrine and Covenants is published; first book of hymns is compiled by Emma Smith
1836	Kirtland Temple is dedicated
1838	Cornerstone is laid for temple in Far West, Missouri
1839–1846	Nauvoo period
1842	Relief Society is organized on March 17
1842–1844	EMMA HALE SMITH, first president of Relief Society; organization is known as Female Relief Society of Nauvoo
1843	Necessity Committee is organized (forerunner of visiting teaching)
1844	Relief Society is disbanded; Joseph and Hyrum Smith are martyred at Carthage Jail
1846	Nauvoo Temple is dedicated; exodus from Nauvoo begins
1846–1848	Winter Quarters
1846–1848	Mexican War; Mormon Battalion

1847–1877	Brigham Young presides over the Church
1847	First pioneer wagon company enters Salt Lake Valley; site for the Salt Lake Temple is designated
1850	University of Deseret (later University of Utah) is established
1852	Plural marriage is publicly announced
1855	Endowment House is dedicated
1856–1860	Handcart pioneer companies arrive in Salt Lake City
1861–1865	U.S. Civil War
1866	Women's auxiliary is reorganized and renamed Female Relief Society
1866–1880	Eliza R. Snow leads all women's auxiliaries
1867	First general conference is held in the Tabernacle
1869	Transcontinental railroad is completed; Susan B. Anthony and Elizabeth C. Stanton organize National Woman's Suffrage Association; Young Ladies' Retrenchment Society (forerunner of Young Women) is organized
1870	Women in Utah receive vote
1872	*Woman's Exponent* is published
1873	Women's organization is renamed Relief Society
1876	Relief Society begins sericulture and grain storage
1877	St. George Temple is dedicated
1877–1887	John Taylor leads the Church
1878	Primary is organized
1880–1887	ELIZA R. SNOW, second president of Relief Society
1880	Leadership is established for Relief Society, Young Ladies' Mutual Improvement Association, and Primary
1882	Relief Society establishes Deseret Hospital
1887	Edmunds-Tucker Act is passed, disenfranchising women
1888–1901	ZINA D. H. YOUNG, third president of Relief Society
1888	Manti Temple is dedicated
1887–1898	Wilford Woodruff presides over the Church
1889	First Relief Society general conference is held

1890	Manifesto is issued, ending plural marriage
1891	Relief Society joins National Council of Women
1892	Relief Society Jubilee
1892	Women's organization is renamed National Women's Relief Society
1893	Salt Lake Temple is dedicated
1896	Utah is granted statehood; women regain vote
1898–1901	Lorenzo Snow, fifth president of Church
1901–1918	Joseph F. Smith, sixth president of Church
1901–1910	BATHSHEBA W. SMITH, fourth president of Relief Society
1901–1920	Nursing school in Salt Lake City is operated by Relief Society; women from various areas are called to attend
1902	Mothers' classes are introduced in Relief Society
1909	Relief Society, YLMIA, and Primary are housed in Bishops' Building
1910–1921	EMMELINE B. WELLS, fifth president of Relief Society
1914–1918	World War I
1914	*Woman's Exponent* is discontinued; uniform course of study begins in Relief Society
1915	*Relief Society Magazine* begins publication
1916	Visiting teaching messages are introduced
1918	Relief Society sells 200,000 bushels of wheat to U.S. government; money generated becomes wheat trust fund
1918–1945	Heber J. Grant, seventh president of Church
1919	Relief Society establishes social services department
1920	Nineteenth Amendment to the U.S. Constitution grants suffrage to women
1921–1928	CLARISSA SMITH WILLAMS, sixth president of Relief Society
1924	Maternity hospital is founded
1928–1939	LOUISE YATES ROBISON, seventh president of Relief Society
1929	Great Depression begins
1930	Centennial of Church

1931	Relief Society adopts blue and gold as its colors
1933	Singing Mothers Chorus is named; monument commemorating organization of Relief Society is dedicated at the site of Red Brick Store in Nauvoo
1936	Church Welfare Plan is inaugurated
1937	Mormon Handicraft is established
1940–1945	AMY BROWN LYMAN, eighth president of Relief Society
1939–1945	World War II
1942	Relief Society Centennial is curtailed by war; Relief Society presents campanile tower for Nauvoo Bell on Temple Square
1945–1951	George Albert Smith, eighth president of Church
1945–1974	BELLE SMITH SPAFFORD, ninth president of Relief Society; name of organization is again Relief Society
1950–1953	Korean War
1951–1970	David O. McKay, ninth president of Church
1956	Relief Society Building is dedicated
1961	Church Correlation is instituted; lesson materials and budgets for Relief Society and other auxiliaries are placed under the direction of the priesthood
1965–1973	Vietnam War
1966	*Relief Society Magazine* is published in Spanish
1970–1972	Joseph Fielding Smith, tenth president of Church
1970	*Relief Society Magazine* is discontinued; local units receive local budget funds, eliminating Relief Society fundraising efforts
1971	All adult LDS women become members of Relief Society; dues are discontinued
1972–1973	Harold B. Lee, eleventh president of Church
1973–1985	Spencer W. Kimball, twelfth president of Church
1974–1984	BARBARA BRADSHAW SMITH, tenth president of Relief Society
1978	Revelation on priesthood is announced; Relief Society Monument to Women in Nauvoo is dedicated; first General Women's Meeting is broadcast

1979	1000th stake is organized
1980	Consolidated meeting schedule begins; Sesquicentennial of Church is celebrated
1982	Sarah M. Kimball home in Nauvoo is dedicated
1984–1990	BARBARA WOODHEAD WINDER, eleventh president of Relief Society
1984	Relief Society, Young Women, and Primary offices are housed together; wives of international area presidencies serve as general board representatives for Relief Society, Young Women, and Primary
1985–1994	Ezra Taft Benson, thirteenth president of Church
1987	Relief Society stake boards are eliminated, providing greater flexibility in ward boards; Relief Society lessons, with emphasis on the scriptures, are coordinated with Gospel Doctrine course of study
1988	Visiting teaching is changed to accommodate world-wide Church
1989	Local Unit Budget is implemented in the United States and Canada
1990	FamilySearch, a program for personal computers, facilitates family history research
1990–1997	ELAINE LOW JACK, twelfth president of Relief Society
1992	Relief Society Sesquicentennial is celebrated through community service projects and satellite broadcast to five continents; Relief Society initiates Gospel Literacy effort
1993	Centennial of the Salt Lake Temple
1994–1995	Howard W. Hunter, fourteenth president of Church
1994	2000th stake is created
1995	Gordon B. Hinckley, fifteenth president of Church Area authority position is announced; Regional Representatives are discontinued; "The Family: A Proclamation to the World" is introduced at general Relief Society meeting
1996	More than half of Church membership resides outside United States

1997–2002	MARY ELLEN WOOD SMOOT, thirteenth president of Relief Society
1997	Building of small temples is announced; area authority seventies (formerly area authorities) comprise Third, Fourth, and Fifth Quorums of Seventy; Sesquicentennial of pioneers' arrival in Salt Lake Valley; Worldwide Pioneer Heritage Service Day
1998	Monticello Utah Temple, the first of smaller temples, is dedicated; Relief Society and priesthood lessons are taught from the same manual—*Teachings of the Presidents of the Church*
1999	Homemaking is changed to home, family, and personal enrichment; Relief Society Declaration is issued; visiting teaching messages include only quotes from Church leaders and scriptural passages for worldwide applicability
2000	General conference is held in the Conference Center; the 100th temple, the Boston Massachusetts Temple, is dedicated
2002	Winter Olympics are held in Salt Lake City; Relief Society assists; Nauvoo Temple is dedicated on the anniversary of Joseph Smith's martyrdom
2002–2007	BONNIE DANSIE PARKIN, fourteenth president of Relief Society
2003	First global satellite training is held for priesthood leaders
2005	18,000 women participate in humanitarian service projects at BYU Women's Conference, cosponsored by the Relief Society
2006	Home, family, and personal enrichment meetings are held quarterly; smaller group activities to meet varying interests are initiated; remodeled Relief Society Building reopens for its 50th anniversary
2007	JULIE BANGERTER BECK, fifteenth president of the Relief Society

APPENDIX B

MEMBERS OF
THE FIRST RELIEF SOCIETY

1. Emma Smith
2. Sarah M. Cleveland
3. Phebe Ann Hawkes
4. Elizabeth Jones
5. Sophia Packard
6. Philindia Merrick
7. Martha Knight
8. Desdemona Fullmer
9. Elizabeth Ann Whitney
10. Leonora Taylor
11. Bathsheba W. Smith
12. Phebe M. Wheeler
13. Elvira A. Cowles
14. Margaret A. Cook
15. Athalia Robinson*
16. Sarah M. Kimball
17. Eliza R. Snow
18. Sophia Robinson
19. Nancy Rigdon*
20. Sophia Marks

*These women, daughters of Sidney Rigdon, followed their father into apostasy, and their names were stricken from the minutes of the Relief Society. For this reason, some accounts list eighteen women present at the first meeting instead of twenty.

INDEX

ABOUT THE AUTHORS

Janet Peterson earned B.A. and M.A. degrees in English from Brigham Young University and has written extensively for the Church magazines. She and LaRene Gaunt have co-authored biographies of the presidents of the Relief Society, Young Women, and Primary organizations. Janet has served in each of these organizations and is currently serving as a member of the Correlation Committee (Materials Evaluation). She and her husband, Larry, have six children and twelve grandchildren.

LaRene Gaunt has served as a president, a teacher, and a visiting teacher in Relief Society. She received a bachelor's degree from Brigham Young University and is an accredited genealogist, a photographer, and an artist. In addition to co-authoring six books, LaRene has worked as an editor at the *Ensign* magazine since 1990. She and her husband, David, are the parents of three children.